THE TROLLE

OF

NEWCASTLE UPON TYNE

1935-1966

including details of the proposed trolleybus operations in Gateshead

by

T. P. CANNEAUX and N. H. HANSON

2nd Edition (revised), 1985

Printed by Wards (Colour Printers), Gateshead, Tyne and Wear.

ISBN 0 902653 29 6

First published by Trolleybooks, 1974.
Second (revised) edition, Newcastle City Libraries, 1985.

Newcastle upon Tyne City Libraries
Central Library
P.O. Box 1MC
Newcastle upon Tyne
NE99 1MC.

This book is dedicated to the memory of
our respective parents.

CONTENTS

THIS PUBLICATION IS IN NO WAY AN OFFICIAL PUBLICATION OF
TYNE AND WEAR PASSENGER TRANSPORT EXECUTIVE

3

PUBLISHER'S NOTE

Fifty years ago, in October 1935, Newcastle Corporation introduced a trolleybus system which served the City well for just over 30 years. Now only a few traction poles remain to mark the passing of one of the most efficient forms of mass transport.

In 1974 the first edition of this history was published by Trolleybooks Ltd as a tribute to, and record of, one of the largest trolleybus systems outside London. It was well received by enthusiasts and the general public and sold out very quickly.

Since the first edition appeared much additional information on Newcastle trolleybuses has come to light as, for example, on the 1948 'Q1 type' 3-axle vehicles. Much of this new information has been incorporated in three totally new chapters, the remainder appearing in note form.

Of the 80 photographs in this volume 66 did not appear in the first edition.

Despite continuing research by the authors there are still points of uncertainty and we hope that readers will contact us with additional information.

We wish to acknowledge the efforts of the Trolleybooks editors, M. J. Russell and J. Whitehead, in the preparation of the first edition.

In recent years, the City Library has been broadening its publishing programme and we are proud, on the occasion of the fiftieth anniversary of Newcastle's trolleybus system, to produce this greatly expanded edition of its history.

FOREWORD

Newcastle's trolleybuses disappeared from the City's streets nearly twenty years ago and there is now a generation of Novocastrians who have grown up with no recollection of this form of public transport. However there are still very many people who recall the refined and efficient service they provided in the City.

It is therefore pleasing to be able to record admiration of the further research which the authors have undertaken to produce this second edition of "The Trolleybuses of Newcastle upon Tyne". The major role played by Newcastle trolleybuses in the life of the City is well demonstrated and in looking back we cannot dismiss the trolleybuses for much of the transport network of today was developed with these vehicles.

It is most appropriate that this book is being published on the 50th Anniversary of the introduction of trolleybuses in Newcastle. This is a book which I commend, not only to public transport professionals and enthusiasts, but to anyone with an interest in the development of Newcastle.

G. ERIC HUTCHINSON, F.C.I.T.
Director of Operations, Tyne and Wear Passenger Transport Executive

INTRODUCTION

It is difficult to believe that Newcastle has been without trolleybuses now since 1966, and that they have disappeared from the City's streets for ever. In 1963 there was still a flourishing system, on which trolleybuses could be seen operating in all parts of the City. Yet the diesel 'bus now reigns supreme. A conversion to diesel 'buses was first discussed seriously in 1963, although in the nineteen-fifties the attitude had been distinctly neutral.

This was a complete contrast to the enthusiasm of the City Council in the nineteen-thirties. Indeed, the trolleybus was essentially a product of that decade although it had its beginnings in the nineteenth century, and the earliest installations in Great Britain were in Leeds and Bradford in 1911. The trolleybus was brought to a modern form in the late nineteen-twenties and widely adopted in the following decade as a tramway replacement vehicle. It was, as J. Joyce has said in his work 'Trolleybus Trails' (Ian Allan, 1963), 'an integral part of the 'thirties scene of suburban semis and mock-Tudor shops.' Newcastle's system followed the pattern, beginning in 1935 and expanding to a healthy size by the outbreak of war in 1939. By that date, over one hundred trolleybuses served routes in both east and west ends of the City. In the latter part of the nineteen-forties, the fleet nearly doubled in size and route mileage increased by about eleven miles, mostly due to conversion of the remaining tramway services.

The trolleybuses hold many memories of their thirty-one year history in the City of Newcastle. Their smooth, silent running and rapid acceleration are sadly missed in these days of Leyland 'Atlantean' motorbus domination! What of a two-mile, six-minute journey up Westgate Road, with a climb to 400 feet above sea level to the west end of the City one winter's night in 1963? Or of the stupendous sight of eighteen trolleybuses, nose to tail, stretched down the West Road, held up by a broken wire at Condercum Road on a summer's evening in 1957? Memories also of an unfortunate crew spending fifteen minutes attempting to disentangle the trolleybooms of their vehicle from the street lighting wires after a dewirement at the automatic frog at the Haymarket; of processions of three-axle vehicles rapidly reducing evening rush-hour crowds in New Bridge Street; of the foggy December day in 1955, when the whole City's power supply was cut off, and trolleybuses were stranded all over the system for much of the day. These and many more pleasant ones, remind us of Newcastle's trolleybuses which served one of the largest systems in Great Britain, for they formed a major part of the City's transport system for three decades.

AUTHORS' NOTES AND ACKNOWLEDGEMENTS

An outline history of the Newcastle trolleybus system was presented by one of the authors in an article in "Buses Illustrated" in the mid-nineteen sixties, and the 1974 edition of "The Trolleybuses of Newcastle upon Tyne" contained much more detailed information on the system. In the ten years since 1974, further facts have come to the surface, together with more photographs, and these are presented in this revised edition.

Much has changed in the British urban transport scene since the first edition was published. Electric traction returned to Tyneside in 1980, when the Tyne & Wear Metro opened, and this light rapid transit system is flourishing today. Blackpool's new trams are attracting widespread interest, and the trolleybus is likely to return to the U.K. very shortly. Doncaster should be the site of South Yorkshire P.T.E.'s initial trolleybus trials, and there are also firm proposals to operate trolleybuses in Rotherham, Leeds, and Bradford.

The authors still reside some 320 miles apart, and once again, the workload for the revised edition has been divided. Tom Canneaux has again checked service and route information, together with vehicle fleet lists, whilst Noel Hanson has researched further detail on the development of the system, and the history of the delivery of the 1948 BUT 6-wheelers (the Q1s). However, there are still a number of uncertainties remaining – for instance, details of early overhead wiring layouts, which we feel will never be solved!

In addition to those persons already thanked for their assistance in preparing the 1974 edition, the authors would like to thank the following for their help with this revised edition:

Messrs. R. C. Davis, A. Fox, F. P. Groves, I. C. Gumm, G. S. Hearse, N. Pollard, J. Ring, K. Stamp, T. Steele, G. Stoyle, Tyne and Wear Archives (R. Potts), Tyne & Wear P.T.E. (especially G. Clayton, E. Hutchinson, A. Neal).

For their help in obtaining photographs, we should like to thank:

Messrs. C. Carter, R. C. Davis, I. C. Gumm, W. J. Haynes, G. S. Hearse, T. Steele, A. Townsin, Tyne & Wear P.T.E., and the manufacturers of Newcastle trolleybuses.

TEXTUAL CORRECTIONS TO 1974 EDITION

All references to "Tyneside P.T.E." should now read "Tyne & Wear P.T.E.".

p.11 Now six bridges. The old Redheugh Bridge is now replaced by the 1982 Redheugh Bridge, and the Queen Elizabeth II Bridge carries Metro tracks across the River Tyne.

p.12 Sentence beginning "It is perhaps unfortunate the Corporation...", should end "... the Wallsend Boundary to Park Road via High Street section...".

p.12 The Undertaking changed its name in 1922, not 1915.

p.13 Tyne & Wear P.T.E. livery now features light blue instead of maroon, and white is substituted for cream.

p.13	para. 4. Only the Tilling-Stevens were petrol-electric.
p.19	Official Routes. Neptune Road is entirely in Wallsend; the Act is incorrect in stating that part is in Newcastle. The Wallsend streets should not include Hadrian Road, as this road starts east of the junction of Park Road and Buddle Street.
p.38	The traverser in Byker Depot has now been removed.
p.39	Allendale Road (Byker) reverser was still regularly used in the early 1950s; mainly for evening rush-hour extras.
p.42	All references to Oaktree Gardens, Walkerville should read Oaktree Avenue.
p.45	Tavistock Place, Jesmond should read Tavistock Road.
p.46	Bewick Street reference should also refer to those streets used as turning loops by trolleybuses.
p.53	Albion Row, Byker, link was constructed by 29 October 1940.
p.53	Melbourne Street link cost £424. Likely built in winter 1940/1.
p.56	There were 18 Bournemouth trolleybuses in London, not 10.
p.75	The siding on the Great North Road outside the Stadium was not constructed until later.
p.76	Town Moor circle: 63 yards refers to the wiring in the enclosed area of the turning circle; the total length of wiring extension from the North Road was c.110 yards (5 chains).
p.81	Service 34b: no eastern terminus is mentioned; it should be St. Nicholas.
p.82	Service 35c. Insert "Blackett Street" between Grainger Street and New Bridge Street.
p.86	The original planned capacity for Slatyford Depot was 100 motorbuses and 185 trolleybuses—sufficient to house the entire postwar trolleybus fleet, bar one vehicle.
p.87	para. 4. Princess Road should read Princes Road.
p.97	Wingrove Depot. 3-axle vehicles usually stood on the right in the depot, 2-axle trolleybuses taking the left hand bay.
p.97	The wartime Karrier W4's *were* stored out of service at Haymarket.
p.97	The roundabout at the west end of Neville Street was in situ by the summer of 1953; from photographic evidence.
p.98	There *were* automatic frogs at the foot of Denton Bank.
p.101	The two traction poles in Wingrove Road were finally removed in 1983.
p.104.	It is now believed Denton Burn Roundabout was constructed in 1959.
p.107	Reference to walking in Neville Street should read westwards, not eastwards.
p.111	Benwell Church is c.200 feet west of Nichol Street sub-terminus, not 200 yards.
p.115	Service 34 rush-hour extras also ran in the reverse direction.
p.117	Bingfield Gardens reverser: it is believed this was reused at the junction of Church Street and Procter Street in Walker.
p.181	para. 3. Some trolleybuses still in prewar livery had sans-serif lettering, instead of their original lettering.
p.181	para. 4. The rear lower panel numbers were soon transferred to the rear wall lower deck cant rail, to allow adverts to be placed on the rear lower panel.

NOTES FOR GUIDANCE

Every area of the country has obscure local derivations of place names and Tyneside is no exception. To assist the reader the following are offered:—

Byker   This district of the City is pronounced as in 'bike'.
Elswick   Another district of the City; the 'w' is silent.
Lonnen   This is a local dialect word meaning lane. Thus, Silver Lonnen is 'the lane leading to the Silverhills area', and Two Ball Lonnen is 'the lane having two pillars each topped with a stone ball at its junction with the West Road'.

To the non-enthusiast, the following terms used in connection with the trolleybus overhead line installations are explained:—

Frogs   These are the overhead 'points' where one line leaves or joins another. They were operated either by hand (the conductor leaving the vehicle and pulling a handle on an adjacent traction pole) or automatically (by the trolleyheads of the vehicle energising or otherwise a solenoid fitted to the overhead line a short distance before the frog, depending on whether the driver of the trolleybus was applying power or not as the trolleyheads passed beneath).
Gantry   Also known as a double bracket arm, this consisted of a tubular support joining two opposite traction poles.
Running wire   The conductor wire along which the trolleyhead ran or slid.
Span wire   The wire erected across the roadway usually between opposite traction poles.

The following abbreviations are used with reference to rolling stock:—

A.E.C.—Associated Equipment Company, Ltd.
B.T-H—British Thomson-Houston Company, Ltd.
B.U.T.—British United Traction Company, Ltd.
E.E.C.—English Electric Company, Ltd.
MV—Metropolitan-Vickers Electrical Company, Ltd.
M.C.C.W.—Metropolitan-Cammell Carriage and Wagon Company, Ltd.
NCB—Northern Coachbuilders, Ltd.

CHAPTER ONE

TRAMS AND EARLY TROLLEYBUS PLANS

Newcastle upon Tyne (note that hyphens are NOT used) is approximately 270 miles from London and 65 miles from the Scottish border. Situated on the north bank of the Tyne, its correct title is The City and County of Newcastle upon Tyne, for it has been a separate county in its own right since 1400 by Charter of King Henry IV and was created a City in 1882. The chief magistrate of the town has borne the title 'mayor' since 1216, and the right to style himself 'Lord Mayor' was conferred in 1906.

The site of Newcastle was of importance in Roman times, being known as Pons Aelius. The name was derived from that of Emperor Publius Aelius Hadrianus, the builder of what we now call Hadrian's Wall. This selfsame gentleman also ordered a bridge to be built at Pons Aelius, which was the lowest bridging point on the river we now call the Tyne. By the Middle Ages the bridge had fallen into disrepair, together with the settlement.

After the Norman Conquest the settlement was re-established, and a new bridge and a castle were erected in 1080. In 1172, Henry II had the castle pulled down and the present keep was built. This is the 'New Castle' which gives the City its present name. By the thirteenth century, the famous coal trade had begun. Colliers, or 'keels', shipped the coal to London, and Newcastle prospered on the lucrative traffic—so much so that the town could afford to build town walls described by Leland as the finest in Europe. Unfortunately very little of them remain now, most being demolished during the nineteenth century expansion of the City.

This expansion was accelerated by the coming of the railways. Wagonways or tramroads had developed to transport coal from the collieries to the river and led George Stephenson to foresee the possibilities of steam power. W. G. Armstrong (later Lord Armstrong) founded his famous Elswick Works, at first for the manufacture of hydraulic cranes and later for big naval guns and warships. The enormous industrial expansion caused the population of Newcastle to rise from 28,294 in 1801 to 215,328 by 1901 and 271,523 in 1917. During the 1914-18 War, Armstrong's employed 70,000 men working in shifts round the clock.

In the nineteen-twenties the Great Depression struck the north-east and Tyneside was particularly badly hit. The closure of shipyards and the Jarrow March are too well known to need amplification here. In spite of these setbacks, Newcastle continued to spread across the countryside in the form of new housing estates, many of which were built by the Council. The tram termini had been at the limits of the built-up area as in 1914, but now houses spread beyond them. The City's population had risen to 298,000 by 1938.

During the last war, Newcastle's industries again increased in production and effort, and the transport services bore a heavy burden. In the nineteen-fifties development was more or less at a standstill, but from the mid-nineteen-sixties a revival can be seen. The central area of the City is being torn apart, far more

10

destruction being caused by developers and road builders than German bombers ever made! Multi-storey office blocks and urban motorways have sprung up in profusion.

Strange to say, the City's population has declined whilst its area has increased. Today the population figure stands at 222,153, but due to the building of overspill estates just outside the City boundary the true size of Newcastle can be assessed as about 420,000 people. Under the 1974 Local Government Reorganisation scheme, Newcastle has become part of the Tyneside Metropolitan County and the population of the enlarged Newcastle will now be about 300,000.

Newcastle first had tramways in 1879, when the Newcastle and Gosforth Tramways and Carriage Company began horse tram services on tracks leased from the Corporation on a twenty-one year basis, the lease expiring on 11th November 1899. Outside the City boundary the Company laid its own lines into the then separate town of Gosforth. By 1893, the Company operated quite an extensive network, running over seventeen miles of track and having 44 cars and 272 horses. In November, 1879, a steam locomotive had been tried on the Jesmond to Blue House section. The experiment was short-lived and the locomotive was sold.

Under the Newcastle upon Tyne Corporation Tramways and Improvement Act, 1899, the City gained powers to run electric tramways. Due to a disagreement between the Corporation and the Company, the horse tram services ceased on 13th April 1901 and the first electric cars apparently did not operate until 16th December 1901. The first rail had been ceremonially laid on 19th April 1900 and 14¾ miles of track were ready by inauguration day. The majority of the main routes were completed by 1904, although other extensions were built up to and during the First World War. These included routes to Fenham (1907), Shieldfield (1912), and Throckley (1915).

Immediately after the First World War, in 1920, other extensions were opened to serve areas which were then outlying villages, such as Forest Hall (1921), West Moor and the east entrance to Gosforth Park (1921), through Gosforth Park (the Gosforth Park Light Railway) (April 1924), and from Fenham to Westerhope (1925). An extension from Slatyford (on the line to Westerhope) along the line of what was many years later to become Silver Lonnen, was opened in 1926.

In the City, new lines included the lengthening of the Elswick Road route from the foot of Condercum Road, along Benwell Lane to Delaval Road, in 1923, the opening of tracks over the High Level Bridge on January 12th, 1923, and the extension of the Westgate Road route from Condercum Road to *Fox & Hounds* in 1925.

No fewer than five bridges connect the centre of Newcastle with Gateshead on the south bank of the Tyne. These are (from west to east) the Redheugh Bridge (1871), the King Edward VII Railway Bridge (1906), the High Level Bridge (1849) which carries the railway on the top deck and the road below, the Swing Bridge (1879), and the New Tyne Bridge (1928) which is usually referred to now as The Tyne Bridge. Three miles upstream, in the west end of the City, are the Scotswood road bridge (1967) and the Scotswood rail bridge (1868).

The extension of the tramways over the High Level Bridge in 1923 established the first link with the lines of the Gateshead and District Tramways Company, a British Electric Traction Company subsidiary, whilst the second was made on

11

10th October 1928 when cars began operating over the New Tyne Bridge, this being the last extension to the Corporation Tramways.

Newcastle Corporation tramcars were housed in three depots. Byker Depot, in the east end of the City, was the main depot and workshops. Haymarket Depot (a former horse tram depot) was in the City centre, and Wingrove Depot was in the west-end of the City. For a short time, another former horse tram depot at Gosforth was used, but this was soon closed.

By the time trolleybuses arrived the existing tramcars were very varied in age and condition. There were all-enclosed front-exit double deckers, and 'Pullmanised' bogie single-deckers. In all, by 1928 three hundred trams ran over $51\frac{1}{4}$ miles of track. The system was the largest tramway undertaking in the north east —indeed the largest between Leeds and Edinburgh.

Originally, the title of the undertaking was 'Newcastle Corporation Tramways', but in 1915 the name was changed to 'Newcastle Corporation Transport and Electricity Undertaking', which more accurately reflected the Corporation's powers to supply current for purposes other than for traction, which it had gained under the Benwell and Fenham Lighting Order 1904.

Another Company with which the Corporation Tramways had through running arrangements was the Tyneside Tramways and Tramroads Company, the title of which, incidentally, was only recently changed to the Tyneside Omnibus Company. This Company ran services in the shipbuilding town of Wallsend, immediately to the east of the City, with services from Wallsend eastwards to North Shields and north-westwards to Gosforth. The latter route was on private right-of-way entirely and connected with the Corporation's tramway lines at Henry Street, Gosforth. The Tyneside Tramways and Tramroads Company abandoned its trams on 6th April 1930 and Newcastle Corporation purchased the section from the City boundary at Walker Road to Wallsend Park Road, together with track northwards from Henry Street up the Great North Road to Gosforth Park Gates. Corporation trams continued to run from Wallsend Boundary on Shields Road over the Company's lines in High Street, Wallsend, to Park Road until 25th May 1930. After that date, a joint service of motorbuses took over. The section from Walker to Wallsend Park Road is relevant because this was incorporated in the first trolleybus route of 1935. It is perhaps unfortunate that the Corporation did not also purchase the Wallsend Boundary to High Street section of tram track from the Company, as this might later have encouraged the construction of a circular trolleybus route linked to what became the trolleybus terminus in Park Road.

The generating station for the Newcastle Corporation tramways was constructed at the Manors, on the eastern edge of the City centre, adjacent to the administrative offices of the undertaking, building work having commenced on 14th January 1900. As well as supplying current to the tramways, the power station supplied electricity to part of the west end, public buildings, and Corporation quays on the Tyne.

Incorporated in the Newcastle upon Tyne Corporation Act, 1911, (an Act which otherwise deals mainly with matters totally unconnected with transport) are certain fascinating and confusing powers which do relate to public transport.

Under Part XIII Paragraph 97 Section 4, the City was empowered to work and use motor omnibuses, but not to manufacture them. Then the Act states that

'Every motor omnibus **moved by electric power*** shall be so equipped and worked as to prevent any interference with telegraphic communication by means of any telegraph line of the Postmaster-General.' This would seem to point to trolleybuses. It will be recalled that Leeds and Bradford inaugurated trolleybus systems in 1911.

Section 6 of the same paragraph, however, categorically defines 'motor omnibus' as 'any stage carriage moved by mechanical power contained in or carried along with such carriage', which would seem to exclude the trolleybus, which is not a prime mover but takes its power from an outside source (namely the power station via the overhead wires). Perhaps the Corporation were contemplating a battery-electric vehicle, for such 'buses did run in the early years of the century. In London during 1907, for example, an open-top double-deck battery 'bus was put into service by the London Electrobus Co. Ltd., operating on a route between Victoria and Liverpool Street Stations via Whitehall and Fleet Street. The Company also owned a charging and power station.

One mention which the trolleybus did receive in Council was on 10th December 1919 during the debate on the Newcastle úpon Tyne Corporation Bill, 1920, Part VI of which related to motorbuses. Alderman Weidner asked whether the Council had thought of taking powers to run trackless trolley cars, as the London County Council had done. The Sheriff replied that powers were held to run horse or mechanical cars and the question of trackless cars had been gone into carefully before, but they 'had come to the conclusion it was not advisable to adopt them—experience had shown they were wise in this decision!' (?). The Town Clerk further stated that it was too late at this stage to include such powers in the proposed Bill.

Motorbus operation had commenced in 1912 on a route which ran to Westerhope, then only a mining village north-north-west of the centre of Newcastle. Mr. G. S. Hearse, author of '*Tramways of Northumberland*',states that almost all the early motorbuses were Tilling-Stevens or Straker-Squire petrol-electric vehicles. One (registered BB 585) is illustrated in his book. In 1919, a Sentinel steam wagon fitted with seats and towing a trailer, was working a service to Burradon, another mining village to the north-east of Newcastle.

By 1925, there were five motorbus services run by the Corporation, to Branch End, Belsay, Gosforth, Hexham and Seaton Sluice. Belsay and Seaton Sluice are fifteen and ten miles respectively from the centre of Newcastle, and Hexham is no less than twenty miles away. By this time, the motorbus services were known officially as the Blue Bus Services. The original livery of saxe blue was changed to one of dark blue in 1929 and this was retained until 1949 when they and the trolleybuses, which when introduced were in a yellow, white and chocolate livery, were all repainted into a new standardised livery of cadmium or chrome yellow, cream and maroon. The latter is still used as it was perpetuated by the Tyne & Wear Passenger Transport Executive, and is, indeed, to be extended to Company vehicles operating within the area. The 1949 change of motorbus livery from blue to yellow, incidentally, it was greeted with dismay by members of the travelling public. It was thought that intending passengers waiting at stops would be confused, it being suggested that it would be difficult to tell if it were a

*Authors' bold

trolleybus or motorbus which was approaching since both were now the same colour! Even today, seemingly colourblind older citizens still refer to Corporation motorbuses as 'Blue Buses'.

The position regarding the motorbus routes had changed by 1930 for great housing expansion had taken place. Areas of the City suburbs out of the reach of the trams were being served by motorbuses. By this date, far from being regarded as feeders to the trams, the motorbus services had become an important part of the undertaking in their own right.

The trams had remained a major part of the Corporation's transport fleet right through the nineteen-twenties although there was mounting criticism of them. In 1928, a great deal of controversy had centred round the decision to lay tracks over the New Tyne Bridge. This would form a second link with the Gateshead and District Tramways Company's system and the alternative route it would provide was essential to relieve the severe loadings on the High Level Bridge which had over 100 tramcars an hour passing over it at this time. The New Tyne Bridge, as well as giving employment to many men in a time of great economic depression, was envisaged as relieving the traffic problems of the central areas of Newcastle and Gateshead. It is not surprising, therefore, that the motoring organisations were vociferous in their protests against the operation of trams over the new bridge, arguing that the idea of the bridge was to relieve traffic congestion, and running trams over it would only add to this, not relieve it.

Many trams were thirty years old and looked shabby when compared with the then rival motorbuses running into the City. In fairness, it must be stated that new B Class tramcars were delivered as late as 1926 and the C Class bogie single-deckers had been rebuilt once, being modernised again in 1932. The B Class trams were fully enclosed, being known as 'Glasshouses', and were relatively up-to-date at the time. The necessity for large-scale track renewal on many routes was approaching, however, and the City Council was seemingly unwilling to commit itself to more heavy expenditure on tramway equipment. It was stated at the March 1932 meeting of the Council that since 1918 no less than £686,000 had been spent on the renewal of tramway plant and equipment. Previously, in 1930, the Council had adopted a policy that 'in every case when the permanent way of a tram route becomes worn out, and must be renewed if a tram service is to be continued, careful consideration must be given to . . . whether the route could be more efficiently served by a form of transport other than trams.' This, then, was the death-knell of the tramway system, although it was to be twenty years before the last Corporation car ran.

Trolleybuses were first considered as tramway replacement vehicles in 1931. In October of that year the Transport and Electricity Committee presented a report to the Council entitled 'Report of the Committee as to the Substitution of Omnibuses for Tramcars on the Osborne Road Route'. It set out the following points:—

1. It is Council policy to substitute for trams if the track is worn out. The track is very bad.

2. In this case it is considered too expensive to renew the track. (Authors' Note: £15,489 was the figure quoted). The Committee had investigated the merits of both motorbuses and trolleybuses very thoroughly, and from all points of view. They came to the conclusion

that motorbuses were better on the following counts:

(a) If trams were removed and motorbuses introduced the route would be able to be extended northwards to serve new estates in the Matthew Bank area comparatively cheaply.

(b) On the other hand, if trolleybuses were to be introduced, expensive capital expenditure would be incurred in the erection of overhead and in obtaining Parliamentary powers in order to carry out the extension.

3. The conversion would require ten motorbuses at a cost of £1,800 each. If the substitution were not successful the motorbuses could still be used on other routes in the City. If, however, trolleybuses were used and the conversion was unsuccessful, the vehicles could NOT be used elsewhere in the City.

(Authors' Note: This decision was reached even after the Chairman, Vice-Chairman, and General Manager had visited trolleybus systems already in operation.)

4. The Committee, therefore, recommends the substitution of motorbuses for tramcars and the extension of the service to Matthew Bank.

This was not the end of the matter. At the Council meeting of 12th December 1931, a Councillor Oates argued that the City's tramways ought to be modernised not abandoned. Needless to say, his protestations fell on deaf ears, but a long debate at that meeting having reached no conclusion, it was finally decided at the Council meeting held on 16th December 1931 that the trams would not be swept away in favour of motorbuses after all, but that the track would be patched up in the interim. At the latter meeting, it was stated that the residents had protested strongly over the proposals to remove their trams. There had also been many letters in the local press on the general subject of trams versus motorbuses. During the debates at both the December Council meetings there was no mention of trolleybuses — all was on the subject of trams and motorbuses, although Mr. G. S. Hearse states in *'Tramways of Northumberland'*, that the Osborne Road trams continued 'pending the consideration of the introduction of trolleybuses at a later date'. It is now known that legal complications arising from the original tramway powers made it impossible to apply for a Provisional Order for trolleybuses, and the cost of applying for a unique Act would have been prohibitive.

CHAPTER TWO

THE TROLLEYBUSES ARE ESTABLISHED

It was another three years before the Corporation Transport again considered trolleybuses, or at least made any firm move towards their adoption. In May 1934, the Transport and Electricity Committee presented another report to the City Council regarding a tramway conversion. This time, however, trolleybuses received more favourable attention.

The report, which was entitled "The Report of the Committee as to Proposals for the Establishment of a Trackless Trolley System on the Wallsend to Westgate Road Tram Route", set out the following points:—

1. It is the policy of the Transport and Electricity Committee, approved by the Council in 1930, that 'in every case when the permanent way of a tram route becomes worn out and must be renewed if a tram service is to be continued . . . careful consideration must be given to . . . whether the route could be more efficiently served by a form of transport other than trams'.

    (Authors' Note: The City Engineer, not the Transport Department, was responsible in Newcastle for maintaining the tram tracks and reported that the cost of complete renewal of the track from Condercum Road at the western end of the route, eastwards via City Road to the City Boundary at Walker (i.e. virtually the whole route) would cost £90,288. This would give an expected life of 20 years. He added that only the track in the east end of the City, in City Road and Walker Road needed replacing. Possibly the reason for quoting the cost of renewing all the track was to lend more weight to the case for abandonment of the trams on this route.)

2. The annual revenue surplus for various types of transport was estimated as follows:—

    (a) Surplus for the existing tram route Condercum Road-Wallsend (with track renewal), together with the existing motorbus service Denton Burn-Cowen's Monument   £6,124
    (b) Surplus for a substitute service Denton Burn-Wallsend of petrol-engined motor omnibuses (Requiring 33 vehicles)   £7,849
    (c) Surplus for a substitute service Denton Burn-Wallsend of heavy oil-engined motor omnibuses (Requiring 33 vehicles)   £7,690
    (d) Surplus for the route using trackless trolleys (Requiring 29 vehicles — 27 service, 2 spare)   £14,813

    (Authors' Note: The Committee recommended the substitution of trackless trolleys. In passing it is interesting to note that the surplus for diesel 'buses was estimated as being less than that for petrol vehicles.)

3. It has been ascertained that no general Act of Parliament is likely to be passed in the present Session, so it would be easy to obtain a Local Act for trolleybus powers.

This report was presented at the Council Meeting on 2nd May 1934, and the debate on the proposal followed at the Meeting held on 8th May 1934.

Before dealing with this debate, it is necessary to trace the history of the mixed tram and motorbus service which was operating on the Wallsend-Westgate Road service at the time. Dealing first with the tram route, double track had been laid up Westgate Road at the start of electric operation in the City, and it terminated on the West Road at its junction with Condercum Road, about half a mile past Wingrove Depot. In the early nineteen-hundreds this was the practical end of the continuously built-up area of the City, at least on the south side of the West Road — on the north side Wingrove Depot was almost the last building before the fields began! After the 1914-18 War, the urban sprawl continued and the line was extended, though only as single track with passing loops, a further half mile to *Fox & Hounds* opening to traffic on 30th January 1925. The new terminus was known initially as *Fox & Hounds* but later it was renamed West Road. In spite of the extension, most trams still terminated at Condercum Road and only certain cars continued to *Fox & Hounds*

Originally, the Westgate Road route was given service number 4 but by 1925 it consisted of the following route numbers and services:—

21 Westgate Road—St. John's Church or Central Station (peak hours only)
22 *Fox & Hounds*—Grainger Street—Pilgrim Street (peak hours only)
23 Westgate Road—City Road—Walker (Church Street)
24 Westgate Road—City Road—Wallsend

By 1930, competing private enterprise motorbuses had begun running into the City from points west, and the General Manager's report for the year ending 31st March 1930 stated that the tram service from Condercum Road to *Fox & Hounds* had, in fact, been withdrawn during the course of the year, as had the service from Two Ball Lonnen (Fenham) to Westerhope, (1¼ miles), and that 'in each case a motorbus service has been substituted.'

The same annual report makes the comment that a new motorbus service from Denton Burn to Haymarket had been introduced on 3rd June 1929. This was presumably the replacement for the *Fox & Hounds* tram service. The western part of the route which this motorbus service covered is known. Beginning in Slatyford Lane, which is on the north side of the West Road, approximately half way between Denton Square and Denton Burn roundabout, it ran along the West Road a short distance eastwards and turned right into Denton Road and followed the subsequent trolleybus route along Whickham View and Ferguson's Lane (alternate 'buses travelling via Pendower, possibly along Pease Avenue, thus forming a 'circle' route in Benwell) to the *Fox & Hounds* and thence travelled eastwards along the West Road and Westgate Road into the City centre. On 7th October 1929, the service was altered to run Denton Burn—Denton Bank—Haymarket. Due to vociferous protests by passengers, this modification lasted only one day. It then reverted to operating via Ferguson's Lane and Old Benwell. The westward extension beyond the tram terminus was to serve new housing estates which had sprung up in the West Benwell and Denton areas. The new service became motorbus service number 2, and is presumably the one referred to in the Transport and Electricity Committee's report of 1934 as 'Denton Burn to Cowen's Monument'. The General Manager's annual report for the year ending 31st March 1936 noted that motorbus revenue for the year had fallen by £7,353 due

17

to the discontinuation of the Denton Burn route and the introduction of trolley-buses.

In the east end, Walker was served by the following tram routes by 1934:—

41 Walker (Church Street)—Byker Bridge—Wrekenton (operated jointly with Gateshead)

42 Walker (Church Street)—Byker Bridge—Pilgrim Street (Rush-hours only)

43 Walker—Welbeck Road—Byker Bridge—Wrekenton (operated jointly with Gateshead)

44 Walker—Welbeck Road—Byker Bridge—Pilgrim Street (Rush-hours only)

Returning to the debate on the proposed introduction of trolleybuses which took place at the Council Meeting of 8th May 1934, the Council was told that there had been a vast improvement in the design of trolleybuses in the last three years (an illusion to the decision on the Osborne Road route?), and photographs of modern trolleybuses were displayed in the Council Chamber. The great advantage of trolleybuses, it was claimed, was that they ran on home produced fuel 'generated at our own power station' and soon to be generated by the new Central Electricity Generating Board, which had undertaken that it would supply electricity over the next ten years at a price somewhat less than that at which Newcastle was able to manufacture it. (History has proved that this hope of cheap current was not to be, and it was later one of the major reasons for the demise of the trolleybus). Increased revenue from trolleybuses was almost assured, the Council were told, for in those towns where trolleybuses had been introduced, earnings had risen on average by 10 per cent. It was considered easier to retrain tram drivers for electric trolleybuses than for motorbuses (this statement being greeted with applause by Councillors) and, finally, unlike motorbuses, there were no fumes and little vibration from trolleybuses.

Not all Councillors were in favour of trolleybuses. A Councillor Percival disputed the wisdom of substituting trolleybuses. He said that oil engine 'buses were the coming thing (prophetic words indeed!), and he produced figures to support his contention. Whereas, he argued, in 1929-30 twenty authorities ran trolleybuses and twenty-two in 1932-3, no less than fifty-four ran diesel 'buses as against only eleven in 1931. He quoted Mr. Pilcher, General Manager of Manchester, who said that diesels were as cheap to run as petrol 'buses, and also quoted figures from 'Commercial Motor' which reported, in its issue of 9th February 1933, that trolleybuses were 3d. per mile dearer to operate than petrol 'buses and that the latter were in turn 1d. a mile dearer to run than diesels.

It was stressed to the Council, however, that it was essential to give consent to apply for Parliamentary powers to run trolleybuses immediately, so that the opportunity to exploit the slack period at Westminster would not be lost. The debate, therefore, continued to discuss trolleybuses. The Council was informed that such vehicles were available with capacities from 54 to 72 seats, and that the estimated cost of the twenty-nine 60-seat trolleybuses which the Undertaking proposed to purchase would be £58,000. The total cost of conversion was estimated at £73,400. The motion to adopt trolleybuses was put to the vote, and was carried.

The decision had been taken. It was now a matter of implementation. The trolleybus Bill was presented to Parliament and received Royal Assent by July 1934, becoming The Newcastle upon Tyne Corporation Act, 1934, as set out below. In setting out the official trolleybus powers in this book it is not intended

18

to reproduce the exact legal language, but merely to give the essential spirit of the text. Nor is it the intention fully to enumerate the whole provision of a particular Act or Provisional Order, but only the official routes over which the Corporation was empowered to work trolley vehicles. Such clauses which refer to protection of the Postmaster General, his power to use the traction poles for telegraph lines, the protection of the various local gas and electricity undertakings, the Corporation's rights to widen the roads over which trolleybuses ran, with the consequent reduction of the pavements, are not mentioned in detail.

The Newcastle upon Tyne Corporation Act, 1934, authorised the following routes to be constructed:—

Route 1: (7 miles 6 furlongs 3 chains). Commencing in the Borough of Wallsend, in Park Road at its junction with High Street and passing along Park Road, into, and along, Hadrian Road, Buddle Street, and Neptune Road, into and along the following streets in the City:—Neptune Road, Fisher Street, White Street, Station Road, Walker Road, Glasshouse Bridge, City Road, Pilgrim Street, Mosley Street, St. Nicholas Square, Collingwood Street, Westgate Road, and West Road to the boundary between the City and Newburn U.D.C. as at 1st June 1934.

Route 2: (1 furlong 2 chains). Wholly in the City, commencing in Collingwood Street at its junction with St. Nicholas Street, passing along St. Nicholas Street, and Westgate Road into and terminating in Collingwood Street at its junction with Westgate Road.

Route 3: (1 mile 3 furlongs 3 chains.) Commencing in West Road at a point 150 yards eastwards of the said City boundary, and passing into and along Denton Road, Whickham View, Ferguson's Lane, Tower View, and Fox-and-Hounds Lane, and terminating in West Road at the junction with Fox-and-Hounds Lane.

Also authorised were turning points, and connecting and depot links.

At Wallsend, the terminus could have been constructed at the junction of Hadrian Road and Park Road, or up to 100ft. north of Vine Street. In fact, in due course, a reverser was erected at Vine Street.

Many of these provisions were repeated in the Newcastle upon Tyne Corporation (General Powers) Act, 1935, which also gave powers to the Corporation to operate trolleybuses over all tram routes, inside or outside the City— in the latter case with the consent of the relevant local authority.

All of the proposed routes in the 1934 Act were implemented, unlike those in later acts and Provisional Orders. An interesting point was made at the August 1934 Council Meeting when a Councillor Graham said the City did well to rid itself of the burden of maintaining tram track, and that trolleybuses with pneumatic tyres could not possibly do the damage that trams with heavy wheels running over iron (sic) rails had. This was counteracted in November 1937 by the City Council granting a sum of £24,658 to remove tracks in Walker and Spital Tongues to include £10,936 to repair 'the flanks of the road' on trolleybus routes. The trolleybuses had pounded the shoulders to pieces!

At their Meeting on 19th December 1934 the Council considered tenders which had been submitted for the supply of the new electric vehicles. The Transport and Electricity Committee informed the Council that eight manufacturers

19

had tendered for the supply of chassis (an indication of the variety of makes available at the time) and nine for the bodywork. The tenders had asked for 30 vehicles, not 29 as earlier envisaged. As a result, orders for chassis were placed as follows:—

a) Ten AEC 664T type chassis with English Electric control equipment, suitable for double-deck bodies £12,110

b) Ten Karrier E6A type chassis with Metrovick control equipment suitable for double-deck bodies £12,215

c) Ten Guy BTX type chassis with Guy-Stevens patent control equipment, suitable for double-deck bodies   ...   £12,315

Based on the tenders for bodywork to be fitted to three-axle chassis the following orders were placed:—

a) Twenty Metro-Cammell all-metal, 60-seat double-deck bodies £19,760

b) Five Brush all-metal, 60-seat double-deck bodies   £4,990

c) Five English Electric all-metal, 60-seat double-deck bodies £4,990

The cost of thirty trolleybuses now totalled £66,380 and the cost of the whole conversion was revised to £93,000. The electrical control equipment quoted for with the Guy BTX chassis is worthy of note in that the vehicles were not delivered as specified, but were built with B.T-H. equipment.

The reason for the choice of three different manufacturers of chassis was apparently the desire to evaluate various types before deciding on a standard type of trolleybus.

Fleet numbers 10-39 were allocated and the vehicles were registered BVK800-829 respectively. Apparently, the reason for starting fleet numbering at 10 and not 1 was due to the desire to coincide last digits of fleet numbers with those of registration numbers, a desire which only came to light after the batch of registration numbers had been allocated. Of the ten A.E.C. 664T's five (10-14) were fitted with English Electric bodies and five (15-19) with Brush bodies. The ten Karrier E6A's (20-29) and the ten Guy BTX's (30-39) shared the twenty Metro-Cammell bodies between them. Metro-Cammell later supplied the bulk of the bodies for the prewar trolleybus fleet—89 out of 113 vehicles—whilst the Brush and English Electric bodies were to remain unique in the ranks of Newcastle's trolleybuses. The only other bodywork manufacturer given anything like large orders in prewar days was Chas. H. Roe Ltd.

The initial thirty vehicles were of the rear-entrance and front-exit arrangement, as were all subsequent prewar trolleybus deliveries in order to be similar to the extensive front-exit tram fleet.

Having ordered the rolling stock the Corporation also sought tenders to convert existing tramway overhead for trolleybus operation, and in February 1935 a tender of £19,625 was accepted from Clough-Smith Ltd., of Westminster, to convert the 7½ miles of existing tramway overhead equipment and to erect new overhead for approximately 2 miles over the Denton Loop. The firm had some considerable experience in tram-to-trolleybus conversions including, locally, that at Darlington in 1927. On 8th April, 1935, work began on the conversion of the overhead.

A week earlier, on 1st April, the Manors Power Station became worked directly by the Central Electricity Generating Board and the responsibility for the generation of electricity was thereby removed from the Corporation.

As it was considered one of the economies of the trolleybus substitution, existing tram standards were utilized as far as possible. From Wallsend terminus westwards to Brighton Grove junction on Westgate Road, and generally on all roads between 26ft. and 37ft. 6ins. in width, gantry cross tubes approximately 3ins. in diameter were used to join the existing tram poles across the width of the road. Gantry construction was a Clough-Smith speciality. It was often adopted so that poles originally designed to support only two running wires as used on tramways could cope with the stresses imposed by four or six wires as used by trolleybuses without risk of distortion. In Newcastle this method enabled no fewer than 500 tramway standards to be reused. All reused tram poles were filled with concrete in which steel rod reinforcement was suspended, and each pole undergoing this treatment received a 'B' prefix to its number. In roads exceeding 37ft. 6ins. wide, such as the West Road beyond Brighton Grove, bracket arms were employed. Past Condercum Road tram terminus the single track section of tramway had only required standards with bracket arms on the south side of the road, so new poles were erected along the north kerb, with bracket arms to support the eastbound trolleybus wiring. In streets under 26ft. wide, for example Fox-and-Hounds Lane (13-15ft.) and Whickham View (20-22ft.), double bracket arms up to 16ft. long were used on one set of poles. In Fox-and-Hounds Lane the poles were mounted on the west kerb, and in Whickham View, on the south kerb, eastwards from Thorntree Drive.

New traction poles were to B.S. 8 of June 1931 and were (depending on location) 31, 33, or 35 feet long having a steel sleeve 2ft. in length and $\frac{3}{8}''$ thick, shrunk on to counteract oxidisation below ground and projected 1ft. above the pavement. The tram poles were painted in the customary green, but on the Denton Loop extension the standards were smartly finished in aluminium, with finials and a section 2ft. above the ground painted black. Clough-Smith Ltd. used standard round-section tramway wire on their contract but on later extensions, which were executed direct by Newcastle Transport overhead gangs, running wire was grooved and known as Portsmouth section (viz. a figure of 8 with a large lower section), which became adopted by virtually all British trolleybus operators in an attempt to reduce trolley wheel noise and radio interference. In later extensions erected by direct labour all fittings were stamped 'NCT' from the undertaking's own foundry in Byker Depot. In 1949 the Corporation converted to 'MTA' standard overhead. At several points in the City centre it was necessary to support the overhead with rosettes either for aesthetic or engineering reasons. Examples (mostly inherited from the trams) were Collingwood Street, and later, Blackett Street and the plinth of the Earl Grey Monument. Many of these rosettes still remain with cut-off ends of span wires still attached. All trolleybus overhead was triple insulated, an additional insulator being fitted between the traction wires, which were spaced at 21 inch gauge.

During the initial 1935 conversion Clough-Smith Ltd.'s gangs generally erected the new trolleybus wires about a foot above the tram wires so that the latter could be simply cut down on conversion day. The task of conversion was facilitated by the fact that it was possible to use spare underground feeder cable conduits laid in 1900 for the electrification of the tramways.

21

Work on the overhead progressed steadily throughout the spring and summer of 1935 and had advanced sufficiently for Clough-Smith Ltd. to deliver a trolleybus for driver training in June 1935. Regrettably nothing is known of the identity of this vehicle at all. Clough-Smith Ltd. may have supplied it specially for the Newcastle contract, or possibly it was one the firm kept for testing installations. Any information from readers would be most welcome. (In point of fact there are four chassis numbers in the Karrier E6 '54 series' sanction which have not been traced—54019 and 54029 -31. At the time these vehicles would have been constructed (1930/31), Karrier and Clough-Smith Ltd. were marketing trolleybuses jointly but the association ceased about 1932).

A temporary set-back in the early summer which was witnessed by Mr. D. Hanson, father of one of the authors, was the demolition of a brand-new traction pole on Denton Bank by a runaway traction engine and trailer which overturned after brushing the pole aside.

This slight mishap did not, of course, prevent the first trial run over the wiring then ready (which was about half the route length) on 31st July 1935.

The first of the new trolleybuses to be delivered was 15, an AEC 664T with Brush body, which arrived on the 24th July 1935. One of the new vehicles on a test run made front page news in the 'Evening Chronicle' for Monday 9th September 1935, when a photograph showed it surrounded by a large crowd with booms lowered 'after a mishap' in Westgate Road.

Huddersfield and Wolverhampton Corporation Transport Departments both sent teams to assist Newcastle in these early, inexperienced days. The first test run over the complete system took place on 17th September 1935. The Corporation were then confident enough to invite a Ministry of Transport inspection, which took place on 23rd and 24th September; the Inspecting Officer being satisfied, the system opened on 1st October 1935.

The following speed limits and instructions were imposed as to the working of the route:—

Speed Limits:

Denton Burn to Wallsend Route

Speed (mph)	Section
25	Denton Bank and West Road between Grange Road and Denton terminus.
15	Westgate Road between Elswick Road and Blenheim Street (Westgate Hill) on downhill journey. Also Westgate Road between Blenheim Street and Tramway Offices, Manors.
10	Descending Fisher Hill (in Walker), and when traversing the turning loop Westgate Road—St. Nicholas Street—Collingwood Street.
5	Under all overhead junctions, at all turning points, at any right-angled turn of intersecting streets, under all railway bridges, and in City Road opposite Keelmans' Hospital (on west-bound journeys).
20	All other places.

Compulsory Stops:

1) Before entering Carville Boundary bridge (on Walker Road).
2) Foot of Westgate Hill, at Blenheim Street junction, descending.

Terminal Movements:

Wallsend:
From City; Passengers to alight in Park Road before the 'bus turns into Vine Street to reverse.
To City; After reversing, 'bus to stand to the north of Vine Street.
Conductors must take up position to the rear when the 'bus is being reversed out of Vine Street into Park Road. (*The terminal point at Wallsend Park Road was altered in later years, as can be seen from the wiring diagram, because reversing out into Park Road became too dangerous in view of increased traffic.*)

Wallsend: Park Road Bridge;
'Buses must be driven through the bridge in the centre of the road, and must not be driven through when another vehicle is passing. In the case of two 'buses approaching, the 'bus proceeding to the City has preference.

Carville Boundary Bridge:
'Buses must not be driven through the bridge while another vehicle is approaching. 'Buses to the City have precedence.

Denton Bank reversing loop:
From City; Before crossing the road to the reversing loop, the conductor must stand in the roadway at the offside of the driver's cab to give warning of, or to, approaching traffic.

Fox-and-Hounds Lane:
'Buses must not pass each other in Fox-and-Hounds Lane until such time as the road is widened. (*The widening of this road is still awaited!*) 'Buses from the City have precedence.

Fox-and-Hounds Reverser, Westgate Road; (*A mistake—actually West Road at this point*).
When about to cross the road to the reverser, conductors must stand on the roadway at the offside of the driver's cab to give warning of, or to, approaching traffic.
Conductors must take up position at the rear when the 'bus is being reversed out of Fox-and-Hounds reverser.

Most of the speed limits were liberally interpreted in the later years!

As can be seen from the Ministry of Transport Regulations, intermediate turning points were provided. From west to east they were as follows:—

a)   The north-west corner of the Denton Loop at the junction of the West Road and Silver Lonnen, where a reverser was provided which could be used by trolleybuses travelling west down Denton Bank from the City. (Referred to as 'Denton Bank Reversing Loop' in the regulations and shown as 'Denton Burn Boundary' on the original destination indicator blinds.) On the building of the extension to Denton Square in 1938, this reverser appears to have been dismantled.

b) A reverser was also provided at the *Fox & Hounds* in Fox-and-Hounds Road so set out that vehicles from the City turned right into that road and then reversed onto the West Road. It directly replaced the tram terminal point at *Fox & Hounds*.

c) In the central area of the City, St. Nicholas' Cathedral loop enabled short-workings from both the east and the west ends to be turned at peak hours.

d) In the City's east end there was a turning circle at the foot of the Church Street, Walker, though this was used all day.

The thirty trolleybuses were stabled at Wingrove Depot, (Wingrove Sheds as they were more usually known), where they occupied the three 'roads' of one of the two bays in the Depot. Initially the three 'roads' in the other bay continued to be occupied by the Elswick Road trams. Continually increasing traffic on the new Westgate Road trolleybus route, however, caused progressively more trolleybuses to be required. By 1938, no fewer than forty-two trolleybuses were using Wingrove Depot, leaving the trams only a track and a half! The Elswick Road trams, incidentally, shared positive traction wires with the trolleybuses up Westgate Hill (i.e. those nearest the centre of the road).

As befitted the inauguration of a completely new form of public transport in the City, the trolleybuses were afforded a Civic Opening Ceremony as had occurred at the opening of electric tramways at the turn of the century.

On the morning of Tuesday 1st October 1935, six of the sparkling new trolleybuses, led by Brush-bodied AEC 664T No. 19 (BVK 809) carrying 'RESERVED' on its blinds, stood at the western end of the route, ready to carry the official party consisting of 230 persons headed by the Lord Mayor, Councillor Dalgliesh, and the Chairman of the Transport and Electricity Committee, Alderman Mayne. In addition to City Councillors, the party included members of other local councils, representatives of the local omnibus and tram companies, and the various contractors connected with the installation, as well as the Press.

After the short opening ceremony, when Mrs. Mayne, wife of the Chairman, purchased the first ticket, the six trolleybuses set off for the eastern terminus at Park Road, Wallsend. As the *Newcastle Journal* reported the next day, 'the trams (were) still running on the route so the trolleybuses proceeded at a low speed'. Besides this obvious reason for their cautious progress, a more compelling one was no doubt the drain on the electricity supply due to six vehicles travelling on one section together. At the boundary between the City and Wallsend, the Mayor of the latter Borough joined the party and the trolleybuses then continued over the last three-quarters of a mile to Park Road terminus. Six trolleybuses turning consecutively on the reverser must have been an imposing sight!

On returning to the centre of Newcastle, lunch was held at the Old Assembly Rooms and in speeches delivered at this function, Councillors were in full praise for the City's new trolleybus system. Later in the day, dinner was held at the Royal Station Hotel.

Unfortunately, the rosy glow of civic pride was to some extent dispelled by the events of the next day, Wednesday, 2nd October. This was the first day of normal full public service and chaos reigned. The *Newcastle Journal* for 3rd October 1935 reported that dislocation of service had occurred 'owing to minor

24

Newcastle Transport's solitary AEC Q-type motorbus (156), delivered in 1933, is pictured here at Byker Depot. Its folding front doors were instrumental in the adoption of such on the City's trolleybus fleet in 1935.   R. C. Davis collection

No. 13, one of five English Electric-bodied AEC 664Ts in the inaugural fleet, basks in the sun at *Fox & Hounds* during the summer of 1936. The reverser is to the right and the tram track is still in place. Note also the silver-painted traction poles carrying an early type of street lighting and the United motorbus topping Denton Bank. The dial of the tramway time-clock can just be discerned above the head of the bystander on the right.

Mrs. E. T. Knowles

25

Five of the initial Guy BTX trolleybuses with Metro-Cammell bodywork lined up for the official photographer at Stephenson's Monument, Westgate Road. The separate front exit door was a feature of the pre-war trolleybus fleet.
Tyne & Wear P.T.E.

A spot of bother outside the Odeon, Pilgrim Street, with a broken wire causing delay to five trolleybuses—Guy BTX No. 330 heads the line-up. The view dates from 1948 and as 330 is without blinds, it is possible that she is being transferred between depots. Behind is another BTX in post-war livery, followed by two new 1948 BUT 9641Ts and a wartime Karrier utility in post-war livery.

G. S. Hearse

Seats on top! The general arrangement on the upper-deck of Metro-Cammell-bodied Karrier E6A No. 25, looking forward. The seats were upholstered in blue leather and the woodwork grained and varnished. The front staircase provided direct access to the front exit doors.

R. C. Davis collection, courtesy M.C.C.W.

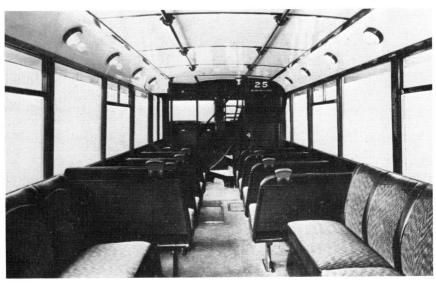

Room inside! The lower-deck of No. 25, again looking forward. Lower-deck seating was upholstered in blue jazz-pattern moquette. Note the fixed ceiling grab-rails for standing passengers and the prominent fleet-number on the front staircase bulkhead.

R. C. Davis collection, courtesy M.C.C.W.

No. 25, at the St. Nicholas sub-terminus of service 4B in prewar days. It features a Metro-Cammell 60-seat body on a Karrier E6A chassis. The Castle Keep towers behind it.

R. C. Davis collection

A prewar scene at the foot of Raby Street on Walker Road, Byker, which was the terminus of tram service 15. G-class tram 185 prepares to depart and will turn left opposite the telephone kiosk into Raby Street on its journey to Westmorland Road, while trolleybus No. 69 waits for it to clear the westbound trolleybus wires.

W. A. Camwell

Learner driver duty for No. 16, an AEC 664T with Brush body, on Denton Bank, West Road. A pre-1939 view.

A. Townsin collection

Another view on Denton Bank, shows No. 15, an AEC 664T with Brush body and No. 20, a Karrier E6A with Metro-Cammell body. The year is 1935 and the scene specially posed for the official photographer.   Tyne & Wear P.T.E.

No. 332 (ex. 32) in prewar livery, as modified during the war, about to turn from Percy Street into Haymarket Depot, followed by a Strachans utility-bodied Guy "Arab" "Blue Bus" and a United Automobile Services Leyland "Titan". about 1947.

Tyne & Wear P.T.E.

A 1948 view of Metro-Cammell bodied No. 372 passing Stephenson's Monument, Westgate Road, bound for Denton Square on route 34B, shows the final livery applied to prewar stock.

C. Carter

Passengers hurry to board No. 13 westbound in Station Road, Walker. This prewar view features one of the five AEC 664Ts of the original fleet with English Electric bodies.

A. Townsin collection

Fenham (Two Ball Lonnen) terminus on 31st July, 1938, showing G-class tram No. 186 on the last day of tram operation on service 31; the Saturday-only service which extended to Westerhope had ceased the previous day. Note the tram taking current from the trolley-bus overhead (erected for the opening of trolleybus service 6 on the next day); the trolley-bus reverser can be discerned in the background. W. A. Camwell

A very interesting view of No. 73 in Barrack Road in 1937, possibly just before the Stanhope Street route commenced operation. This vehicle appears to be in blue livery and any information from readers would be welcome. Tram track and overhead are in evidence; also, on the left can be seen the St. James' Park loop with side gantries erected prior to receiving the running wire.   Mrs. M. Swart

No. 13 stands gleaming in the yard at the English Electric factory before delivery to Newcastle in 1935. It has an AEC 664T chassis.   GEC Traction

faults and delays', when 'the service came into full operation for the first time'. Hundreds of intending passengers were kept waiting on the West Road and Westgate Road. Many gave up waiting and walked into the City, giving rise, the newspaper commented, to scenes similar to those seen during the General Strike nine years before. By evening, schedules were running 20-30 minutes late and vehicles were running in batches of two or three. Alderman Mayne was quoted as saying 'give drivers and trollybuses (sic) time to settle down'. An old employee once said that the inaugural trolleybus stock was underpowered. 80 h.p. motors were fitted and this may have been a major factor in slow running, although drivers would be understandably cautious during the first week or so. In point of fact, timetables were erratic, especially at noon and at about 5 p.m., due to nervous drivers being slow and also to frequent dewirements, which were put down originally to bad driving but subsequently found to be due to faulty overhead. Early comments from the passengers on the vehicles themselves spoke of the comfort and silence of the trolleybuses after the motorbuses and, especially, the trams.

The new trolleybus services were as follows:—
DENTON BURN BOUNDARY (4B) (having turned via Denton Loop consisting of Denton Road, Whickham View, Ferguson's Lane, Tower View, and Fox-and-Hounds Lane or reverse)—West Road—FOX-&-HOUNDS (4) (4A) (4C) (reverser)—West Road—Westgate Road—Collingwood Street—St. Nicholas Square—ST. NICHOLAS CATHEDRAL (turning via loop Collingwood Street—St. Nicholas Street—Westgate Road (4B) (4C) (4D))—Mosley Street — Pilgrim Street — City Road — Glasshouse Bridge—Walker Road to WALKER (CHURCH STREET) (foot of) (turning circle) (4A) (4D) OR via Station Road—White Street—Fisher Street—Neptune Road—Buddle Street—Hadrian Road—WALLSEND PARK ROAD (Vine Street) (reverser) (4) (4D) and return.
4, 4A, 4B operated daily and 4C, 4D operated Monday-Friday peak hours only.
It is believed that the last trams on the routes to be replaced had run on 1st October 1935 as follows:

21 Westgate Road—St. John's Church or Central Station (Rush-hours only).
22 *Fox & Hounds*—Grainger Street—Pilgrim Street (Rush-hours only)
23 Westgate Road—City Road—Walker (Church Street)
24 Westgate Road—City Road—Wallsend
42 Walker (Church Street)—Byker Bridge—Pilgrim Street (Rush-hours only).

At the same time the Walker section only of tram service 41 (Walker (Church Street)—Byker Bridge—Wrekenton), operated jointly with Gateshead and District Tramways Company, was abandoned, and the jointly-operated service 43 was cut back to Welbeck Road.
A mile of double track from the Big Lamp to Wingrove Sheds had to be maintained for another nine years to give Elswick Road trams access to the depot. These gained the Elswick Road tracks by using a single connecting curve at the top of Westgate Hill (the Big Lamp), leading from the inward line on Westgate Road to the inward line on Elswick Road, each end of which was approached by

a trailing crossover to give access to the outward tracks. This curve was also used for storing temporarily disabled trams. The trolleybuses had no similar wiring provision here and would have had to be shunted round from Elswick Road to Westgate Road if it was necessary to travel west up the latter road. In order to transfer trolleybuses from Wingrove depot to Byker Works for maintenance and repair they were invariably towed. There was no use of trailing skates in Newcastle.

Once drivers had become used to their new charges and had gained experience, the system settled down to normal working through the winter of 1935-36, although one handicap which became apparent very quickly was the lack of traction batteries. Accidents, mishaps, and traffic delays must have created great difficulties for the drivers if their trolleybuses had no means of negotiating these other than when on the overhead lines, and at the City Council Meeting of 9th November, 1935 authorisation was given to fit traction batteries to the existing fleet at a cost of £3,269 after the Transport and Electricity Committee had presented a report on the necessity of fitting such batteries. The Council also approved the fitting of traction batteries to all future trolleybuses.

The Council's optimism with regard to the increase in traffic which trolley-buses were expected to generate was more than fully justified. Indeed, the increase was positively embarrassing. Passenger loading increased by as much as 25 per cent and in January 1936 the Transport Undertaking was forced to apply to the Northern Traffic Commissioners for temporary licences to operate motorbuses at peak hours on the trolleybus routes. The licences were valid for six months only, just long enough to allow extra trolleybuses to be ordered and delivered.

An additional trolleybus was delivered on 21st December 1935—40(CVK 52), a Karrier E6A with a Metro-Cammell 60-seat body. No authorisation by the Council for this vehicle has been traced. The trolleybus fleet strength thus rose to thirty-one vehicles.

In April 1936, to cope with the acute peak-hour traffic, the Council authorised, on the recommendation of the Transport and Electricity Committee, the purchase of six additional trolleybuses—three Karrier E6As and three Guy BTXs, all six to be fitted with Metro-Cammell 60-seat dual-entrance bodies at a total cost of £15,365. The Corporation was told that both manufacturers were prepared to regard this purchase as an extension of the original contract, which presumably meant that there would be no price increase. It will be noticed that AEC were not asked to supply, possibly due to the difficulty in guaranteeing delivery dates, which were important since the motorbus licences were only valid for six months. The vehicles were duly delivered and entered service as 41-43 (Karrier E6A) and 44-46 (Guy BTX) in December 1936, and were registered DTN141-146.

CHAPTER THREE

PRE-WAR EXPANSION

Newcastle Corporation Transport Department was now committed to converting its tram routes to trolleybus operation and in September 1936 the next service to be converted was agreed. This was to be the Brighton Grove—Stanhope Street—Shields Road—Welbeck Road (Walker) tram route, again an east-west cross-city route. This ran from Brighton Grove, just off the Westgate Road, about a mile from the City centre, and passed along Stanhope Street, the main thoroughfare of the Arthur's Hill area and consisting mainly of late nineteenth-century terraced houses and little corner shops. It then emerged onto Barrack Road and passed alongside St. James' Park, the Newcastle United Football Club ground, and thence into the City centre via Gallowgate. The route then struck directly east through the central area, leaving it by New Bridge Street, into the east-end over Byker Bridge, and climbed up Shields Road, the shopping centre for this part of Newcastle. After half a mile or so the route swung right into Union Road, and shortly afterwards turned left into the long straight Welbeck Road which dropped steadily down to the River Tyne at Walker. The route terminated at a junction with the Westgate—Wallsend route at Fisher Street. Approximately a quarter of a mile before this, another line diverged down Church Street, the main street of the former Walker village, also to join the Wallsend route after half a mile.

The route had been worked by trams, but over the years there were changes both in the route numbering and the linkings of the east and west-end sections formerly terminating in the City centre. Surprisingly, it has been impossible to determine precise details as to the situation when trolleybuses replaced trams on these routes, though the following information can be given.

In 1925 the west-end routes had been worked by the following tram services:

25 Stanhope Street—Pilgrim Street (Saturdays only)

26 Stanhope Street—Heworth (Joint service with Gateshead and District Tramways Company—ceased well before 1937)

27 Stanhope Street—Byker Bridge—Wallsend (Rush-hours only)

Also in 1925, the following services were operating from the east-end:—

41 Walker (Church Street)—Byker Bridge—Wrekenton (Joint with Gateshead)

42 Walker (Church Street)—Byker Bridge—Pilgrim Street (Rush-hours only)

43 Walker—Welbeck Road—Byker Bridge—Wrekenton (Joint with Gateshead)

44 Walker—Welbeck Road—Byker Bridge—Pilgrim Street (Rush-hours only)

As already mentioned, joint services 41 and 43 were cut back to City and Welbeck Road respectively when the inaugural trolleybus route to Walker was introduced and service 42 was withdrawn.

Route 27 had been worked jointly with the Tyneside Tramways and Tram-roads Company, whose cars at one time reversed on Westgate Road after their journey up Stanhope Street, and indeed there is an old photograph in the Local History Collection of the City Libraries showing one performing this manoeuvre. As previously mentioned the Tyneside trams ceased to run in 1930 when the Company converted to motorbuses. The latter only ran into the centre of New-castle (to Croft Street), and not up into the west-end.

A Committee Report to the full Council still set out the relative costs of the conversion to the three forms of transport which could be substituted for trams, although it was obvious that trolleybuses were the expected substitute. The figures were as follows:—

(a) Surplus Revenue expected from working the route with trams £9,119
(b) Surplus Revenue from petrol 'buses (57-seats)   £3,151
(c) Surplus Revenue from 'heavy oil-engine' 'buses (57-seats)   £5,354
(d) Surplus Revenue from 'heavy oil-engine' 'buses (52-seats)   £6,193
(e) Surplus Revenue from trolleybuses (60-seats)   £9,046

The next section of the report immediately stated that the cost of twenty-five trolleybuses, the number deemed necessary, was estimated at £61,250, and the conversion of the overhead at £11,000. The Council approved the conversion of the route to trolleybus operation with little opposition.

The Provisional Order for the conversion of the Stanhope Street routes was confirmed on 25th March 1937 under the General Powers Act, 1935. It set out the following routes:—

Route 1: (2 furlongs 5.4 chains.) Commencing in Westgate Road at its junction with Brighton Grove and passing in a northerly direction, into and along Brighton Grove, thence along Crossley Terrace in an easterly direction into and along Dilston Road and in a westerly direction into and along Callerton Place, terminating in Brighton Grove at its junction with Callerton Place.

Route 2: (4 miles, 3 furlongs, 6.93 chains.) Commencing in Stanhope Street at its junction with Crossley Terrace, by a junction with proposed Route 1, and passing in an easterly direction along Stanhope Street, Barrack Road, Gallowgate, Blackett Street, New Bridge Street, Byker Bridge, Shields Road West, Shields Road, into and in a southerly direction, along Union Road, Bothal Street, easterly along Welbeck Road, termi-nating at the junction of Welbeck Road with White Street and Fisher Street.

Route 3: (4 furlongs, 4.8 chains.) Commencing in Welbeck Road at its junction with Church Street by a junction with proposed Route 2, passing in a southerly direction along Church Street to a terminus at the junction of Church Street with Walker Road and Station Road.

Route 4: (4 furlongs, 1 chain.) Commencing in New Bridge Street at its junc-tion with Market Street, by a junction with proposed Route 2, and proceeding in a south-westerly direction along Market Street and Grainger Street and terminating in Westgate Road at its junction with Grainger Street.

Route 5: (6.35 chains.) Commencing in Pilgrim Street at its junction with Blackett Street in a southerly direction along Pilgrim Street to its junction with Market Street and terminating there.

Route 6: (2 furlongs, 4.5 chains.) Commencing in Shields Road at its junction with Union Road and in a northerly and easterly direction along Shields Road to the north entrance of Byker Tramway Depot.

Route 7: (1 furlong, 9 chains.) Commencing in the Fossway at the southern entrance to Byker Tramway Depot, and in a westerly direction along the Fossway to a junction with proposed route 6.

Route 8: (3 chains.) An unnamed back lane connection between the Fossway and Union Road.

In November 1936 the twenty-five vehicles were ordered after sanction by the Council as follows:—

(a)	9 AEC 664T chassis with English Electric control equipment	£12,537
(b)	8 Karrier E6A chassis with Metro-Vick equipment	£11,152
(c)	8 Guy BTX chassis with Guy-Stevens patent equipment	£11,104
(d)	25 Metro-Cammell all-metal, double-deck bodies	£28,275

Total £63,068

As the mid-nineteen thirties' trolleybus boom continued, manufacturers scrambled to design and produce trolleybus chassis. Crossley Motors, Ltd. of Manchester did so at this time, building an example of both a 2-axle and a 3-axle vehicle for demonstration purposes. At the end of June 1937 Crossley loaned Newcastle Transport their 3-axle TDD6 prototype which was fitted with a Metro-Cammell 68-seat body. It was in Newcastle for nine days. Perhaps the Undertaking were not very impressed! Later it ran as a demonstrator until June 1938 in Ashton-under-Lyne, in which fleet it was numbered 58 and by whom it was subsequently purchased. Its fleet number is quoted as 58 in official Newcastle lists, leading one to believe that it was in the Ashton livery of dark blue and white with red bands when in Newcastle.

By March 1937 a further six trolleybuses were required for the existing Westgate Road services to cope with still increasing traffic. Orders were therefore placed being equally divided between AEC (type 664T), Guy (type BTX), and Karrier (type E6A), with Metro-Cammell supplying all six metal bodies, at a total cost of £15,136. These, together with the twenty-five vehicles on order for the Stanhope Street conversion, became 47-77, (ETN 47-77), being delivered mainly between July and September 1937.

In March 1937 the General Manager's Report noted that the overhead conversion of the Stanhope Street services was well under way. No new construction (as opposed to conversion of ex-tram wiring) was required apart from a single line of wiring at Brighton Grove terminus. Span wires were used in Stanhope Street itself, as well as in Shields Road, although Welbeck Road employed gantries. One point at which a rather specialised overhead arrangement was required was at Byker Bridge in the east end. The deep Ouseburn valley cuts across the main traffic arteries on its course to the Tyne. To enable the railway and road to cross the valley, two viaducts exist—Ouseburn Viaduct, the rail bridge built for the Newcastle and North Shields Railway in the 1860s, and Byker Bridge, built for road traffic in the 1880s. Both are approximately 80 feet high. Byker Bridge has been referred to as the highest and longest ever traversed by trolleybuses in the United Kingdom and the traction poles were elaborately stayed to achieve rigidity, using gantries and bracing wires.

One new wiring feature was the St. James' Park loop, to cope with football traffic from the Newcastle United football ground in Barrack Road. A photograph taken about the time when the Stanhope Street services were converted shows the bracket arms on the island separating the service road from Barrack Road ready for the wires of the loop, so it must have been inserted at a slightly later date.

It was stated that the wires in Market Street and Grainger Street (proposed Route 4 above, connecting the new route with the existing Westgate Road service) would enable services to be operated between Westgate and Walker via Shields Road as was done prewar, although not as an all-day working. Proposed Route 5, which would bring trolleybuses onto the A1 trunk road in Newcastle for the first time, was a link forming part of a turning point for rush-hour short-workings from the east end. A turning circle was in due course provided at the junction of Welbeck Road and White Street (a continuation of Walker Road), in Walker, while proposed Route 3 was adopted and wiring connections made to the existing turning circle for Wallsend services at the foot of Church Street, Walker.

Proposed Routes 6, 7, and 8 of the Provisional Order were to give connection to Byker Depot, proposed Route 7 being the Depot exit wiring and proposed Route 8 a vital link to get vehicles from the Depot to the eastern terminus of the route. The trams had used the same narrow lane and the track survived for many years. Thus trolleybuses penetrated Byker Depot for the first time. Byker Depot, together with the Central Workshops and adjacent 'bus garage, was, and still is, the largest of the undertaking, covering $14\frac{1}{2}$ acres today, although the original tram depot covered only 13 acres. Car Sheds built in 1901 had accommodation for eighty trams on eight roads, and facilities existed in the workshops for heavy repairs, both electrical and mechanical, and for bodywork including the building of tram bodies. A traverser (which is still there) was installed for moving complete vehicles in the paintshop. The layout of the original trolleybus wiring accommodation in the depot is as yet not known to the authors, although one would estimate that twenty-five trolleybuses required $2\frac{1}{2}$ roads (ten per road). Any further information on the wiring layout in the depot at this time would be welcome.

At his official inspection, the Ministry of Transport Inspecting Officer imposed the following conditions for operating the new route:—

Speed Limits: Brighton Grove to Church Street and Welbeck Road via Stanhope Street, Blackett Street, Shields Road and Union Road route.

Speed (mph.)	Section
25	(i) Welbeck Road, Church Street, and in Shields Road between the junction of Union Road and Byker Bridge.
	(ii) New Bridge Street between Byker Bridge and the railway underbridge adjacent to Manors Station.
15	(i) While passing over Byker Bridge.
	(ii) While passing over the railway bridge adjacent to Manors Station.
20	Elsewhere (Subject to existing standard restrictions of 5 mph,

and 5 mph to apply to passing under the railway bridge in Welbeck Road.)

Terminal Movements, etc.: Allendale Road Reverser must be only used when an inspector is in attendance to warn road traffic.

The rather unusual reverser at Allendale Road was shown as 'Byker' on destination indicators but was seldom used, at least in postwar years, possibly because it involved trolleybuses reversing at right angles across a busy road junction.

The new trolleybus services began operating on 19th September 1937 as follows, extending the route mileage to about 14 miles.

BRIGHTON GROVE (loop via Dilston Road, Callerton Place, and Brighton Grove) (5A) (5B)—Crossley Terrace—Stanhope Street—Barrack Road—Gallowgate—Blackett Street—PILGRIM STREET (loop via New Bridge Street, Pilgrim Street, Market Street) (5C)—New Bridge Street—Byker Bridge—Shields Road West—Shields Road—Union Road—Bothal Street—Welbeck Road—WELBECK ROAD (east end) (turning circle) (5B)—Church Street—WALKER (CHURCH STREET) (foot of) (turning circle) (5A) (5C) and return. The 5A and 5B operated daily whilst the 5C operated Monday to Friday peak-hours only. Additional journeys were also operated between PILGRIM STREET and WALKER (WEST-BOURNE AVENUE) (reverser) outward via Market Street and New Bridge Street and inward to Pilgrim Street from New Bridge Street. This operated Monday to Saturday as a part-day extra service and was also operated as a special evening service to cover Greyhound and dirt-track race meetings at Brough Park Stadium.

It is believed that tram service 43 (Welbeck Road—Byker Bridge—Wrekenton), operated jointly with Gateshead and District, was cut back to the City and 44 (Welbeck Road—Byker Bridge—Pilgrim Street) was abandoned completely, together with the tram services to Stanhope Street.

At the City Council Meeting in September 1937 (as the Stanhope Street services commenced operation), more proposed conversions were discussed and it was noticeable that for the first time, when the Council's authorisation for abandonment of a tram service was given, conversion to trolleybuses was assumed by the Committee. The tone of the Report to the Council was of just a further stage in the expansion of the trolleybus network with no apparent need to justify or argue the case for tram abandonment. The debate by the Council fully bears this out. Firm proposals were made for the conversion of three tram routes, together with tentative plans for two others.

The new routes on which the Transport and Electricity Committee proposed to operate trolleybuses were:—

(a) Central Station—Osborne Road (Jesmond) (estimated to require nine vehicles).

(b) Pilgrim Street — Wallsend Boundary (Walkerville) (estimated to require five vehicles).

(c) Central Station—Two Ball Lonnen (Fenham) (estimated to require ten vehicles).

The Committee asked the Council to apply for a Provisional Order for these and certain other routes, including the Westerhope Tramroad and the Westmorland Road tram route, together with the Armstrong Road motorbus route, although the three routes tabulated above were the only ones on which it was intended to operate trolleybuses in the immediate future.

In October 1937 the Council authorised the placing of orders for the twenty-four vehicles required as follows:—

14	Karrier E6A chassis	£21,602
10	Guy BTX chassis	£15,260
24	Metro-Cammell all-metal 60-seat bodies	£27,840
	Total	£64,702

The placing of repeat orders with the manufacturers was stated to be official policy in the interests of standardisation of vehicle types. These vehicles became 85-108 (FVK 85-108) when delivered in the late summer of 1938, for in addition to the above a further six trolleybuses which became numbered 79-84 (FVK 79-84) were ordered for the Westgate Road services to cope with the still increasing traffic, tenders having been accepted from AEC Ltd. of £9,252 for six 664T. type chassis, and from Chas. H. Roe Ltd. of £6,720 for six teak-framed bodies. Also delivered in the late summer of 1938, these were the first Newcastle trolleybuses to have Roe bodywork fitted. This manufacturer was destined to supply a substantial number to the undertaking in the next few years and the choice was probably influenced by the devious arrival of 78.

Two Guy BTX chassis were shown at the 1937 Commercial Motor Show, one of which was fitted with a standard Newcastle-type front-exit 60-seat body but built by Roe. The two were later inspected and purchased by Newcastle Transport. The already complete vehicle was delivered in December 1937, becoming 78 (FBB 78), and entered service in January 1938. The unbodied chassis was sent to Northern Coachbuilders Ltd.'s factory in Claremont Road, Spital Tongues, Newcastle and it emerged in November 1938 sporting a handsome metal framed body as 109 (FVK 109). Council authorisation was not given until January 1938, (after 78 had entered service) for purchase of the two Guy BTX chassis, at £1,388 and £1,493, together with one Roe body at £1,095 and one NCB body at £1,160 a total of £5,136.

On 13th September 1937 a two-axle Willowbrook-bodied Daimler CTM4 demonstrator, finished in red-and-cream livery and registered CWK 67, arrived in the City and entered service on 17th September 1937. Newcastle Transport gave it a slightly longer trial than the Crossley 3-axle demonstrator loaned the previous year, for CWK 67 ran until 17th November 1937 and returned to Daimler on 19th November. It was later demonstrated elsewhere, and after initial loan it was purchased during 1938 by nearby South Shields Corporation (a trolleybus convert which had inaugurated services in 1936) becoming their 234. During the debate on the purchase of the 24 trolleybuses for the 1938 conversions, an Alderman Chapman, referring to the demonstrators, asked if the proposed vehicles were of the same type as the 'yellow 'buses', and hoped the Corporation were not going to buy any of the 'red 'buses'. Alderman Mayne, Chairman of the Transport Committee, replied that the Corporation had asked the makers of the 'red 'bus' to give a trial run but did not propose to buy any of this type.

At a Special Meeting on 17th November 1937, the Corporation set out the draft of the Provisional Order for the proposed conversions under the General Powers Act, 1935, as outlined at the September meeting. These were as follows:—

Route 1: (1 mile, 7 furlongs, 0 chains.) Commencing in Osborne Road at its junction with Lonsdale Terrace, and passing along Osborne Road, Jesmond Road, Great North Road, Barras Bridge and Northumberland Street and terminating at the junction of Northumberland Street and Blackett Street by a junction with route 2 of the 1937 Order.

Route 2: (1 furlong.) Commencing in Osborne Road at its junction with Lonsdale Terrace, by a junction with Route 1, along Lonsdale Terrace, Tavistock Road and terminating in Osborne Road by a junction with Route 1.

Route 3: (9.7 chains.) Commencing in Grainger Street at Grey's Monument, and in a southerly direction along Grainger Street to its junction with Market Street and terminating there.

Route 4: (4.8 chains.) Commencing in Westgate Road at its junction with Grainger Street West, and in a southerly direction along Grainger Street West and terminating at the junction of that street and Neville Street.

Route 5: (1 mile, 1 furlong.) Commencing in Shields Road at Byker Tramway Depot and in an easterly direction along Shields Road to the boundary of the City with the Borough of Wallsend.

Route 6: (3 furlongs.) Commencing in Shields Road at its junction with Rowantree Road along Rowantree Road, Lilac Road to the junction of Lilac Road with Shields Road and terminating there.

Route 7: (3 miles.) Commencing in Barrack Road at its junction with Stanhope Street and in a westerly direction along Barrack Road, Ponteland Road, Fenham Hall Drive and onto Tramroad 45 (the Westerhope Tramroad) to its terminus at Westerhope.

Route 8: (5 furlongs.) Commencing in Pease Avenue at its junction with Fox-and-Hounds Lane and in a northerly direction along Pease Avenue across West Road and into Two Ball Lonnen, along that road to its junction with Fenham Hall Drive, and terminating there.

Route 9: (3 miles, 7 furlongs.) Commencing at the junction of Whickham View with Denton Road and in a southerly direction along Denton Road, easterly along Armstrong Road, St. John's Road, Gluehouse Lane, Westmorland Road and Neville Street to its junction with Westgate Road and terminating there.

Route 10: (5.7 chains.) Bewick Street along its length from Clayton Street West, to Neville Street.

Route 11: (1 furlong.) Commencing in Clayton Street West at its junction with Westgate Road and along Clayton Road West to its junction with Neville Street and terminating there.

Route 12: (2 furlongs.) Commencing at the junction of West Road and Denton Road and westerly along West Road and terminating at the junction of West Road and Copperas Lane. (Denton Square.)

Route 13: (3 furlongs.) Commencing in Melbourne Street at its junction with City Road and north-easterly along Melbourne Street and Stepney Lane, to terminate at the junction of Stepney Lane with New Bridge Street.

Route 14: (1 furlong.) Commencing in Pilgrim Street at its junction with Market Street and in a southerly direction along Pilgrim Street to a terminus at the junction of Pilgrim Street with Mosley Street.

Route 15: (5.3 chains.) Commencing in Northumberland Street at its junction with Haymarket, and in a westerly direction across Haymarket and Percy Street to Georges Place and the entrance to Haymarket Depot.

Route 16: (2 furlongs.) Commencing in College Avenue south-westerly along College Avenue from the western entrance to Haymarket Depot, and south-easterly along St. Thomas' Street along Percy Street to Barras Bridge.

This application for powers was subsequently confirmed by the Newcastle upon Tyne Corporation (Trolley Vehicles) Order Confirmation Act, 1938.

Examining these powers in some detail, they contain several interesting unrealised proposals. Proposed Route 1 formed the basis of the Osborne Road service, whilst proposed Rouse 2 was the Osborne Road terminal loop of single road wiring along a square of side streets which would extend the trolleybuses a mere 50 yards beyond the end of the tram tracks at St. George's Church.

Proposed Routes 3 and 4 were links in the central area and would see (in 1938) wiring along the whole length of Grainger Street.

From the existing Byker Depot access wiring in Shields Road, proposed Route 5 extended eastwards to the Wallsend Boundary, whilst proposed Route 6 was to have been a diversion into part of Walkerville housing estate parallel to the LNER's Coast loop line, and was intended to be a turning loop. The Walkerville Residents' Association protested vehemently, however, pointing out that there were a number of services passing the estate. Proposed Route 6 was, therefore, never built and the Wallsend Boundary services in the event turned at a reverser in Oaktree Gardens, on the north side of Shields Road.

Part of proposed Route 7 was to become service 6 to Fenham. In addition, it was decided to seek powers to operate trolleybuses westwards beyond the proposed Two Ball Lonnen terminus of this service to what was then the village of Westerhope but which is now a suburb of Newcastle with several large housing estates. This was to be on the right-of-way of the tramway sleeper track of Westerhope Tramroad, then running partially through fields along the line of the present Netherby Drive and alongside Stanfordham Road to Westerhope, where it terminated just past Ellesmere Avenue. It would, therefore, be necessary to construct a roadway on which to run trolleybuses. This was authorised late in 1937 to be 'built up to 20 feet from the centre-line of the tramroad' from Two Ball Lonnen west to Silver Lonnen. Had the trolleybuses been extended beyond here, on the line of the tramroad, in later years they would have passed through the forecourt of the Slatyford Depot, as this intruded onto the tramway right-of-way.

In proposed Route 8, Newcastle Transport sought, in Pease Avenue, a bypass for the bottleneck at Fox-and-Hounds Lane. Such relief was denied to them for the powers were never implemented. Fox-and-Hounds Lane is still literally a lane, so narrow that two trolleybuses could not pass each other. In spite of the Ministry of Transport Regulations stating that 'trolleybuses FROM the City have precedence', in practise, it was more usual for the trolleybuses from the City to wait at the top of Fox-and-Hounds Lane for east-bound trolleybuses coming up from Old Benwell. Pease Avenue itself, in Pendower estate, had at this time been in existence for about ten years, but it is not apparent as to why this trolleybus wiring extension was never built.

The remainder of proposed Route 8, Two Ball Lonnen, would have linked the existing West Road service with the new Fenham route and was perhaps intended to facilitate the introduction of circular workings via the West Road and Fenham. This half mile link was never built.

Proposed Rouse 9 was extremely interesting as a 'might-have-been', and the tram and motorbus services which operated over it are worth some mention. It is simpler to deal with the streets in reverse order to that previously given. Therefore, starting at Neville Street (which was the only part of the proposed route actually built), this formed the centre of the tramway system and eventually several trolleybus routes terminated near here. The remainder, namely Westmorland Road, Gluehouse Lane, St. John's Road, Armstrong Road and Denton Road, would have entailed the conversion and extension of the short, one mile long Westmorland Road tram route operating into this part of Elswick in the west end. The outer terminus of this route was at the dead-end of Westmorland Road facing the east wall of St. John's (Elswick) Cemetery. To extend trolleybuses the $2\frac{1}{2}$ miles along St. John's Road, Armstrong Road and up Denton Road in order to join the Denton loop, as proposed, would have entailed making a connection between Westmorland Road and St. John's Road at the south-east corner of the cemetery. The Provisional Order mentions Gluehouse Lane, now West View, as the link, but this would have involved two right-angled turns and the passage of a very short steep section of this road which runs along the east side of the cemetery. This no doubt had a great deal to do with the Undertaking's later reluctance to wire this route for trolleybus operation. Gluehouse Lane at this point was already the terminus of two motorbus services—10 (St. John's Road—Armstrong Road—Denton Burn), and 15 (St. John's Road—Armstrong Road—Cowgate [Morris Works]) which had commenced operation in 1936.

What actually happened was that when the Westmorland Road tram route was finally abandoned, on 2nd July 1939, these services were linked along Westmorland Road with motorbus services from Central Station to Heaton (Simonside Terrace) and Central Station to Walker (Stack Hotel). The reason for the two year delay was the construction of a link road, becoming part of St. John's Road, rising from St. John's Road to Westmorland Road to obviate the two right-angled turns previously mentioned. Thus only motorbuses (present services 1 and 2) used the specially-built link road, never trolleybuses.

Proposed Routes 10 and 11, together with Neville Street, formed a turning loop round St. Mary's Roman Catholic Cathedral. This arrangement remained until the construction of the traffic roundabout at the western end of Neville Street in 1953, which trolleybuses then turned around instead.

Proposed Route 12 was an extension from Denton Burn to Denton Square and commenced operation on the 24th April 1938, some time before the Osborne Road, Fenham, and Wallsend Boundary services. At Denton Square, a turning circle was specially constructed on privately-owned ground on the south side of the West Road, just east of Copperas Lane, which street forms the City boundary at this point. This cleared standing trolleybuses from the busy A69 West Road to Carlisle. The Undertaking showed considerable foresight in providing such turning facilities for the West Road was reconstructed as a dual carriageway in the nineteen-fifties, starting westward from the City boundary at Denton Square. This extension continued to be operated until final trolleybus abandonment in October 1966.

Turning again to the Central area, proposed Routes 13 to 16 covered two links and an access for trolleybuses to the Haymarket Depot. Proposed Route 13 was not actually implemented until after declaration of war, when Melbourne Street was seen to be a potentially valuable emergency connection on the eastern edge of the City centre between City Road, at the Manors, and New Bridge Street at Red Barns. It was hardly ever used afterwards, except on enthusiasts' tours and in emergencies, having no regular service use.

Proposed Route 14 was along Pilgrim Street southwards from the junction with Market Street on the 1938 routes to its junction with Mosley Street and the Denton-Wallsend route. It was never wired for trolleybuses. The tram wires here, which were last used in March 1950, were retained as trolleybus feeders until October 1966, being taken down in the following month.

With the introduction of proposed Routes 15 and 16 trolleybuses finally penetrated Haymarket Depot and trolleybus wiring was provided into all three Newcastle Transport depots. Proposed Route 15 was a connection to the depot from a point on the Osborne Road route whilst proposed Route 16 covered the depot exit wiring. Vehicles on the Osborne Road service became stabled here, thus saving a long trek into the east end to Byker Depot.

The General Manager's Report for the Financial Year Ending 31st March 1938 stated that a new mercury-arc rectifier substation at the foot of Welbeck Road was 'virtually complete and ready to open'. This station helped to take the extra load the trolleybuses were imposing on the successful Wallsend route, as well as the Stanhope Street and Welbeck Road service.

The first of the routes set out in the Provisional Order of 1938 to commence operation was the extension to Denton Square which opened on 24th April 1938, as already mentioned. Span wire construction was used for the overhead and the Ministry of Transport Inspecting Officer imposed the following condition on terminal movements:—

Denton Square Turning Circle:

> When starting from this circle, conductors must be on the main road, and ready to signal the driver.

As a result of the extension to Denton Square, a variation to the 4 Group of routes was introduced. Service 4B was extended over the new section and the section was also used by a peak-hour only service running PILGRIM STREET— DENTON SQUARE and one journey by June 1939 running at 6.34 a.m. Denton Square—City Road—Walker Road—Wallsend. A new service numbered 5 was introduced simultaneously which ran as follows:—

DENTON SQUARE (Copperas Lane) (turning circle)—West Road— Fox-and-Hounds—Westgate Road—Brighton Grove—Crossley Terrace Stanhope Street—Barrack Road—Gallowgate—Blackett Street and as 5 group to WALKER (CHURCH STREET) and return, operating daily.

On Monday 1st August 1938, service 6 (Central Station—Fenham [Two Ball Lonnen]) was the first of a trio of new services to open. It replaced tram service 31 (covering the same route), which ceased the previous Sunday, 31st July 1938, (see illustration), whilst on Saturday 30th July 1938 tram service 32 (Central Station—Westerhope), which operated only on Saturdays, also ran for the last time. Having been suspended during 1929 (week day service from 29th April; Saturday/Sunday service from 13th December) and motorbuses substituted between Stamfordham Road and Westerhope, the trams had been reinstated in 1936, as the 'buses were grossly overloaded with Saturday shoppers travelling into the City centre. The tram track and overhead had remained in situ in the interim and there must have been some spectacular sparks flying every Saturday when the first tram of the day set off beyond Fenham terminus!

New trolleybus service 6 operated as follows:—

FENHAM (Two Ball Lonnen) (reverser)—Fenham Hall Drive—Ponteland Road—Barrack Road—Gallowgate—Blackett Street—Grainger Street— Grainger Street West—Neville Street—CENTRAL STATION thence via a loop of Bewick Street, Clayton Street West, Neville Street and return. This service operated daily.

Upon conversion to trolleybuses, motorbuses were still left to serve Westerhope as trolleybuses only ran as far as Two Ball Lonnen. The reverser in Ovington Grove can just be seen in the illustration.

A month later, on 2nd September 1938, the other two new trolleybus services commenced, numbered 9 and 12, and operated as follows:—

9. OSBORNE ROAD (Jesmond) (having turned via Tavistock Place and Lonsdale Terrace)—Osborne Road—Jesmond Road—Barras Bridge— Northumberland Street—Pilgrim Street—Market Street—Grainger Street—Grainger Street West—Neville Street—CENTRAL STATION thence via a loop of Bewick Street, Clayton Street West, Neville Street, and return. The service was operated daily at a frequency of 4-6 mins.

12. WALLSEND BOUNDARY (Walkerville) (Oaktree Gardens) (reverser)—Shields Road—Shields Road West—Byker Bridge—New Bridge Street—Blackett Street—Grainger Street—Grainger Street West Neville Street—CENTRAL STATION thence via loop Bewick Street, Clayton Street, Neville Street, and return. This service was operated daily at a frequency of 10 mins.

Additional journeys were also operated between WALLSEND BOUNDARY and PILGRIM STREET, running inwards via New Bridge Street, and outwards via Market Street and New Bridge Street.

These replaced tram routes 38 (Central Station—Osborne Road), and 22 (new number) (Benwell—Wallsend Boundary), together with route 13 (Scotswood Bridge—Wallsend Boundary) which ran on Saturdays only.

So it was that, seven years after the controversy, the Osborne Road tram service was finally converted to trolleybus and not motorbus operation and trolleybuses penetrated the north-eastern part of Newcastle for the first time.

The Ministry of Transport Inspecting Officer imposed the following conditions:—

Speed Limits:

Speed (mph)	Section
25	Fenham Hall Drive and in Barrack Road, north of Hunter's Road junction (until the roadway is reconstructed).
20	Tavistock Road, Lonsdale Terrace, and Osborne Road turning loop.

| 10 | Under Skew Railway Bridge, Walkerville. |
| 30 | All other places, subject to standard restrictions of 5 mph. |

Compulsory Stop: In Fenham Hall Drive before crossing Two Ball Lonnen.

These routes to Fenham, Jesmond, and Walkerville were mainly of span wire construction, supported on the original tramway standards except at junctions. Bewick Street was the only street not formerly served by trams.

The routes served three entirely different areas of the City. Service 6, after leaving the Stanhope Street service in Barrack Road, skirted the edge of the Town Moor running in almost rural surroundings until, at Wingrove Road junction on Fenham Hall Drive, it entered Fenham itself, which consisted of large houses and a convent school, whilst a rash of nineteen-thirties semi-detached properties continued up to the terminus. Service 9 ran into a substantially Victorian-built suburb of large houses, at that time very select, whilst service 12 passed along Shields Road, the east-end shopping centre (between Byker Bridge and Union Road junction), before turning into the industrial part of Shields Road flanked by C. & A. Parsons' huge engineering works, and finally, for the last half-mile, running into then recent housing development.

With these services converted, trolleybus route mileage expanded to 22.20 miles, whilst tram route mileage had shrunk from approximately 51 miles to 31 miles in less than three years.

CHAPTER FOUR

DIGRESSION TO GATESHEAD

On the south bank of the River Tyne, opposite Newcastle, stands the town of Gateshead. Public transport was provided throughout the area, (which might be more broadly termed 'Greater Gateshead'), mainly by the Gateshead & District Tramways Company, a subsidiary of the British Electric Traction Company. During the latter part of the nineteen-thirties the extensive cross-river services mentioned in Chapter 1 were being maintained jointly with Newcastle Transport, and Gateshead & District cars penetrated largely into northern and north-eastern areas of Newcastle. Services extending into the west end had ceased in 1927.

Its larger neighbour being committed to a policy of replacing trams with trolleybuses, and it being considered essential for the two systems to maintain joint services, Gateshead, therefore, seemed forced to convert to trolleybus operation if through running were to continue.

There had been several early attempts to operate trolleybuses in Gateshead, all of which had come to nothing.

The Company had, in their Gateshead & District Tramways Act, 1909, obtained powers to run 'omnibuses, carriages, motor cars, or **carriages worked on the trolley system without rails'***, as well as powers to extend the existing tramways. These powers were intended to be used to run trackless trolleys over the High Level Bridge, at that time a toll bridge owned by the North Eastern Railway Company. The latter effectively stifled this idea by promptly imposing a toll of 2d per ton, or fraction thereof, on motor omnibuses.

In the North Eastern Railway Bill, 1914, the railway company itself attempted to obtain powers to run trolleybuses over the bridge. Both the Gateshead & District Tramways Company and Newcastle Transport opposed this Clause, the former on the grounds of competition, and the latter on the grounds that they were the tramway authority for the City, and the Clause was rejected by Parliament at Committee Stage.

In 1920, Durham County Council promoted a Parliamentary Bill to construct the Durham County Council Tramways. Included in this were proposed trolleybus routes. One was from Gateshead Station (the south end of the High Level Bridge), along Bensham Road in Gateshead to Sunniside and Consett, whilst another was from Heworth tram terminus (on the east side of Gateshead) to Washington. This Bill was rejected by the House of Commons. In passing it is interesting to note that nearby Tynemouth Corporation had been granted trolleybus powers in 1919, but they were never implemented.

During the nineteen-thirties, relations between the Company and Gateshead Corporation were not good. Gateshead Corporation had the usual option to purchase the tramway undertaking as set out in the Tramways Act, 1870. In 1936, the Company stated that they considered their services were satisfactory, and did not believe it necessary to improve or extend the existing network; if the Corporation did not want trams, the Company would substitute petrol 'buses. The Corporation considered the purchase of the tramway system in December 1936, it being

*Authors' bold

thought necessary in order to retain control over transport services in the area by working the Newcastle and Gateshead tramways as one. In reply, the Company's parent, the Northern General Transport Company, applied to the Traffic Commissioners for powers to run motorbuses over the tram routes in Gateshead. Gateshead Corporation retaliated by promoting the Gateshead Corporation Bill in 1937. This proposed the purchase of the Company and conversion of the tramways to trolleybus operation. In addition, the proposed trolleybus system would extend into several parts of 'Greater Gateshead' beyond the existing tram termini. This would have given the town a trolleybus system with 18.74 miles of route against the tramway route mileage of 12.66. Gateshead Corporation even went so far as to obtain estimates of the cost of substituting trolleybuses for the trams. These were prepared jointly by Mr. T. P. Easton, Newcastle's General Manager, and the Town Clerk of Gateshead, and were as follows:—

65 double-deck trolleybuses at £2,500 each	£162,500
12½ miles of overhead conversion	£25,912
2 mercury-arc rectifier substations	£9,000
New negative feeder cables	£3,000
Total	£200,412

Mr. Easton stated that new feeder conduits would be necessary, since no spares were already in existence as had been the case in Newcastle. It will be seen that these estimates did not cover the cost of any extensions but it will be seen that Gateshead Corporation appeared to be very much in favour of a trolleybus system.

The Company stated that since Newcastle was converting to trolleybuses they would probably have to follow suit, but they could foresee difficulties with Wellington Street railway bridge in the centre of the town.

The Company themselves promoted a rival trolleybus Bill designed to forestall the Corporation takeover of the tramway undertaking but no extensions beyond the tram termini were proposed, although application could have been made to the Ministry of Transport for a Provisional Order to make such extensions.

Although the Company's proposals became law as the Gateshead & District Tramways and Trolley Vehicles Act, 1938, Gateshead Corporation still thought that the Company's main intention was to let Northern run motorbuses over the existing tram system. The Act itself mentioned the through-running of trams with Newcastle Transport and the City's intention to abandon 'a large part of its tramways' and to convert to trolleybuses. It also stated: 'it is expedient that the Company be authorised to run trolley vehicles along the routes of tramways and light railways, and to enter into working agreements with other operators of trolley vehicles'. The main powers obtained were as follows:—

1. The Company may provide, equip and maintain trolley vehicles, and work and run same (a) along any tramway routes or part thereof; and (b) with the consent of the Minister, along any street or road in the Borough, Felling Urban District or Whickham Urban District which the Company thinks it necessary or convenient to use . . .

for turning points or connecting links to a depot, garage building, or land belonging to the Company, providing it is not more than ½ mile in length.

2. The Company to submit plans to the Minister, the Police Authority, and the Local Authority before equipping any trolley vehicle route with a turning point.

3. The Minister is empowered to make a Provisional Order to allow further routes.

4. The Company is empowered to erect trolley vehicle electrical equipment, and to use the existing tramway equipment.

5. The powers to be exercised within ten years.

6. The Company to provide adequate clearances at colliery companies' level crossings for the overhead.

7. The Company not to abandon any tramway without first substituting a trolley vehicle route, and not to abandon a joint tramway route without the consent of Newcastle Corporation. The Company to negotiate with Newcastle as to the type of transport on the joint routes.

8. The Company not to oppose Newcastle if the latter seeks powers before 1st December 1943 to run trolley vehicles over the Tyne or High Level Bridges.

Nothing was done towards abandoning the trams, and the War intervened the following year effectively stopping any plans for some time. As a result, the trams soldiered on for another thirteen years.

CHAPTER FIVE

WARTIME TWILIGHT

In February 1939, the Newcastle Transport and Electricity Committee presented to the full Council a report which considered 'the further development of the trolley vehicle system', and the General Manager, Mr. T. P. Easton, made a very sweeping recommendation on this subject, involving the scrapping of 250 trams and 31½ miles of track.

At the March Council Meeting, the Report was debated and the Corporation in effect announced their plans regarding the extension of the trolleybus system. It can be realised, from comments made during the Council Meetings and published in the Council Proceedings, that the Corporation was anxious to rid the City of its tramway system. They were reluctant, however, to abandon the large Corporation-owned electrical feeder network and the capital invested in it, hence the wide-ranging plans for trolleybus conversion.

In the climate prevailing in prewar days, it was not unusual to make ambitious plans to convert ALL existing tram routes to trolleybus operation. In Newcastle the only tram routes to be excepted from the plan were the Gosforth Park Light Railway, where the trams ran through Gosforth Park, 5 miles north of the City centre, on reserved track away from any road, the Spital Tongues route, serving a small area one mile north west of the City centre, which really had insufficient traffic potential for electric traction (and which in any case had been converted to motorbus operation in April 1936); and the Westmorland Road route, dealt with earlier.

This massive conversion to trolleybus operation was estimated at the time to cost £392,272. The Undertaking did not propose to borrow money for this, but to pay for it out of operating profits over the next five years, this being cheaper than borrowing. There was opposition from some Councillors to the effect that a great burden had been placed on the Corporation for strengthening roads—£121,000 to date—and the remainder of the debate was mainly financial.

The level of fares at this time is of interest. In 1938-9, the fare structure ranged from ½d. to 4½d. An indication of the average length of a journey is that most fares were issued at 1½d. giving a journey of about 2 miles. These figures were basically the same as at the end of the first financial year of traffic, on 31st March 1936, indicating the stability of prices during this period.

In March 1939, Newcastle purchased a demonstration trolleybus, DHP 112, a Daimler CTM6 three-axle vehicle fitted with a Metro-Cammell 60-seat front-exit body. This vehicle had been running in the City on loan from the manufacturers but in Newcastle Transport livery as number 112 since 14th March 1938. It remained the only Daimler in the fleet, (indeed it was one of only three CTM6's built before the war), and its Coventry registration number betrayed its demonstrator origin. It had been offered to Newcastle Transport in October 1936 for test purposes before the manufacturers put the type on the market, although it was not operated in the City until two years after this. Daimler must have been anxious for orders, for they did not charge Newcastle any hiring costs! Now, in

1939, Daimler were prepared to sell it to Newcastle at £2,683. The Council were told that this was the price the makers had quoted for each of a batch of six vehicles which they would be prepared to build for the Undertaking. No such batch was ever built, and 112 remained unique in Newcastle.

This still leaves unresolved the matter of the blank fleet numbers 110 and 111, which has puzzled transport historians for years. It is possible that these numbers were allocated to further demonstrators but this is unlikely as none are recorded in official Byker Depot records whereas the Crossley and CWK 67 are recorded. It is difficult to relate them to these two vehicles for the numbers would have been well out of sequence at the time they were operated. One possible explanation may be that for some reason the numbers 110 and 111 were allocated "posthumously" to the two demonstrators previously on hire and since departed, for official Byker depot records for these two vehicles do not quote a fleet number —indeed the Crossley vehicle is even recorded as being Ashton-under-Lyne 58. Alternatively, and this seems the most likely, DHP 112 was so very nearly but not quite the registration number required to "agree" with the next blank fleet number. The undertaking would have had no control over the issue of the registration number to Daimler by the Coventry licensing authority; they could of course have re-registered the vehicle in order to make fleet and registration numbers "agree" and have numbered the vehicle 110 with subsequent deliveries starting at 111. They appear to have chosen, however, to leave things as they were, and simply to have omitted fleet numbers 110 and 111 in order to issue 112 to DHP 112, possibly bearing in mind the two demonstrators loaned previously. Any further light which can be shed on this subject would be most welcome.

The final batch of trolleybuses purchased before the outbreak of War, again to cope with increased traffic, were twelve Karrier E6A's, six of which were fitted with 60-seat teak-framed bodies by Charles H. Roe Ltd. (113-118, registered HVK 113-118), and six with all-metal bodies of the same capacity by Metro-Cammell (119-124, registered HVK 119-124). The twelve were ordered in April 1939 at a cost of £17,688 for the chassis, £6,858 for the Metro-Cammell bodies, and £6,618 for the Roe bodies, a total of £31,164. They were delivered between December 1939 and April 1940, except for 116 which did not arrive until 14th December 1940.

Also in April 1939, the Council was recommended to implement the Undertaking's plans to convert yet another tram route, the Elswick Road service. This was about 2½ miles long in the west-end where it forked left off Westgate Road at the Big Lamp junction at the top of Westgate Hill and passed through the suburbs of Elswick and Benwell, along Elswick Road, Adelaide Terrace, and Benwell Lane, to its terminus in West Benwell at Delaval Road. New housing estates had sprung up in West Benwell along Whickham View beyond the tram terminus, and it was intended to extend the trolleybus wires along Whickham View to connect with the Denton Loop at the junction of that street with Ferguson's Lane.

The conversion was estimated to cost £54,000 for the vehicles, and £7,290 for the overhead. In May 1939 it was proposed to order the twenty vehicles for the route, but the Council were warned of the possibility of a delay in delivery, a warning borne out by subsequent events.

51

In September 1939, plans for the conversion of the Elswick Road tram route were shelved temporarily, in view of the outbreak of War and the uncertain situation, but powers to operate trolleybuses were nevertheless sought, these being confirmed in 1940 as under:—

Route 1: (2 miles 2 furlongs.) Commencing in Whickham View at its junction with Ferguson's Lane, and easterly along Whickham View, Benwell Lane, Adelaide Terrace, and Elswick Road to the junction of Elswick Road with Westgate Road and terminating there.

Route 2: (2 furlongs 8 chains.) Commencing in Buckingham Street at its junction with Westgate Road, and north-easterly along Buckingham Street and Heber Street to the junction of Heber Street with Gallowgate and terminating there.

Route 3: (2 furlongs 5 chains.) Commencing in Clayton Street at its junction with Westgate Road, and north-easterly along Clayton Street to a terminus at the junction of Clayton Street and Blackett Street.

At the Big Lamp a diversion from the tram route was projected, for the wires were to cross the junction and go down Buckingham Street and Heber Street to Barrack Road, which already carried the wires of the Fenham and Stanhope Street routes. An eleven-storey office block now straddles Heber Street at its former meeting with Barrack Road. Both Buckingham Street and Heber Street were narrow and fairly steep, scarcely ideal for trolleybus operation and this diversion would have added a half mile to the Elswick Road route.

In the City centre, trolleybuses entering via Gallowgate from Barrack Road were intended to use Blackett Street, Grainger Street, and Westgate Road as a clockwise turning loop to relieve traffic congestion in Clayton Street which was used by the trams. Trolleybuses entering the central area via Westgate Hill would have used Clayton Street, Blackett Street, Grainger Street, and Westgate Road, leaving by Westgate Hill. In view of this projected arrangement eastbound single-road wiring only was possibly intended in Buckingham Street and Heber Street.

CHAPTER SIX

TROLLEYBUSES IN WARTIME

The first feature to disappear from both trams and trolleybuses (and certain motorbuses) at the outbreak of War was the postal-box facility. This had been available on late-night trolleybuses operating on routes 4B, 6, 9 and 12 (but not 5) as successors to the trams. It was a facility not restored after hostilities ceased.

Private cars and motor transport in general became sparse as the War progressed, due to the scarcity of petrol and rubber. Public transport reigned supreme, and trams became king of the road once more.

The biggest disruption to public transport during the War was not so much air raids, as the effects of the blackout. The absence of street lights and the requirements for headlights to be masked made driving very difficult, and indeed dangerous at times, and as far as passenger vehicles were concerned, life became very tedious for platform staff.

At first, windows were painted out, black or blue, but conditions inside the vehicles were so gloomy in daylight that the paint was removed, and at night dimmed interior lights were allowed, shrouded so as to throw a pool of light to the gangway floor. This dim illumination led to Newcastle Transport being deprived of not inconsiderable sums of revenue due to dishonest passengers tendering foreign coins, etc. to conductors, relying on the poor light to aid them in their deception. From 23rd October 1940, three lights per deck and a platform light were allowed during blackouts.

To aid pedestrians and traffic finding their way in the blackout, traction poles had their lowest third painted white. Trolleybuses had the front part of the front wings and an area at the foot of the rear panels painted white at first. Later, this white area was extended to all wings together with a narrow band along the bottom edge of the vehicles' side panels. Canopy Masks were fitted over frogs and crossings to prevent arcing being visible from the air. Dewirements were to be avoided at all costs—finding TWO wires in total darkness, and fitting trolley heads back on them, was a difficult procedure!

Surprisingly, Newcastle did not suffer heavily from air raids, even though the country's biggest concentration of ship-building was to be found on Tyneside. Nevertheless, as a precaution, Newcastle Transport took steps to prevent dislocation should the trolleybus network become damaged. As mentioned earlier, Melbourne Street was wired in 1940 to provide an alternative link between the eastern and western sections of the system in case the bridge carrying New Bridge Street over the railway at Manors was destroyed or damaged. This connection was used a number of times, one occasion being after the air raid which destroyed the New Bridge Street Goods Station of the LNER, on 1st September 1941. This building was the largest covered goods station in the country, and was filled with inflammable foodstuffs. When hit by incendiary bombs, it burned for a week. The trolleybus wires in New Bridge Street were cut and the tram service halted.

The Ministry of Transport gave sanction for another emergency link in October 1940 and this was constructed in 1941, along Albion Row in the east-end suburb of Byker, linking Shields Road with City Road. It provided a connection between those streets in case Byker Bridge was hit. This link was built at a cost of £650 from materials in stock and was 680 yards long, suspended from double bracket arms. Unlike Melbourne Street, it was not normally connected up to the main wires, but was only intended to be linked up to the wires in Shields Road and City Road if an emergency occurred. It remained unused until 1956, when it was dismantled.

Meanwhile, by March 1940, a new high tension feeder from the Manors to Westgate sub-station, via Westmorland Road had been laid. This was to ensure power supplies in case of breakdown in the Westgate Road high tension feeder, and to help supply the proposed sub-station at Back Northbourne Street for the projected Elswick Road route. Additional feeder cables from Westgate sub-station to Denton Bank were also laid to cope with increased traffic. Emergency power supplies were not forgotten. Arrangements were made with the Newcastle and District Electric Lighting Co. (DISCO) to supply current for traction purposes to the west end should Corporation-owned feeder equipment be hit, and vice versa, whilst the North Eastern Electric Supply Co. (NESCO) Byker station was to provide a similar service for trams and trolleybuses in the east end.

In September 1940, a German bomber, possibly mistaking the ribbon of the West Road for the Tyne, pitched a string of light bombs, nine in all, along the line of the road from Benwell Grove westwards to Condercum Road. Four of these produced craters in the road surface and trolleybuses had to negotiate these the next morning.

By December 1940, last tram and trolleybus journeys were brought forward to end at 10 p.m. in order to save power. Motorbuses were already finishing earlier than electric transport.

In February 1941, a severe blizzard struck the north-east and transport was completely paralysed, all main routes being blocked for some time. March 1941 saw the retirement of the General Manager, Mr. T. P. Easton, who had stayed on for an extra six months; Mr. H. C. Godsmark, formerly of Huddersfield, took over. Mr. Easton's opinions regarding trolleybuses were echoed by the new General Manager, for Mr. Godsmark quickly announced that it was still the intention to convert all tram routes to trolleybus operation after the war.

On 30th June 1941, Service 12 (Wallsend Boundary—Central Station) was extended via Grainger Street—Westgate Road—West Road—*Fox-&-Hounds*— Fox-and-Hounds Lane—Tower View—Ferguson's Lane and Whickham View (where a new turning circle was provided), operating daily.

On 1st September 1941 an unexploded bomb prevented trolleybuses from proceeding east of Skew Bridge, Walkergate, about $\frac{1}{4}$ mile west of Wallsend Boundary terminus, and a temporary diversion via Welbeck Road to Westbourne Avenue reverser, about $\frac{1}{2}$ mile south, was substituted. During the period 1st to 5th September 1941, when the LNER New Bridge Street Goods Station was hit (see earlier) New Bridge Street was closed; services were curtailed and diverted and motorbuses covered the affected part of the route.

In October 1941, new signs were erected to show tram and trolleybus drivers where to cut off power in order to avoid arcing from the overhead. Also at this time, queue barriers were appearing at stops in the City centre due to increasing use being made of public transport in the wartime conditions. Queues were separated for different services for the first time.

November 1941 saw three events of interest. The increasing number of passengers had made it necessary for the Undertaking to look around for additional vehicles. Trolleybuses built for use in South Africa were about to enter service in London and the Undertaking is reported to have investigated the possibility of obtaining similar vehicles for use in Newcastle, but nothing came of this. However, Newcastle Transport did order through the Ministry of War Transport (not the manufacturers) the vehicles intended for the Elswick Road conversion. These were to be twenty Karrier E6A chassis at £1,474 each, ten Roe bodies at £1,190 each and ten Metro-Cammell bodies at £1,230 each, an order totalling £53,680. The order was confirmed by the Council in December 1941.

The third event of November 1941 was the extension, on the 23rd of that month, of the Fenham route a short distance beyond its existing terminus at Two Ball Lonnen. Growing traffic demands from the residents of Stamfordham Road Estate necessitated the extension of the wiring along Netherby Drive to a new terminus at Bingfield Gardens, at the foot of Netherby Drive, $\frac{1}{3}$ mile farther west. The new terminus was still shown as "Fenham" on destination indicators until the end of the system although it was actually on the edge of the Slatyford area. The motorbuses continued to run along Stamfordham Road, and the Two Ball Lonnen reverser at Ovington Grove was removed at this time.

Volunteer auxiliary conductors, known locally as "Platform Guards", were introduced on 15th December 1941 on trams, trolleybuses and motorbuses. They were issued with an arm brassard, and it was their function to call out stopping places (especially in the blackout), to signal drivers, and to register the numbers of passengers boarding, thus fulfilling a useful function.

April 1942 saw, with the introduction of Double Summer Time, an attempt to get the tram and trolleybus services extended to 10.30 p.m., but the crews refused and approached the Ministry of War Transport in protest.

Also in April 1942, the same Government Department offered seven Karrier W4, two-axle chassis, with bodies by an unspecified manufacturer, at a total cost of £18,844. This was in part answer to the previous year's order for twenty Karrier E6As which Newcastle was destined never to receive. The offer of the seven utility vehicles was, therefore, accepted, but Newcastle Transport had to wait a long time for them to materialise—in fact until the Spring of 1944—when they entered service as Nos. 125—131 (JTN 955—961). They were the first two-axle trolleybuses owned and when delivered, fitted with Park Royal utility bodies, their austere finish and unfamiliar layout were in strong contrast with the pre-war trolleybuses.

Meanwhile, five Brighton Corporation AEC 661T two-axle vehicles, 11—15 (FUF11—15), with Weymann 54-seat bodies and dating from 1939, were hired in May 1942. Some entered service in June and others in September, mainly on route 9, but they were returned to Brighton during September and October. The red livery of these Brighton vehicles contrasted with the City's own electric vehicles, and the public noticed.

Still desperate for trolleybuses, the Corporation next approached the Bradford undertaking, who had ten old trolleybuses available for disposal. These were English Electric type E11 three-axle vehicles with 56-seat English Electric bodies and dated from 1929/32! Newcastle sent a party to the Yorkshire city to inspect the vehicles in October 1942 and decided to purchase them. Only nine were prepared for service, and of these, three were never licensed. Six entered service in March and April 1943 and the tenth was cannibalised for spares. They took blank Newcastle fleet numbers 1—9, the tenth being given number 0. In actual fact their advanced age necessitated a limited use, mainly as rush-hour extras, usually on the Westbourne Avenue (Walker)—Pilgrim Street short working, but they have also been reported as used on the Elswick Road services when this was newly converted. Their role was only a stop-gap but they lasted until December 1948. All ten cost only £2,000.

Bournemouth Corporation Transport, like Brighton, had been experiencing a fall in traffic due to the War and the restriction on visits to the South Coast which was designated a Prohibited Area due to the proximity to occupied France, so they were able to loan ten of their well-known Sunbeam MS2 trolleybuses to London in December 1940. When the capital's position eased nine were returned to Bournemouth in November 1941. Newcastle Transport gratefully received nine on loan in September 1942 and five of them stayed until 1945. The other four were transferred to nearby South Shields, where they were referred to as "Newcastle Trolleys". The Park Royal front-exit bodies were similar in style to the standard Newcastle trolleybus layout and while in Newcastle they operated frequently on the Wallsend—Westgate Road route. They were, of course, in Bournemouth livery.

The *Newcastle Journal* for the 8th June 1942 reported an unusual incident which had occurred on the previous Saturday, the 6th. At about 3 p.m., Driver R. Walton of Ovington Grove, Fenham, was driving an eastbound trolleybus down Westgate Road towards the City centre. On the shallow descent of Arthurs Hill the vehicle had to stop to lower its booms in order to pass under a section of overhead which was under repair. Having passed this, Driver Walton discovered that the emergency brake(?) was not acting. The vehicle "gathered speed at an alarming rate". Mrs. M. Golds of Benwell, the conductress, prevented passengers leaving their seats. At the Big Lamp, Driver Walton discovered that the road ahead was blocked by vehicles and pedestrians, and he faced the prospect of running down Westgate Hill, a steep gradient, to certain disaster in the City centre. He therefore swung the trolleybus across Elswick Road into Summerhill Street. The down gradient in this side street was rendered more difficult to negotiate by brick air-raid shelters erected in the roadway, and he was forced to run on the pavement to avoid them. At the foot of Summerhill Street he turned right into Cross Parade and right again, uphill into York Street. Here the gradient reduced the speed and Driver Walton was able to bring the runaway to a stand at the kerb, unscathed, in Elswick Road. On 6th July, the Transport Committee voted awards to Driver Walton (who had 31 years service) of £10, Mrs. Golds £5 and an off-duty conductor, who assisted Mrs. Golds, £5.

On 21st December 1942, an additional sub-station on Walker Road was brought into use to cope with still further increased traffic.

Slowly the quota of vehicles for the Elswick Road conversion was being built up. In February 1943, the Ministry of War Transport offered a further five Karrier W4s at a cost of £14,260, including bodies. The body-builder had, again, not been decided at this stage, but as with the previous batch, Park Royal supplied the utility 56-seat bodies. These trolleybuses, which became Nos. 132—136, (JTN 962—966), were delivered with 125—131 in April 1944. A further six Karrier W4s were then offered, two being built with Weymann bodies at £1,175

The yard of Brush coachworks is the setting for No. 16, as it stands with its front exit doors open: a 1935 view.   Brush

Tarpaulins protect the roof of No. 15, an AEC 664T, under tow from the Brush factory at Loughborough in 1935.   Brush

This enigmatic photograph of No. 10 appears to have been taken at Byker Depot in prewar days. The origin of the damage is unknown, but could have resulted from being crushed between two trams.

Tyne & Wear P.T.E.

The Church Street, Walker, terminus frames a Karrier E6A with Metro-Cammell body c.1936. The vehicle appears to be in non-standard (blue?) livery.   Tyne & Wear P.T.E.

Delivered in 1940, this Roe-bodied Karrier E6A is seen at Central Station in immediate postwar livery, having been renumbered from 118 to 418. The other trolleybus is in prewar livery as modified during wartime, whilst the motorbus is a Corporation "Blue Bus".   Tyne & Wear P.T.E.

A rare view of Karrier E6A No. 40. This vehicle had a Metro-Cammell body and is seen climbing Denton Bank c.1936.   Tyne & Wear P.T.E.

59

An official view of No. 109 outside the Spital Tongues premises of Northern Coachbuilders Ltd. The Guy chassis had been exhibited at the 1937 Commercial Show and was later purchased by Newcastle Corporation Transport; it became the first Newcastle trolleybus to receive a body by this manufacturer.   Northern Coachbuilders

Central Station terminus is the location for this view of No. 105. On this occasion the vehicle is in modified prewar livery, featuring grey roof, and white wheel arches.
W. J. Haynes

A postwar view of 414, ex. No. 114, at the Central Station terminus of route 36 to Fenham. The vehicle is a Karrier E6A with Roe body.   C. Carter

No. 121 undergoing the obligatory tilt test at the Metro-Cammell factory in 1940. This Karrier E6A was one of the last batch of trolleybuses delivered to prewar body design.
Metro-Cammell

A Day at the Races: Neville Street in the fine summer of 1947 is the setting as two trolleybuses and a Newcastle "Blue Bus" negotiate the crowds waiting for Gosforth Park bound trams. *Newcastle Chronicle & Journal*

Market Street, looking east, Summer 1947? Ex-Bradford English Electric 6-wheeler in wartime grey, turns left on a Pilgrim Street short working. B & F Class trams and prewar trolleybuses shift rush-hour crowds. The only known photograph of one of the ex-Bradford trolleybuses in service in Newcastle. *N. Hanson collection*

The Great Blizzard, February, 1941, and troops are clearing snow in Gallowgate. Three trolleybuses, including one on service 5c(?) are trapped in drifts.

Newcastle Chronicle & Journal

This view shows that the Park Royal utility bodies of Newcastle's first batch of wartime Karrier W's did not have rear destination indicators. No. 427 is seen at the junction of Wingrove Road/ Westgate Road. Both the 4-wheeler and a prewar 6-wheeler have become dewired on the Wingrove Depot exit wiring, c.1947.   G. S. Hearse

Four Brighton Corporation AEC 661T trolleybuses with Weymann bodies built in 1939 were loaned to Newcastle for a brief period in 1942 to cover wartime shortages. No photograph of one in service in Newcastle seems to exist and Brighton No. 15, one of those which did venture north, is seen here back in its home town at the Old Steine terminus in 1959.   L.T.P.S.

Denton Square terminus, c.1947, is the suburban location for Guy BTX/Roe No. 378. The vehicle is still in prewar livery but with grey roof, and is on service 4B to St. Nicholas Cathedral.   Newcastle City Libraries and four with Park Royal bodies at £1,250. These were delivered in March 1945 as Nos. 137—142, (JVK 277—282).

Although it had been decided earlier in the war that the conversion of the Elswick Road route should be held back until peace returned, the route was in fact turned over from tramcar operation on 11th June 1944. So ended the working of the Elswick Road tramcars up Westgate Road to the Wingrove Sheds from the Big Lamp. Certain cars from other routes continued to use Wingrove depot until March 1945, and it is believed that a number of Scotswood trams were crewed from there due to a shortage of depot space elsewhere, as no trams were being scrapped.

The wiring for trolleybuses on the route differed from the original intention. The link from the Big Lamp to Barrack Road (along Buckingham Street and Heber Street) was not carried out at all. It is now known that due to their narrowness, the consent of the Minister was required if Buckingham Street and Heber Street were to be wired up, so the Corporation may have decided to forego this part in order to convert the route to trolleybuses without delay. In the City centre, vehicles operating the newly-converted service used Clayton Street, Grainger Street and Westgate Road as their terminal loop, as the trams had done. The standing point was at Eldon Square siding, although "Monument" (i.e. the Earl Grey Monument at the junction of Blackett Street and Grainger Street) was shown on the destination screens. At the outer end of the route, Denton Road Terminus became the westernmost destination, while Delaval Road (the ultimate tram terminus), Benwell and (½ mile east) Nichol Street, Benwell ("Benwell Church" on the indicators) became sub-termini (see Chapter 11—"Beneath Ten Miles of Trolleybus Wires"). The only new traction poles required had been at terminal points and junctions, and on the Whickham View link. This had been important, since steel was scarce at the time. Span wires were predominant.

The new services operated as follows:—
DENTON ROAD TERMINUS (junction of Denton Road and Whickham View) (turning circle) (3)—Whickham View—DELAVAL ROAD (junction of Benwell Lane with Delaval Road) (3A) Benwell Lane—BENWELL CHURCH (reverser at junction of Adelaide Terrace and Nichol Street) (3B)—Adelaide Terrace—Elswick Road—Westgate Road—Clayton Street —MONUMENT (Eldon Square) (3) (3A) (3B) and return via Grainger Street to Westgate Road, operating daily.

These replaced tram services 34 (Delaval Road—Monument) and 35 (foot of Condercum Road—Monument), and this conversion all but cleared trams from the west end of the City. Only the Central Station—Scotswood—Throckley route remained. Trolleybus Service 12 was at the same time cut back from Denton Road terminus to *Fox & Hounds*. Public reaction was however, too strong and the service was re-extended through to Denton Road terminus with effect from Monday 31st July 1944, running until replaced by new service 32 on 1st November 1948.

The new trolleybus services were once again well received, and in his Annual Report, the General Manager mentioned the exceptionally fast accelerative powers of the Karrier W4's on the route. The new service had been in operation just over a year when peace was declared in August 1945, and the battered transport services could begin the task of returning to normal.

65

CHAPTER SEVEN

GATESHEAD AGAIN

At this time some developments took place in regard to the long-proposed trolleybus conversions in Gateshead. In order to safeguard Newcastle Corporation's interest under the Gateshead & District Tramways and Trolley Vehicles Act 1938, the Newcastle General Manager mentioned the necessity for applying for Provisional Powers to operate trolleybuses over the Tyne and High Level Bridges before December 1943 when powers expired, in order, it was hoped, to commit the Company to trolleybus operation.

In a letter to Newcastle Transport dated 29th September 1943, the Company noted that the City intended to apply for a Provisional Order for the High Level and Tyne Bridges connections, but it was surprised, as it had been the Company's opinion that "owing to the peculiar characteristics of the joint routes . . . motor omnibuses are more suitable for through services between Newcastle and Gateshead". There were, the Company said, also difficulties regarding labour and materials due to the War, if such a conversion to trolleybuses were to be implemented.

Notwithstanding, on 1st November 1943, the local authorities of Newcastle, Gateshead and Felling (covering the east side of Gateshead) together with the Gateshead Company, agreed to apply for such a Provisional Order. They stated though, that single-deck trolleybuses (illustrations show 3-axle) would probably have to be used due to "serious difficulties" with low railway bridges in Gateshead. The Company stated that it was not happy about the prospect of running single-deck trolleybuses due to their low load factor compared with the existing trams, yet considered single-deck "oil engine" motorbuses more suitable for the Saltwell Park, Bensham, Dunston and Low Fell routes—i.e. those operating over the High Level Bridge.

The B.E.T.-owned Company also pointed out that there were serious difficulties in trying to operate double-deck trolleybuses up West Street due to the low clearance of West Street bridge. To overcome similar problems at Hills Street Bridge, where it would only be possible to operate one trolleybus through at a time because of the steep pitch of the arch (trams had interlaced track here), it might be necessary to use Half Moon Lane (parallel to Hills Street) and Hills Street as one-way streets in opposite directions with one road of wiring in each.

By May 1944, the Company's opinion was that Tyne Bridge services should be converted to trolleybuses and that High Level services should be converted to motorbuses. Gateshead Corporation and Newcastle Transport, however, still considered that trolleybuses were suitable for all Gateshead routes and asked the Minister of War Transport to intervene to break the deadlock over the question of trolleybuses on the High Level Bridge services.

In March 1944, the City's Town Clerk wrote to the General Manager of the Gateshead Company informing him that Newcastle Council had decided that tram services over the Tyne Bridge should be converted to trolleybus operation as soon as possible, and that their respective experts should meet to decide the feasibility of operating trolleybuses over the High Level Bridge.

The next month, Mr. D. P. Morrison, the General Manager of Bournemouth Corporation Transport, completed a report he had prepared with Mr. Godsmark (Newcastle's General Manager) for the Gateshead Company on the feasibility of running trolleybuses in Gateshead. He made the following points:

(1) The operation of double-deck trolleybuses over the Tyne Bridge to Heworth and Wrekenton, in the east and south-east of Gateshead, posed no problems and should be proceeded with.

(2) The operation of double-deck trolleybuses over the High Level Bridge and in Wellington Street, Gateshead, however, would be difficult. The services were at present run by single-deck bogie trams.

(3) In order to run "high-bridge" type double-deck trolleybuses, it would be necessary to raise the West Street railway bridge by five feet, or lower the roadway, and Mr. Morrison thought there was little likelihood of this (see Chapter 8). The headroom on the road deck of High Level Bridge, seventeen feet, although restricted, was adequate.

(4) The single-deck trams in use had twice the capacity of single-deck trolleybuses. There would, therefore, be difficulty in handling large crowds.

(5) The only possible turning points for trolleybuses in this part of Gateshead town centre were (for High Level services) Hudson Street and (for Tyne Bridge services) Half Moon Lane. Both were inconvenient and would cause congestion. Therefore, he concluded, single-deck trolleybuses were not adequate for traffic demands.

(6) He recommended single-deck motorbuses.

This report was discussed at a meeting in April 1944 at Manors, Newcastle Transport's Head Office, between Mr. Morrison, Newcastle and Gateshead Corporations, and the Gateshead Company's representatives. Mr. Morrison stated that many trolleybus conversions had been carried out in unsuitable areas, and he thought single-deck trolleybuses in Gateshead would be just such an unsuitable conversion, because of insufficient carrying capacity and inadequate bridge clearances.

During the meeting the possibility of changes in Ministry of Transport regulations was mentioned, and the prospect of three-axle, 30 feet long, 7ft. 6ins. wide single-deck trolleybuses carrying 58-60 passengers was also suggested. It was pointed out, though, that under existing size regulations it would take two-single-deck trolleybuses to match the 80-passenger capacity of a single-deck tramcar of the bogie type. Mr. Godsmark pointed out that although individual trolleybuses might be smaller than individual trams, the trolleybuses were faster and, therefore, (to use a modern term) there would be more "throughput" of vehicles.

It was agreed to approach the LNER regarding raising West Street railway bridge to ease the height restrictions. An illustration was shown to the meeting of the proposed overhead wiring layout at Gateshead Station (at the Gateshead end of the High Level) in Wellington Street, incorporating a siding to allow rush-hour extras to load.

No real agreement was reached between the experts at the meeting and it ended on an inconclusive note, perhaps hinting at the future.

At a further meeting of the Joint Committee of Newcastle and Gateshead Corporations concerned with the proposed trolleybus routes, held on 3rd October 1944, it was stated that all the equipment necessary for the conversion of the routes was available and it was possible to effect the conversion by 1948.

CHAPTER EIGHT

THE IMMEDIATE POSTWAR PERIOD

During the 1943-44 Session of Parliament, Newcastle Transport had applied for powers to run trolleybuses over the High Level and Tyne Bridges, thus safeguarding its interests as allowed for in the 1938 Gateshead Act. These powers were granted in 1945 and confirmed in the Newcastle upon Tyne (Trolley Vehicles) Order Confirmation Act, 1945, as follows:

Route 1: (3 furlongs) Commencing in Pilgrim Street, at the junction with Mosley Street and south along Pilgrim Street, over the New Tyne Bridge and terminating in the County Borough of Gateshead, in High Street, by a junction with the existing tramway of the Gateshead & District Tramways Company at a point opposite the northeast corner of Hills Street.

Route 2: (2 furlongs.) Commencing in St. Nicholas Street at a point 0.9 chains north-west of its junction with Westgate Road by a junction with Route 2 of the Act of 1935 and passing south over the High Level Bridge and its approaches and along Wellington Street in the County Borough of Gateshead and terminating by a junction with the existing tramway 0.8 chains south-east of the junction of Wellington Street and Hudson Street.

Route 3: (5 furlongs.) Commencing in Percy Street at the junction with St. Thomas Street by a junction with Route 16 of the Order of 1938 and passing along Percy Street, Newgate Street, Bigg Market and Groat Market and St. Nicholas Street, terminating in that street 1.13 chains south of the junction with Collingwood Street by a junction with Route 2 of the Act of 1935.

Proposed Route 3 ran southwards from the exit wiring of the Haymarket Depot, down to St. Nicholas Cathedral, but only the Percy Street/Newgate Street part (to Grainger Street junction) was actually constructed, and was in fact the only part of the Act ever carried out. Newgate Street and Percy Street were therefore wired up much later for trolleybus operation than other streets in the Central area. A similar situation had applied with regard to the trams.

Newcastle was now seemingly ready to run joint trolleybus services with the Gateshead Company. Newcastle Transport was to pay for all the works under the Act, including erection of all wiring to High Level and Tyne Bridge junctions with the Gateshead tramways, and all would be owned by Newcastle Corporation, even though the centre of the river was the boundary between the City and Gateshead. In March 1945, presumably in readiness for trolleybus operation, the LNER agreed to raise West Street bridge in Gateshead at a cost of £7,500.

The General Manager, Mr. Godsmark, wasted no time after peace was declared in making arrangements for the long-awaited expansion of the trolleybus network and the consequent destruction of the tramway system. Formal powers for the conversion of the remaining tram services, together with several new routes, were set out in the Newcastle upon Tyne Corporation Act, 1946. These were as follows:—

Route 1: (3 miles 7 furlongs.) Commencing in the Great North Road in the Rural District of Castle Ward 6.2 chains north of the main entrance to Gosforth Park, by a junction with route 8 of this Act and passing south along the Great North Road, High Street, Great North Road and terminating in Great North Road in the City at its junction with Jesmond Road.

Route 2: (6 miles 4 furlongs.) Commencing in Newburn Road in the Urban District of Newburn 0.5 chains south of its junction with Hexham Road (as West Road is called at this point) passing along Newburn Road, Church Bank, High Street, Lemington Road, Northumberland Road, Tyne View and Scotswood Road and terminating in Scotswood Road in the City at the junctions of Neville Street and Clayton Street West, by a junction with routes 9 and 11 of the Order of 1938.

Route 3: (3 furlongs.) Commencing in the Urban District of Newburn in Lemington Road at the junction of Northumberland Road by a junction with Route 2 of this Act and terminating in Scotswood Road, Lemington by a junction with Route 2 opposite Holy Saviour's Church.

Route 4: (1 mile 2 furlongs.) Commencing in Jesmond Road at its junction with Osborne Road, passing along Jesmond Road, Benton Bank and Stephenson Road and terminating at either Chillingham Road or Benton Road at their junction with Stephenson Road by a junction with Route 7.

Route 5: (4 furlongs.) Commencing in Shields Road at its junction with Raby Street passing along Raby Street and terminating in Walker Road at its junction with Raby Street.

Route 6: (7 furlongs.) Commencing in New Bridge Street at its junction with Clarence Street, passing along Clarence Street, Portland Road and Sandyford Road and terminating in Jesmond Road at its junction with Sandyford Road.

Route 7: (4 miles.) Commencing in Shields Road at its junction with Chillingham Road and passing along Chillingham Road, Benton Road, Benton Lane, Park Terrace and Great Lime Road and terminating at a point 6.4 chains north west of East Gosforth Lodge by a junction with Route 8.

Route 8: (1 mile 2 furlongs.) Commencing in Great North Road by a junction with Route 1, passing through High Gosforth Park and terminating in Great Lime Road by a junction with Route 7. (This was the Gosforth Park Light Railway's course through the Park.)

Route 9: (1 mile.) Commencing in Shields Road at its junction with Heaton Road, passing along Heaton Road and terminating in Stephenson Road at its junction with Heaton Road.

Route 10: (1 mile 1 furlong.) Commencing in Longbenton U.D.C. at

69

Benton Four Lane Ends and passing along Benton and Whitley main roads, Station Road and terminating in Station Road (Forest Hall) at a point 1.2 chains north of Benton View junction.

Route 11: (1 mile 1 furlong.) Commencing in Ponteland Road at its junction with Fenham Hall Drive and passing along Ponteland Road, Stamfordham Road, Two Ball Lonnen and terminating in Two Ball Lonnen at its junction with Fenham Hall Drive.

Route 12: (6 furlongs 9 chains.) Commencing in Stamfordham Road or Ponteland Road or Two Ball Lonnen at their junction with Route 11, passing along Stamfordham Road and terminating in Stamfordham Road at its junction with Blakelaw Road and Pooley Road.

Route 13: (1 mile 7 furlongs.) Commencing at the junction of Ponteland Road and Stamfordham Road, passing along Ponteland Road to the City boundary (at Kenton Bank Foot).

Route 14: (1 mile 2 furlongs.) Commencing in Fossway at the south entrance to Byker tram depot and passing easterly along Fossway and Maurice Road and terminating in Neptune Road, Wallsend, by a junction with the route of 1935.

Route 15: (5 furlongs 2 chains.) Commencing in Osborne Road at its junction with Lonsdale Terrace, passing along Osborne Road, Jesmond Dene Road and Matthew Bank to the City boundary.

Route 16: (2 miles 3 furlongs.) Commencing in Stephenson Road at its junction with Newton Road, passing along Newton Road, Freeman Road and Benton Park Road to Benton, Four Lane Ends.

Also authorised were the usual links and depot accesses thought necessary.

In addition, Newcastle Transport was obliged to erect a turning point for trolleybuses at, or near, the tram terminus at Henry Street, Gosforth. Proposed Routes, 11, 12, 13, 14, 15, and 16 were to be constructed within five years. Similarly, proposed Route 8 was to be built within seven years.

In order to continue the service that the trams had provided to Gosforth Park racecourse on race days, powers were given to run special trolleybuses via West Moor to the race course on such days. To work trolleybuses into the Park, the Corporation was empowered to abandon the Gosforth Park Light Railway and to construct a road along the right-of-way as described under proposed Route 8.

There were provisions for the protection of Longbenton U.D.C., through whose area the proposed Forest Hall and West Moor routes passed. Therefore, on proposed Route 7 (to West Moor and the East Gates of Gosforth Park) and proposed Route 10 (to Forest Hall) only certain agreed fares were to be charged. If a loss was made, provision was made for the fares to be increased in the following financial year, provided two months notice was given to Longbenton U.D.C.

Clauses were also included which protected Wallsend Corporation and the Tyneside Tramways and Tramroads Company (Proposed Route 14—reference to Maurice Road, which is the name the Fossway takes in Wallsend for its last few yards).

70

Borrowing powers were also given to finance the provisions of the Act, including £40,000 for roadworks, £215,000 for electrical works and £570,000 for vehicles.

The sections of the proposed routes actually opened were Routes 1, 4, 7 (Benton Road only), 9, 15 (excluding part of Osborne Road) and 16 (excluding the High Heaton section of Newton Road and Freeman Road). The Fossway section only of proposed route 14 was eventually wired in 1957 as a result of the Heaton Works Light Railway Order, 1956 (see Chapter 9), not as part of the provisions of the 1946 Act.

The powers embodied in the above Act were very comprehensive, and would have increased route mileage from $24\frac{3}{4}$ to $44\frac{1}{2}$, had they all been implemented. They covered the conversion of all the remaining tram routes operated wholly north of the river, which were mainly in the north-eastern suburbs and in the east-end (apart from the long Throckley route through the west-end) and the extension of trolleybuses over roads not previously served by electric traction—viz, proposed routes 11, 12, 13, 14, 15, and 16.

Proposed route 11 would have carried the wires on up Ponteland Road through the Cowgate area and then south again to rejoin the Fenham route at Fenham Hall Drive junction. Proposed Route 12 was a partial revival of the pre-war plans to convert the former Westerhope tram route. However, its inner end was to come from Cowgate via Stamfordham Road, not directly along the line of the tramway. It will be noticed that proposed route 12 was to stop short of Westerhope at Pooley Road junction to serve Blakelaw Estate which was being built at that time.

Proposed Route 13 was more ambitious, nearly two miles long, from Cowgate all the way to the City boundary at Kenton Bank Foot. It would have passed through a built-up area for approximately the first mile, to Kenton Bar, but then would have run through open fields to the small detached suburban community of Kenton Bank Foot—hardly ideal traffic potential! In addition the route would have terminated at the foot of an incline, under a railway bridge, on a bend on the A696 major road to Scotland! The built-up area has advanced since then of course, and at the time of writing (1972) a "New Town" estate is to be built to cover the remaining fields.

Proposed routes 12 and 13 would have required extensive alteration to the overhead in the 1950s, had they been built, as sections of Ponteland Road and Stamfordham Road were re-constructed as dual-carriageway, the new west-bound carriageway of Stamfordham Road being constructed on part of the track-bed of the former Westerhope Tramroad.

Proposed route 2 (City—Scotswood—Lemington—Newburn—Throckley) was a tram route. The outer part was converted to motorbus operation in June 1946, after a decision made in October 1945, although this was stated at the time to be only a temporary measure, pending introduction of trolleybuses. It left trams running only the Scotswood—City section until October 1948 (rush-hour extras until 11th September 1949). It was necessary to use single-deck motor-buses at first, due to two weak railway bridges in Lemington. The trams had been able to by-pass the area on reserved track, which in proposed route 3 of the 1946 Act it was proposed to make into a roadway over which trolleybuses would operate. The roadway is there now, but it has never seen a trolleybus.

As with the Kenton Bank Foot route, the Act only empowered the Corporation to run to an awkward terminal point, 11 yards short of the West Road junction at Throckley in front of the Lyric Cinema, which was the former tram terminus. Where trolleybuses could have turned is a mystery, for the road is only about 30 feet wide and there is no convenient side street for a reverser. Present day motorbus services cross over the West Road and use a wide stretch of road in a housing estate on the other side as their standing point.

Proposed route 5, which covered the existing Raby Street tram route in the east-end suburb of Byker, became motorbus operated, whilst proposed route 6 covered the Shieldfield/Sandyford tram route, connecting New Bridge Street and Jesmond Road. Proposed route 7 also covered an existing tram route and would have gone through the north-eastern suburbs to West Moor and the east entrance of Gosforth Park, an exit for the trolleybuses being provided from the Park in proposed Route 8, which was the conversion of the Gosforth Park Light Railway into a road. This would have enabled trolleybus services to have been worked through the Park to and from the Great North Road as had the trams. It was intended to work these Race Specials through Heaton and West Moor via Chillingham Road and Benton Road. It would have been interesting to see trolleybuses dealing with the race crowds at Gosforth Park Grandstand, but it was not to be. Today, Tyne & Wear P.T.E. motorbuses handle race traffic on a large expanse of tarmac where the Grandstand Tramway Station used to be in the Park, from a point marked with "Q here for Buses" notices. It is believed that a difference of opinion with the Ministry of Transport regarding the £25,000 cost of providing the roadway through the Park and the cost of strengthening a tram-way bridge in the Park, prevented the Gosforth Park Light Railway and the West Moor route being converted to trolleybus operation. As a consequence of the failure to get the Gosforth Park and West Moor routes converted to trolley-buses, proposed route 10 to Forest Hall became motorbus worked.

Proposed routes 15 and 16 are interesting in that sections were not built and other sections became links for wiring seemingly not authorised by the Act! As can be seen from the overhead map, the short section of proposed route 15 at the north end of Osborne Road, Jesmond, was not wired, although the traction poles and section boxes were put up and were in situ until 1968. The section of wiring in Jesmond Dene Road between the Great North Road and the top of Osborne Road does not appear in the Act. Presumably this length of wiring was erected under the broad heading of "links thought necessary".

To cope with this enormous projected expansion of the trolleybus system Newcastle Transport initially ordered, in February 1946, thirty-six two-axle Karrier chassis with Metro-Cammell bodies at £3,786 each, a total of £136,296. The Council were warned of the probability of long delays in delivery, hence the need to order at this time. The vehicles were delivered, mostly in early 1949, as Sunbeam F4s with fleet numbers 443—478 (LBB 43—78). The existing trolleybus fleet had been renumbered by adding 300 to existing numbers in 1946, to avoid duplicating with motorbus fleet numbers. 1946 saw once again, a change of General Manager, as Mr. Frank S. Taylor inherited the trolleybus conversion operation, and he remained in the post until his retirement in 1968.

There were several meetings held during 1946 regarding the Gateshead trolleybuses. At one, on 7th August, between the two Corporations, the Town Clerk of Gateshead raised the matter of the extension of the new form of trans-port beyond the existing tram termini after conversion. Newcastle stated that they were only concerned with the actual conversion of existing routes and that

Gateshead Corporation should bring this matter to the Company's notice if they required extensions.

At a meeting held on the 3rd October, several items of importance were discussed. The police had refused permission to run trolleybuses wider than 7 feet 6 inches over the High Level Bridge, and at this meeting the decision was accepted by both Newcastle and Gateshead Corporations. One wonders why, therefore, that the 8ft. wide B.U.T. three-axle stock of both 1948 and 1950 carried both "Gateshead Station" and "Dunston" on their destination blinds, since to reach these points would entail a journey over the High Level Bridge. Also at the October meeting, Newcastle asked the Gateshead Company to give details of the vehicles they had ordered for the proposed conversion, which the City was eager to pursue. They were surprised to learn that no trolleybuses had been ordered. The Company gave as their reasons the fact that a formal through running agreement had not yet been signed, and the decision by the police not to allow 8ft. wide vehicles over the High Level had not been taken until August.

The turning points for trolleybuses in the centre of Gateshead were also discussed. Those for the Tyne Bridge services had, it was stated, already been agreed. For the High Level Bridge routes there were three possibilities:

(a)   Wellington Street/Hudson Street, to which the police objected.

(b)   Running up West Street to the Shipley Art Gallery (about 1 mile) and turning there, if West Street railway bridge was raised in the next 3-4 months, and the Company were ready to alter the overhead (suggested by Gateshead Corporation, upon which Newcastle Transport stated they could not help with this extension to the overhead line as they were fully committed).

(c)   A turning loop of the High Level and Tyne Bridges, by which, after coming over the High Level, trolleybuses would turn left into Half Moon Lane (parallel to Hills Street) and return to Newcastle via Tyne Bridge.

The Company were not very enthusiastic. First, they stated that they were not expecting the delivery of any new trolleybuses before 1948 or early 1949, and in any event, they could not agree to Newcastle trolleybuses running up West Street to the Shipley Art Gallery under their wires. Nor could they even agree to the City's vehicles coming over the High Level to turn at Wellington Street. They suggested turning such vehicles in the centre of Newcastle and this is what happened on conversion of the Gosforth route in April 1948. Finally, it was stated that the only route on which the police were prepared to allow 8 ft. wide trolleybuses was that to Low Fell.

November 1946 witnessed several events of importance. First, 50 further vehicles were ordered for the new extensions, well in advance to counter the long waiting-lists manufacturers had at this time for both home and export orders. Twenty were to be B.U.T. 9641T three-axle vehicles with Metro-Cammell 8ft. wide 70-seat bodies (479—498) and thirty were to be Sunbeam S7 three-axle vehicles with Northern Coachbuilders 7ft. 6ins. wide 70-seat bodies (499—528). The B.U.T. chassis cost £48,649 and their MCW bodies £55,400, whilst the Sunbeam chassis cost £76,043 and their NCB bodies £77,850.

The B.U.T's were under construction for London Transport, but were diverted to Newcastle, being described by the General Manager as "the largest,

73

most modern road passenger vehicles in the country". There were 97 being built for the capital in 1948, but by arrangement with the manufacturers and their would-be owners, twenty were diverted to the north-east to ease Newcastle's acute trolleybus shortage. They were delivered in the spring of 1948, followed by the Sunbeam S7s in the late autumn of that year (i.e. before the delivery of the two-axle Sunbeam F4s) and were registered in one block (LTN 479—528).

In preparation for the proposed conversion, the Undertaking began building sub-stations to supplement those already existing for the trams. One such was planned and built for the North Road—Gosforth Park route at Broadway West, about 3½ miles north of the City centre. In November 1946 conversion of the West Moor tram sub-station on Benton Lane was authorised, it being intended to install a mercury-arc rectifier in place of the rotary convertors. In May 1947, the building of a new sub-station at Cartington Terrace, in North Heaton, was authorised to provide power for the intended trolleybus services on Chillingham and Heaton Roads. It could be (and was) used by trams until the trolleybuses arrived. In addition, it was originally intended to construct a new sub-station for the South Gosforth route in Grandstand Road, near the junction of the Great North Road and Jesmond Dene Road. Unfortunately, a site was not available but an alternative location was found at Matthew Bank. At South Gosforth itself, another distribution point was erected in Benton Park Road near the old Tyneside Company's cutting. In all 1,200 Kw capacity of mercury-arc rectifier plant was installed for these conversions and use was again made of spare cable conduits provided on the original tramway routes to carry the extra feeders, so avoiding the normal expense of excavation and backfilling.

Another event of November 1946 instilled a note of doom into all these plans of expansion, although it was not heeded at the time. A Councillor King said in Council that trolleybuses were liable to cause stoppages in the streets "as the trams had done" and asked if it was wise to use trolleybuses "which cause traffic blocks", and should the Corporation not be using "more mobile oil 'buses?"

December 1946 saw an event which would seemingly reinforce the view that Gateshead and District were soon to substitute trolleybuses for their trams. An agreement was proposed between Newcastle Transport and the Company which dealt with the through running of Gateshead trolleybuses and which was to remain in force for a period of ten years. Mutual assistance was to be given in case of breakdowns.

The routes which it was proposed to operate were those covering the joint tram services in operation at that time and were as follows (Gateshead termini quoted first):

Low Fell to Gosforth
Low Fell to Central Station
Dunston to Central Station
Bensham to Central Station
Saltwell Park to Blackett Street (Monument)
Wrekenton to Barras Bridge
Heworth to Chillingham Road (Heaton)

At the same time powers were sought to abandon the tram tracks in Great

North Road, Newcastle, and to lay the way open for trolleybus conversion. In spite of this move, considerable relaying of tracks and repoling was taking place on the Gateshead tramway system during 1947-48, much of it using equipment purchased secondhand from Salford, Oldham and elsewhere.

In order to run trolleybuses over the proposed new routes in Newcastle, a large contract for supply of overhead equipment and cables was placed early in 1947. This included 517 traction poles (380 medium, 105 heavy and 32 extra-heavy), 100 bracket arms and 22 miles of traction running wire, in addition to insulators, ears, span wire and other fittings.

At Gosforth, plans were made in January 1947 for a sub-terminus at Holly-wood Avenue, to replace the tram terminus at Henry Street and to serve the Gosforth Greyhound Stadium and Rugby Ground. Considerable siding space was erected, sufficient to hold fifteen trolleybuses for Stadium crowds. A long siding outside the North Road entrance was also built. In February 1947 authorisation was given for the purchase of land from the High Gosforth Park Company Ltd., for a turning point on the Great North Road (the future Gosforth Park terminus) and for the expense of altering a traffic island at Polwarth Drive, for the same purpose.

The weather, as in 1941, played a cruel role at this point. The winter of 1946-47 was the worst for many years, snow and ice remaining for many weeks. On Thursday, 13th March, a heavy blizzard struck the north-east and seriously dislocated all transport services, both road and rail. Even the tram services were curtailed.

In 1947, modifications were made to the Haymarket Depot to enable a third bay to be made available for trolleybuses. To do this, a new doorway in the College Avenue (now King's Road) end of the building was necessary. An air-raid shelter was filled in, between the footpath in College Avenue and the depot, and the ground surfaced. In addition, adjustment of levels was necessary between the road and the depot. This depot was of small area and capacity and extremely cramped, with tight curves in the tracks. It was approached from Georges Lane, a short, narrow thoroughfare off the Haymarket, and was originally a horse-tram depot with adjacent stables. The stable portion had had a new, higher roof fitted on electrification of the tramways and it was this part which had the sharp curves. It would appear that the total number of roads was only five and that trolleybuses used three of these in the former stable part. The remaining two were used by trams and in the nineteen fifties by motorbuses and/or for storing out-of-service trolleybuses. Our thanks must go, in passing, to Mr. G. S. Hearse for clarifying certain elusive points on this depot.

Meanwhile in July 1947, Gateshead obtained an extension for a further three years of their 1938 powers. Once again, this apparently further reinforced plans for trolleybus operation.

To replace pre-war vehicles and to further cater for the proposed vast expansion of Newcastle's system and the conversion of the Gateshead joint routes, fifty more trolleybuses were ordered in October 1947. It may appear questionable to the reader that trolleybuses only seven or eight years old should be replaced, when one considers that a pre-war trolleybus had a life of 12-15 years. Apparently the early demise of pre-war stock was founded on accountancy reasons. At this time it was cheaper to buy new vehicles out of revenue than to run existing stock until worn out, the logic being that the above course was better than purchasing replacements with borrowed money, possibly at high rates of interest, some years later.

The new stock was to be of the two-axle type, twenty-five Sunbeam F4s (529—533) and a similar number of B.U.T. 9611Ts (554—578). All were to be fitted with Northern Coachbuilders' 56-seat, 7ft. 6ins. wide bodies. This firm was, in this immediate post war period, extremely busy building bodies for transport undertakings all over the country. They had been engaged in the production of wings and parts for Barracuda aircraft during the war and after cessation of hostilities had quickly turned over to peacetime work. 'Buses were completed at the Newcastle factory in Claremont Road, Spital Tongues, but chassis were stored at the Company's premises at Cramlington, Northumberland, about nine miles north-east of the City centre. These premises were an old airship hangar and Northern Coachbuilders carried out tilt tests there on a machine built in their own workshops. Some bodies were actually built at Cramlington. The illustration shows a batch of the Sunbeam 6-wheelers under construction at Spital Tongues in June 1948.

An interesting and unique short-working point on the planned Gosforth Park route produced a great deal of controversy in Council during January 1948. This was the famous "Town Moor" turning circle in Grandstand Road, opposite Jesmond Dene Road junction. It consisted of 63 yards of wiring, on the left of the North Road, which then turned on to the Town Moor on the south side of Grandstand Road and back to the Great North Road, thus forming a circle. The section let into the Moor was railed off and gates were placed at its entrance and exit to Grandstand Road. The terminus was intended to be used on the occasion of exhibitions, fairs and shows held on the Town Moor, but especially for "The Hoppings", the giant Race Week Fair held every year during the last week in June. The purpose of this specially-built turning circle, costing £3,100, was to prevent the dislocation of the regular North Road service by specials, for the nearest existing turning point was at Hollywood Avenue. The Town Moor circle reduced empty running and the number of vehicles required to operate the service. Some Councillors opposed its building on the grounds that yet another piece of open space was being taken from the Moor, which is held in trust 'in perpetuity' by the City on the proviso that it is never to be built on. The built-up area completely surrounds the 900 acres of the Town Moor and extends far beyond it, yet the Moor remains refreshingly open.

During the next month, a further new sub-station was authorised in the west-end, to be built in Barrack Road beside the south-east corner of Fenham Barracks, for the proposed extensions of the Fenham route, which would take place "as soon as the necessary vehicles are available". Although the Fenham route was not extended under the 1946 Act, the sub-station was built; it is now a vandalised shell. West Moor sub-station, unused after the trams were withdrawn, had its yard used as a store for traction poles until the early nineteen sixties. The conversion of the overhead on the Gosforth route was described as 'virtually complete' by 31st March 1948 and preparatory work on the West Jesmond and Benton routes had commenced and was expected to be ready by "late 1948".

The first of the B.U.T. 9641T three-axle vehicles (believed to be 482) was delivered on 17th February 1948 and the remainder continued to arrive from

Metro-Cammell's Birmingham premises, to be stored at Byker depot ready for the first conversion, that of the Gosforth Park route. Two of the last four arrived on 8th April after a two-day tow. The illustrations show 482 on arrival and some of the batch newly-delivered. During 1948, the trolleybus capacity of Byker depot was increased to accommodate 40 more vehicles.

The contrast between the new B.U.T. 9641Ts (30ft. long, 8ft. wide with 70 seats) and the trams they replaced must have been enormous. The tramcars were all at least 22 years old, and their maintenance had been neglected during the war giving them a shoddy appearance, whilst the track had been allowed to deteriorate to a very poor condition—a revelation indeed when the trolleybuses took over.

The last tramcar to Gosforth, B class No. 290, ran on the night of Saturday 16th April 1948 following which the removal of redundant tram wires began in pouring rain during the night of Saturday and Sunday, 16th and 17th April. In the last few months, trams had used newly-erected trolleybus overhead, but not in the conventional way. Both up and down tram tracks were on the east side of the carriageway of the Great North Road north of Gosforth Stadium. New northbound trolleybus wires had been erected over the west side of the road, but it was necessary only to erect a negative wire on the southbound side, the southbound tram wire being used as the trolleybus positive. This left the northbound tram wire in the centre of each span wire, and it was this that had to be removed.

The Gosforth Park trolleybus route opened with a civic ceremony on 18th April 1948. As mentioned there were four turning points, as follows (going north):—Town Moor, Hollywood Avenue, Polwarth Drive and Gosforth Park Gates (actually West Gates). As can be seen from the indicator blind details, "North Gosforth" was also carried but not used, and it is possible that if all the powers had been implemented, this would have been used to describe the actual terminus at West Gates, and "Gosforth Park" used for the race course itself, in the Park. At Gosforth Park Gates, where the trams had a special entrance to the Gosforth Park Light Railway, a turning circle for trolleybuses was erected. For almost one year, prior to the inauguration of the trolleybus system in Glasgow in April 1949, this became the northernmost trolleybus terminus in the British Isles, being approximately 24 miles north of Belfast's Glengormley terminus. At Polwarth Drive's junction with the Great North Road, another circle was provided to serve Brunton Park Estate, replacing a tramway crossover at this point.

From Barras Bridge junction with Jesmond Road, where the 1938 wires of the Osborne Road route diverged, the new trolleybus wires ran in a northerly direction up the A1 trunk road with the open space of Town Moor on the left, and glimpses through the trees of the houses in Jesmond on the right. After about two miles, the route crossed the City boundary into Gosforth, which is in Northumberland. After threading the busy High Street, which fulfils an out-of-town shopping area function for north Newcastle, the route continued, passing over the branch railway line to Ponteland (closed to passengers 1929) at Three Mile Bridge. North of this the section of tramway to Gosforth Park Gates was, until 1930, owned by the Tyneside Company, and was bought by Newcastle Corporation on the cessation of tram operation by the Company, as mentioned earlier in the text. The remaining two miles ran nearly to Wideopen and were in due course flanked by exclusive housing estates built in the nineteen fifties.

The new trolleybus services operated as follows:
Services 31 and 31A
CENTRAL STATION (31) (31A)—Neville Street—Grainger Street West
—Grainger Street—Market Street—Pilgrim Street—Northumberland Street
—Barras Bridge—Great North Road—Gosforth High Street—Great North
Road—GOSFORTH PARK (31) (turning circle) OR POLWARTH
DRIVE (31A) (turning circle) and return. Operated daily.
Service 31B
CENTRAL STATION—Neville Street—Grainger Street West—Grainger
Street—Newgate Street—Percy Street—Haymarket—Barras Bridge—Great
North Road—Gosforth High Street—Great North Road—HOLLYWOOD
AVENUE (elongated turning circle with siding in lay-by in Hollywood
Avenue itself) and return. Operated weekdays only.

All ran to a 10 minute frequency, and it should be noted that these were in an entirely new block of service numbers, a harbinger of things to come. They replaced the following tram services:
00 Gosforth Park Circle.
10 Central Station—Gosforth Park (or sub-termini)
30 Low Fell—Gosforth (Henry Street), worked jointly with Gateshead and District Tramways Co.

The earlier intention, as quoted in *Modern Transport* for 3rd August 1946, had been that the tram track would continue to be used by Gateshead trams as far as Henry Street, Gosforth, and the wires were altered to eliminate conflict between terminating trams and passing trolleybuses at this point. At a late stage, this was changed.

Gateshead trams still continued to operate the southern section of service 30 but ran only to Newcastle Central Station, and it now became necessary for the traveller to change from tram to trolleybus to travel from Low Fell to Gosforth. In addition, several other joint tram services were affected by the Gosforth conversion. Cars from Saltwell Park in Gateshead now terminated at Central Station instead of the Monument, and the Heworth—Chillingham Road circular service was split, trams from Heworth now terminating at Haymarket, with Newcastle cars from Chillingham Road and Shieldfield terminating at Pilgrim Street.

In June 1948, Mr. Morrison's fears of 1944 regarding the raising of West Street railway bridge in Gateshead were dispelled. At a cost of £15,000 the bridge was lifted 4 feet by hydraulic jacks, to give a clearance of 16 feet 6 inches. This was still not enough for double-deck trams, but now gave just sufficient clearance for double-deck trolleybuses, as well as any type of single-deck tramcar.

With reference to the new Gosforth Park route the *Newcastle Journal* reported on 15th July 1948 that the residents of "Gosforth Garden Village" in Hollywood Avenue were protesting against a proposal to extend trolleybuses along that road into the estate. This proposal resulted from a request by Gosforth U.D.C. in June 1948 to switch motorbus service 10 to Grange Estate and extend the trolleybuses from the Stadium terminus to the eastern end of Hollywood Avenue with the ultimate desire that they could be run along Broadway West to Grange Estate, about ¼ mile to the north on the west side of the Great North Road. By September 1948, after the local residents' protests, the Hollywood Avenue extension scheme was dropped.

On 19th November 1948 the General Manager gave the Town Clerk the estimated cost of extending trolleybuses along Broadway West into Grange Estate, which was then being built. The figure was £1,900, using materials in stock and the Department's own labour, and the extension would be built under Section 4 of the 1946 Act. The Ministry of Transport was approached for permission, this being given on 21st January 1949. There was, however, a delay of two years before the extension finally opened, and the matter is, therefore, taken up later in correct chronological sequence.

In the summer of 1948, at the same time that the Hollywood Avenue residents were protesting, the Transport Committee was reporting to the Council on the necessity to replace the existing tower wagons in view of the increased amount of overhead work occasioned by the conversion scheme. The tower wagon fleet at the time consisted of seven A.E.Cs (which were 23 years old and believed to have been converted from single-deck motorbuses) and two small Morris vehicles 16 years old. It was proposed to replace all of these with eight Karrier CK3 chassis similar to one already in service, the chassis to cost £4,817. In October 1948 an order was placed with Eagle hydraulic towers for these chassis, at a total cost of £6,924. The order was not exclusively for the Transport Department, some vehicles being for use of the City Lighting Department. All service vehicles were finished in Post Office red with straw-coloured Gill-Sans lettering.

Returning once again to the Gateshead saga, the 1938 plans, Newcastle's Order of 1945 for trolleybuses over the two bridges and frequent reports and statements in the press—even as late as 1948—still indicated that Gateshead and District would convert to trolleybuses. Newcastle was building up its post-war trolleybus fleet, and in readiness had added Gateshead destinations to indicator blinds (see Appendix E) and had arranged wiring (e.g. at the Newcastle end of the High Level Bridge) for easy erection of links. Gateshead and District was reported early in 1948 to have estimated the cost of converting to trolleybus operation as £750,000 (£600,000 to £700,000 being mentioned at other times). Press reports even mentioned that the Company had ordered eighty-three 56-seat two-axle trolleybuses, costing £250,000, whilst other reports rumoured seventy vehicles, a rather low figure considering that about 75 trams were to be replaced, but this has been officially refuted. The figure may have been merely an accurate estimate of the number of vehicles needed.

Finally, the Gateshead Company made a volte-face and in the Gateshead and District Tramways Act 1950, abandoned its powers to operate trolleybuses and took motorbus powers, at the same time changing its name to Gateshead and District Omnibus Company. In *Modern Tramway* for January 1950, Mr. J. H. Price wrote (and we quote with his permission) "The Gateshead and District Tramways Company have decided to close their tramway routes across the Tyne Bridge by 31st March 1950. This is by agreement with Newcastle Corporation, who are anxious to get rid of the small amount of tramway operation to which they are still committed by reason of the old established arrangements for through running onto the Gateshead system . . . The Company is a member of the British Electric Traction Group; this vast organisation, in spite of its name, is nowadays one of our biggest operators of motorbuses. It is therefore, not surprising that the trolleybuses have not been forthcoming and that the Company prefer to keep the trams running until the Corporation give way and consent to have 'buses instead. It is also not surprising that the Company have been quick to seize on the opportunity accorded them by Newcastle Corporation, whose love of trolleybuses is outweighed by their dislike of trams, and who, to get rid of the last vestige of rail traction in their department are willing to agree to the substitution of 'buses. According to the Company, conversion of the routes concerned to trolleybus operation could not be brought about in less than two or three years, and this is longer than Newcastle are willing to wait."

Thus when the last Newcastle trams were withdrawn on 4th March 1950 from the Wrekenton services, Newcastle Transport began running motorbuses over the Tyne Bridge to Wrekenton and Heworth, in Gateshead. The Gateshead Company could still, however, by reason of joint running agreements, operate trams to Newcastle Central Station. Thus Newcastle Transport was credited with 0.53 miles(!) of track in 1950 due to the operation of Gateshead trams over the High Level Bridge on the Low Fell, Saltwell Park, Bensham and Dunston routes.

This situation did not last long. Gateshead introduced its own diesel 'buses, Guy Arabs with Park Royal 7ft. 6ins. wide, 56-seat bodies, on the Bensham and Saltwell Park services on 4th March 1951 and on the Low Fell route on 8th April 1951. The through service between Gosforth and Low Fell was never restored. The Teams route closed in July 1951 and finally the last route, Central Station —Dunston, succumbed on 4th August 1951. Tyneside was without trams.

No longer could passengers, (including one of the authors, then of tender age), waiting for a westbound 34 trolleybus at Stephenson's Monument, watch the absorbing sight of Gateshead's bogie single-deckers arriving at their Central Station terminus and turning their trolleys ready to return south over the High Level Bridge; or at Haymarket terminus, whilst waiting for a No. 8 Circle 'bus, see cars coming and going on the stub track in Claremont Road.

The probable reasons for the Company's final decision not to operate trolleybuses were the fact that British Electric Traction, which controlled the Gateshead Company, were, in spite of their name, mainly motorbus operators, not trolleybus operators, and that the 1948 Transport Act envisaged a regional "takeover" of both municipal and private 'bus operators, which would have meant the Company would have to hand over several hundred thousand pounds' worth of new trolleybus equipment to the Government. A fuller discussion is given in Mr. G. S. Hearse's *"The Tramways of Gateshead"* (author, 1965).

The next stage in the Newcastle tramway replacement scheme took place on 1st November 1948, after delivery of the three-axle NCB-bodied Sunbeam S7's, when many new trolleybus and motorbus routes commenced operation. At the same time, the opportunity was taken to revise completely the numbering of trolleybus services. Instead of trams, trolleybuses and motorbuses each having their own series of route numbers, which led to duplication, the trolleybus service numbers were now integrated into the general motorbus series. The groups of trolleybus services numbered 3, 4, and 5 were renumbered by the addition of 30, thus becoming 33, 34, and 35, etc. The recently introduced 31 group of services remained unaltered.

A full list of the new and revised existing services is as follows:

32   **New Service** FENHAM (Bingfield Gardens) (reverser)—Netherby Drive—Fenham Hall Drive—Ponteland Road—Barrack Road—Gallowgate—Blackett Street—New Bridge Street—Byker Bridge—Shields Road

West—Shields Road—WALLSEND BOUNDARY (Walkerville) (Oak Tree Gardens) (reverser) and return. Operated Daily.

Additional Journeys Operated
PILGRIM STREET—Market Street—New Bridge Street—Byker Bridge —Shields Road West—Shields Road—WALLSEND BOUNDARY (Walkerville) (Oak Tree Gardens) (reverser) and return. Operated Mon.-Sat., early mornings and peak-hours.

33	**Renumbered and Extended Service** (based on former 3)
33A	DENTON ROAD TERMINUS (junction Denton Road/Whickham
33B	View) (turning circle) (33) Whickham View—DELAVAL ROAD (junction Benwell Lane/Delaval Road) (33A) Benwell Lane—BENWELL CHURCH (reverser at junction of Adelaide Terrace/Nichol Street) (33B)—Adelaide Terrace—Elswick Road—Westgate Road—Grainger Street—Market Street—Pilgrim Street—Northumberland Street—Barras Bridge—Jesmond Road—Osborne Road—and via turning loop of Tavistock Place, Lonsdale Terrace and OSBORNE ROAD (Jesmond) (33) (33A) (33B) and return. Operated Daily.

Additional Journeys Operated
Service 33B from DELAVAL ROAD (junction of Benwell Lane/Delaval Road)—Benwell Lane—Adelaide Terrace—Elswick Road—Westgate Road—Clayton Street—MONUMENT (Eldon Square) and return via Grainger Street to Westgate Road. Operated Mon.-Sat. early mornings and Mon.-Fri. peak-hours only.

34	**Renumbered Service** (former 4, 4A, 4B)
34A	DENTON SQUARE (junction of West Road/ Copperas Lane) (turning circle) (34B)—West Road—*Fox & Hounds* (34) (34A)—West Road —Westgate Road—Collingwood Street—St. Nicholas Square—ST. NICHOLAS CATHEDRAL (turning via loop Collingwood Street—St. Nicholas Street—Westgate Road) (34)—Mosley Street—Pilgrim Street —City Road—Glasshouse Bridge—Walker Road to WALKER (CHURCH STREET) (foot of) (turning circle) (34A) or via Station Road—White Street—Fisher Street—Neptune Road—Buddle Street—Hadrian Road—WALLSEND PARK ROAD (Vine Street) (reverser) (34) and return. Operated Mon.-Sat.
34B	

On Sundays, a through service, DENTON SQUARE—WALLSEND PARK ROAD was operated with additional journeys ST. NICHOLAS CATHEDRAL—WALKER (Church Street) and return.

35	**Renumbered and Extended Services**
35A	DENTON SQUARE (junction of West Road/Copperas Lane) (35)— West Road—Westgate Road—BRIGHTON GROVE (35A) (35B)— Crossley Terrace—Stanhope Street—Barrack Road—Gallowgate— Blackett Street—New Bridge Street—Byker Bridge—Shields Road West —Shields Road—Union Road—Bothal Street—Welbeck Road—WELBECK ROAD (east end of) (turning circle) (35) (35B) or thence Church Street—WALKER (Church Street) (foot of) (35) (35A) and return. Operated Daily.
35B	

35C	**New Service**
	DELAVAL ROAD (junction of Benwell Lane/Delaval Road)—Benwell

Lane—Adelaide Terrace—Elswick Road—Westgate Road—Grainger Street—(westbound: Market Street)—New Bridge Street—Byker Bridge —Shields Road West—Shields Road—Union Road—Bothal Street—Welbeck Road—WALKER (WESTBOURNE AVENUE) (reverser) and return. Operated Daily.

Additional Journeys Operated
BENWELL CHURCH (reverser at junction of Adelaide Terrace/Nichol Street)—Adelaide Terrace—Elswick Road—Westgate Road—Clayton Street—MONUMENT (Eldon Square) and return via loop Blackett Street—Grainger Street—Westgate Road.
WALKER (WESTBOURNE AVENUE) (reverser)—Welbeck Road—Bothal Street—Union Road—Shields Road—Shields Road West—Byker Bridge—New Bridge Street—PILGRIM STREET, returning via Market Street—New Bridge Street. Operated Weekday morning peak-hours only.

36 **Renumbered Service** (former 6)
CENTRAL STATION—Neville Street—Grainger Street West—Grainger Street—Blackett Street—Gallowgate—Barrack Road—Ponteland Road —Fenham Hall Drive—Netherby Drive—FENHAM (Bingfield Gardens) (reverser) and return. Operated Daily.

38 **New Service**
DENTON ROAD TERMINUS (junction of Denton Road/Whickham View) (turning circle)—Whickham View—Fergusons Lane—Fox-and-Hounds Lane—West Road—Westgate Road—Grainger Street—Market Street—Pilgrim Street—Northumberland Street—Barras Bridge—Jesmond Road—Benton Bank—Stephenson Road—Benton Road—BENTON ROAD (SWARLAND AVENUE) (turning circle) and return. Operated Daily.

39 **New Service**
MONUMENT (Eldon Square)—Blackett Street—Northumberland Street—Barras Bridge—Jesmond Road—Benton Bank—Stephenson Road —Benton Road—Benton Park Road—Haddrick's Mill Road—Matthew Bank—Jesmond Dene Road—Great North Road—Barras Bridge—Haymarket—Percy Street—MONUMENT (Eldon Square). Circular service operated in both directions Daily.

To enable the new services to operate, a vast irregular circle of trolleybus wiring had been constructed in the north-eastern suburbs. From opposite the Town Moor circle, overhead diverged from the North Road along Jesmond Dene Road to South Gosforth, with a reverser for short-workings at Matthew Bank (Beatty Avenue) (removed in the early 1950's) and after briefly straying outside the City boundary, along Benton Park Road to Four Lane Ends, Benton. Traction poles on Jesmond Dene Road had been in place for some considerable time before trolleybus services commenced and it is believed that they came from the Newburn—Throckley section of the Throckley tram route. The first few yards of Jesmond Dene Road eastwards from the North Road had been a tramway stub terminal.

On Benton Park Road, a quarter-mile long siding was constructed on the south side of the road over an equally long layby, to serve the Ministry of Pensions and National Insurance national headquarters. All this section from the

North Road to Four Lane Ends was fresh ground for electric road transport. At Four Lane Ends, the Forest Hall and West Moor tram routes diverged, but these became motorbus operated. From this point (again briefly outside the City boundary) the trolleybus wires turned south, down Benton Road to Chillingham Road Ends. As can be seen from the overhead map, there was a turning circle at Swarland Avenue and another siding for Ministry traffic.

At Chillingham Road Ends the trolleybus overhead turned west and ran via Benton Bank to join the 1938 wiring of the Osborne Road route at Jesmond station. To return to Chillingham Road Ends; it is here that the Newcastle to Tynemouth Coast Road begins and it will be seen from the destination blind Appendix that post war trolleybuses carried "Coast Road" as a destination, and also "via Coast Road". No definite plans for an extension are known, but assured traffic from Wills' Tobacco Factory, ½ mile east, just inside the City boundary, may have been a reason.

31st October 1948 had seen the withdrawal of various tram services including the West Moor and Forest Hall routes, and the short-lived service from New Bridge Street to Chillingham Road via Byker Bridge, which had only commenced on the 18th April 1948. 4th December 1948 saw the end of the Raby Street trams reversing on the crossover on the short stub of track remaining on Walker Road, the northern terminus of the route having been cut back to Newton Road with effect from 31st October 1948. The Forest Hall tram overhead, outward from Benton Four Lane Ends, remained only 3-6 months after abandonment. The overhead installations on the West Moor route remained for about a year, however, in order to allow cars to be taken to Gosforth Park for scrapping. Similarly, the northbound tram traction wire on Benton Road was left in place, trams proceeding from Byker depot along Chillingham Road. Indeed, a great deal of Chillingham Road tram overhead was left in place from about Simonside Terrace northwards to Chillingham Road Ends for trolleybus feeder facilities to Benton Road until about 1960.

On 16th January 1949, additional trolleybus services were introduced following the erection of overhead along Heaton Road (proposed route 9 of the 1946 Act), whilst others were revised, only some ten weeks after their introduction on 1st November 1948, as follows:—

37 **New Service**

DENTON ROAD TERMINUS (Junction of Denton Road/Whickham View) (turning circle)—Whickham View—Ferguson's Lane—Fox-and-Hounds Lane—West Road—Westgate Road—Grainger Street—Blackett Street—New Bridge Street—Byker Bridge—Shields Road West—Shields Road—Heaton Road—Stephenson Road—Benton Road—BENTON ROAD (Swarland Avenue) (turning circle) and return. Operated Daily.

39 **Revised Service**

CENTRAL STATION—Neville Street—Grainger Street West—Grainger Street—Market Street—Pilgrim Street—Northumberland Street—Barras Bridge—Jesmond Road—Benton Bank—Stephenson Road—Benton Road—Benton Park Road—Haddrick's Mill Road—Matthew Bank—Jesmond Dene Road—Great North Road—Barras Bridge—Northumberland Street—Pilgrim Street—Market Street—Grainger Street—

Grainger Street West—Neville Street—CENTRAL STATION. Circular Service operated in one direction only as above. Daily.

40 **New Service**
CENTRAL STATION—Neville Street—Grainger Street West—Grainger Street— Market Street—Pilgrim Street—Northumberland Street— Barras Bridge—Great North Road—Jesmond Dene Road—Matthew Bank—Haddrick's Mill Road—Benton Park Road—Benton Road— Stephenson Road—Benton Bank—Jesmond Road—Barras Bridge— Northumberland Street—Pilgrim Street—Market Street—Grainger Street —Grainger Street West—Neville Street—CENTRAL STATION. Circular service operated in one direction only as above. Daily.

41 **New Service**
CENTRAL STATION—Neville Street—Grainger Street West—Grainger Street—Market Street—Pilgrim Street—Northumberland Street— Barras Bridge—Jesmond Road—Benton Bank—Stephenson Road—Heaton Road—Shields Road—Shields Road West—Byker Bridge—New Bridge Street—Market Street—Grainger Street—Grainger Street West—Neville Street—CENTRAL STATION.Circular service operated in one direction only as above. Daily.

42 **New Service**
CENTRAL STATION—Neville Street—Grainger Street West—Grainger Street—Blackett Street—New Bridge Street—Byker Bridge—Shields Road West—Shields Road—Heaton Road—Stephenson Road—Benton Bank—Jesmond Road—Barras Bridge—Northumberland Street—Pilgrim Street—Market Street—Grainger Street—Grainger Street West—Neville Street—CENTRAL STATION. Circular service operated in one direction only as above. Daily.

As a consequence of the introduction of the new 39 and 40 services, the temporary route 39, Eldon Square to Benton, was discontinued. Following this, apart from a rush-hour only service from Vickers' Elswick Works, (Scotswood Road—City—Byker Bridge—Byker) this left only the joint tram services on which no car proceeded beyond the City from the south. Motorbuses now covered Chillingham Road.

These were to be the last extensions under the 1946 Act and they raised the trolleybus route mileage to 35.039 served by 221 vehicles. Many pre-war trolleybuses were still in stock and 443-478 were being delivered at this time. All the post-war trolleybuses were fitted with carbon insert trolleyheads from new, whereas pre-war and wartime vehicles had trolleywheels at first.

During the early part of 1949, several Glasgow Corporation Transport motorbus instructors came south to Newcastle, their nearest trolleybus system, to be trained to drive trolleybuses, in order to be able to instruct Glasgow personnel for that city's inauguration of its trolleybus system in April 1949.

Newcastle's last tram ran, as mentioned earlier, on 4th March 1950. Thus was the tramcar swept from Newcastle, while seventeen months later Gateshead and District ran the last car on Tyneside.

A month after the Benton and Heaton circular services came into operation, Newcastle Transport ordered what were to be the last trolleybuses supplied to the undertaking. They were 50 further B.U.T. 9641T three-axle vehicles, 8ft. wide with Metro-Cammell 70-seat bodies, which on delivery became Nos. 579—628

(NBB 579—628), bought at a cost of £283,829. Delivered in 1950, they were perhaps the best-looking trolleybuses in Newcastle's fleet, and in our opinion, the most handsome double-deck trolleybuses built in this country. 628 was the highest-numbered vehicle in Newcastle Transport's fleet.

In 1949, the decision was taken to standardise the livery of all passenger vehicles. Prior to this, trams, trolleybuses and motorbuses had all been different colours. Both motor and trolleybuses now appeared in chrome yellow, a colour developed from the shade of the trams' rocker panels, and very smart they looked too. In order to avoid confusion amongst intending passengers due to the new livery, new motorbuses were fitted with two circular metal discs, one in the front upper-deck nearside window and the other in the near-side lower-deck window nearest the platform, inscribed "MB" (Motorbus). These were removed once the passengers became accustomed to the new colours.

The General Manager's Report for 1948-49 mentioned the debating point in transport circles of the relative merits of diesel and electric traction. The main difficulties with the use of electricity were the high cost of current and the heavy capital cost of equipment, and these put trolleybuses at a disadvantage. "However," he continued, "a serious problem may arise if the whole country's . . . transport . . . were dependent on imported fuel oil." Words worthy of consideration! Nevertheless fares in 1948-49 were still reasonable, ranging from ½d. to 6d., the most common fare being 1½d.

Meanwhile, all through the summer of 1949, brand new NCB-bodied B.U.T. 9611T two-axle vehicles were rolling out of Claremont Road Factory and into traffic. This enabled older stock to be withdrawn and sixty-eight were disposed of in 1949-50, reducing the fleet to 204.

CHAPTER NINE

THE STAGNANT FIFTIES

As the new decade dawned, things looked very bright for Newcastle's trolleybus system. The revitalisation of the last two years had doubled the network's size compared with 1939. The trams had all been replaced, and Newcastle Transport now had only trolleybuses and motorbuses. In many places, but especially in the central area, pedestrian refuge islands were being positioned now that the centre of the road did not have to be kept clear for trams. This, it was claimed, increased road safety. Tram track was lifted immediately following tramway abandonment in some places, but in others it was still in situ many years later—for instance, part of the stretch of single track between Condercum Road and *Fox & Hounds* was not removed until 1960.

New vehicles were rapidly replacing ageing pre-war and wartime trolleybuses, worn out prematurely by overwork and undermaintenance during the War. The new NCB-bodied Sunbeam F4 two-axle vehicles, which like the B.U.T. 9611T's were of pleasing design, were entering service during the first three months of 1950. There was then a gap of only one month before the first of the repeat order of B.U.T. 9641T three-axle trolleybuses arrived, and these magnificent vehicles continued to stream into traffic at approximately monthly intervals —622 and 624—628 being the last, on 1st November 1950. 628 had been exhibited at the 1950 Commercial Motor Show and on its journey north it apparently stopped off for a week at Tees-side, where the Tees-side Railless Traction Board (as it was then) tried it on their system in the eastern outskirts of Middlesbrough.

The trolleybus overhead on the Gosforth Park extensions had remained unaltered since the conversion of April 1948, but in the summer of 1950 work began on widening the Great North Road northwards from Three Mile Bridge nearly to the terminus. In particular, West Gosforth railway bridge over the Ponteland branch was doubled in width to the west, and the overhead required alteration.

About this time the Undertaking began to feel the necessity for a new depot in the west of the City. A more modern depot than Wingrove was needed, and with the western termini of routes being well beyond the depot, a considerable amount of dead mileage had resulted. Some accommodation for motorbuses in the west end was also required as Wingrove only stabled trolleybuses and there was no room to extend. Further, considerable congestion was caused on Westgate Road, especially by westbound trolleybuses, due to crew changing at lunch times. Often large numbers of trolleybuses would be held up as no overtaking loops were provided.

Steel was still in short supply in 1950, and Newcastle Transport was extremely fortunate to locate a hangar formerly used for Sunderland flying-boats at Calgarth, Lake Windermere, and available for disposal. The framework was purchased for £9,500. It had been dismantled at Calgarth by 3rd June 1950, and was transported to Newcastle and erected on a prepared site at Slatyford, between Slatyford Lane and Silver Lonnen, near Stamfordham Road, between 26th June and September. The preparation of the site and the erection of the steelwork cost an additional £20,351. Sufficient land was purchased for any further extensions. The work of completion was put to tender, and a figure of £153,000 accepted. At one time it was intended to have an open-wall building but this idea was not very popular. The Ministry of Transport, due to restrictions on capital expenditure at this period, would not sanction the completion; therefore the gaunt skeleton steel frame of the unfinished depot towered over the area for some years until the financial position eased.

From April to October 1951 there were further alterations to the Great North Road on the north side of Gosforth, and Newcastle Transport found itself unable, through roadworks, to use Hollywood Avenue terminus on a regular basis. Therefore, with the co-operation of the Ministry of Transport and Northumberland County Council, an alternative turning point was found at Polwarth Drive, ¾-mile to the north of Gosforth Stadium, and the County Council paid the cost of the extra running.

On 4th May 1951, Gosforth U.D.C. informed Newcastle Transport that the roadway in Broadway West was now "ready for 'bus traffic" and would they please build the route. The new area to be served included Grange Estate and some large Government office buildings. The new extension, about ¼ mile long, was via Broadway West to Kielder Way, where the trolleybuses turned around a triangular-shaped green. The route was over concrete roadway and span wire construction was used to support the overhead. The new service commenced on Sunday, 28th October 1951 and was numbered 31A, replacing the service to Polwarth Drive, and brought route mileage up to a total of 35.429 miles. It had a frequency of 12 minutes, with 15 minutes on Sundays, and ran via Northumberland Street. Service 31B also began to run to Grange Estate, but via Newgate Street and Percy Street. Irrespective of final destination, 31B's always ran via Percy Street on weekdays, but there was no Sunday service on this route.

At this period, there were suggestions that trolleybuses might be extended from the existing Polwarth Drive turning circle in a north westerly direction along Polwarth Drive itself to the centre of Brunton Park Estate at Princess Road. Although nothing came of this due to objections from residents, motorbuses, when they took over from trolleybuses in this area in February 1964, did in fact operate to this point.

The final trolleybus powers which Newcastle obtained were embodied in the Newcastle upon Tyne Corporation Act, 1952, and were as follows:—

Route 1: (1 mile 3 furlongs 3.16 chains.) Commencing in Silver Lonnen, at a junction with Netherby Drive, by a junction with Route 7 authorised by the Newcastle upon Tyne Corporation (Trolley Vehicles) Order, 1936, scheduled to, and confirmed by the Newcastle upon Tyne Corporation (Trolley Vehicles) Order Confirmation Act, 1938, passing in a north-easterly direction along Silver Lonnen and north-west along Stamfordham Road and terminating in the Urban District of Newburn at the junction of Stamfordham Road with Beaumont Terrace.

Route 2: (2 furlongs 6.27 chains.) Commencing in the Urban District of Gosforth at Broadway West, by a junction with an existing trolley vehicle turning point in that road, passing west and south along

Broadway West and then south along Wansbeck Road and terminating in Wansbeck Road at its junction with Park Avenue.

The route powers above were to be implemented within ten years, and powers were also given to increase fares on the Gosforth route with the consent of Gosforth U.D.C., and to abandon certain light railways authorised in 1922 and 1923.

In this Act, a third attempt was made to extend the trolleybus network to Westerhope. This time they would have gone nearly to the western end of the area, some 400 yards past the end of the former Westerhope tramroad. Newcastle Transport owned 0.7 acres of land, the roadbed of the tramroad, as well as 0.4 acres at Gosforth. The trolleybuses, however, would have reached Westerhope using public roads, for no mention is made of attempting to follow the tramway. Indeed, as can be seen from the maps, a tortuous dog-leg is described to get from Bingfield Gardens terminus to Stamfordham Road.

The second route proposed in the Act was to extend the new Grange Estate route farther into the estate, along the remainder of Broadway West to a shopping area, thus tapping more traffic. It would have been the only penetration in any depth of trolleybuses into the north-western suburbs, a part of Newcastle consequently dominated by motorbuses.

Unfortunately, neither of the provisions of this Act were implemented, and the City's last trolleybus powers remained unused. Westerhope never did get its trolleybuses in spite of all the attempts over the years.

About this period, 552, one of the NCB-bodied Sunbeam F4 two-axle vehicles, had a slight mishap in Bewick Street. While standing at Central Station terminus with a full load of passengers it ran away backwards across Neville Street and collided with a sand bin in front of the station portico. Luckily no other vehicle was involved.

1953 was the year of the Coronation of Queen Elizabeth II, and all over the country local festivities were arranged and events took place to mark the occasion. Newcastle Transport was not lacking in ideas and in fact provided a noteworthy display. All traction poles were repainted, some in the City centre becoming a puce colour, and this turned out to be the last general repaint they received. The poles were used for the hanging of bunting, flags, shields, etc., as Coronation Day approached. In order to bring the event "to the people" as it were, four vehicles were decorated. Two were motorbuses, an NCB-bodied A.E.C. Regent III and a Willowbrook-bodied Daimler single-decker. The other two were trolleybuses, 450, a Metro-Cammell-bodied Sunbeam F4 two-axle vehicle, and 596, a B.U.T. 9641T three-axle vehicle. (See illustration.) All were finished in gold, and carried suitable portraits, shields, and the like. The trolleybuses operated over all routes so that everyone had a chance to see them, although, strange to say, neither of the authors can recall them!

By this time, the old tramway time clocks which were placed at outlying termini (e.g. *Fox-&-Hounds,* Two Ball Lonnen), had fallen into disuse, although the cases remained for many years, that at Two Ball Lonnen until the traction poles in Netherby Drive were removed in May 1966. However, there were time-keepers who despatched trolleybuses in sequence from certain points, for instance in Osborne Road. (Incidentally, Osborne Road's power was often low since there was no feeder point near, and if two trolleybuses were in the section maximum speed would be limited to 15-18 m.p.h.).

Through the medium of an ex-driver, Mr. I. C. Gumm, it is possible, at

Prewar tower wagons remove the now redundant tram overhead, 31st October 1948, at Benton Four Lane Ends, ready for the new trolleybus service to commence the next day.

Newcastle Chronicle & Journal

Sunbeam F4 No. 463 with Metro-Cammell body and BUT 9641T No. 621 (note short front wings) pass on the narrow Whickham View, Denton Burn in the late 1950s. Note the double bracket arms supporting the overhead wiring.　　　　　　　R. F. Mack

Exhibited at the 1948 Commercial Vehicle Show, Sunbeam F4/Metro-Cammell No. 468 uniquely featured a staircase window. As can be seen in this view, taken at Central Station terminus, this was later blocked off. R. F. Mack

Five trolleybuses (that nearest the camera being No. 455 Sunbeam F4/Metro-Cammell) await crowds of shipyard workmen from Walker Naval Yard. The trolleybuses are standing at the Walker terminus near the foot of Church Street. Late 1950s. R. F. Mack

A sad sight, in 1963, at Dunston Autospares scrapyard in Gateshead as a number of Sunbeam F4/Metro-Cammell vehicles wait to be broken up.

Newcastle Chronicle & Journal

Trolleybuses on parade! Here are all twenty of the batch diverted from London Transport in 1948, allowing the Newcastle Undertaking to open the Gosforth Park group of routes in April of that year.

Tyne & Wear P.T.E.

Shortly after delivery No. 482 (probably the first of the 1948 BUT 9641T's to arrive) is posed alongside prewar Guy BTX No. 400 on the test track at Byker Depot.

Tyne & Wear P.T.E.

The lower saloon of No. 484 looking forward, c.1948. Note the London Transport type bell-cord and wooden duck-boarding. The Metro-Cammell body fitted to this BUT 9641T was diverted from London Transport.   Tyne & Wear P.T.E.

Fares please! the scene is taken inside the lower deck of No. 482, a 1948 BUT 9641T, with the conductor in deep discussion with an Inspector.　　　　　Tyne & Wear P.T.E.

The cab interior of 8ft. wide BUT 9641T No. 484 before delivery to Newcastle in 1948. These vehicles opened the Gosforth Park route in April of that year.　Tyne & Wear P.T.E.

What might have been! This view, taken at Gosforth Park terminus in later years shows that Gateshead termini were featured on Newcastle destination blinds. The London-style indicators of Metro-Cammell bodies BUT 9641T No. 483 of 1948 are clearly seen in this view, 25th January 1964.   T. Steele

The late afternoon sunshine highlights the London-style bodywork of BUT 9641T No. 496, as it stands at the Central Station terminus of route 31, c.1948.   C. Carter

A rear view, looking eastwards up Denton Bank, West Road, at Denton Burn Roundabout, showing No. 489 working a service 35 journey from Denton Square to Welbeck Road. Note the intricate wiring and the masked destination display, 2nd February 1964.   Late D. Hanson

A press photograph, taken in 1954 to draw attention to the traffic congestion caused by parked vehicles at the junction of Grainger Street with Market Street, show a number of trolleybuses. No. 490, a BUT of 1948, crawls out ahead of Sunbeam S7 No. 527. No 454, a Sunbeam F4 bound for Wingrove Depot, passes a sister vehicle bound for the same destination although travelling in the opposite direction.   Newcastle Chronicle & Journal

The solid lines of the Northern Coachbuilders bodywork are well shown in this view of Sunbeam S7, No. 515. The trolleybus is standing with its booms lowered in Clayton Street West near the Central Station, c.1950.   C. Carter

The marks of the tram tracks in Benton Road are still visible in this view of Sunbeam S7 No. 514, at Swarland Avenue terminus, c.1951.   I. C. Gumm

this point, to give an outline of vehicle allocation and services operated from Wingrove Depot, and therefore an idea of the operation of the system in the 1953-4 period. At this time there were usually 72 trolleybuses garaged here using all 6 roads as follows:—499-538, 580-4, 586-90, 609-17, (618-9 at irregular intervals) and some of 466-78. They worked the following services:—
33—joint with Byker.
34 and 34A—joint with Byker.
34B—(Denton Square—St. Nicholas)—solely by Wingrove.
35—one turn only (to Brighton Grove, until about 6 p.m.).
32/36—joint with Byker.
37/38—ten scheduled, plus two from Byker.

In addition, the depot worked the occasional Greyhound ("Dog") Special to Hollywood Avenue.

The depot had limited running repair facilities and a small work-shop, but any major repairs had to be dealt with at Byker. In the early nineteen fifties trolleybuses still carried day duty running numbers, a legacy from the trams, and these were positioned in metal holders at each side cab window. The highest such numbered duty from Wingrove was 73. This involved a journey to Swarland Avenue on service 38, then back via Heaton Road and Shields Road to Wallsend Boundary, finally returning to the west end showing in the front windscreen, "Hospital Special", via Stanhope Street, (for visitors to Newcastle General Hospital, just short of the depot), and then into the depot itself.

In the autumn (perhaps as late as November) of 1953, a traffic roundabout was constructed at the west end of Neville Street where it joined Clayton Street West, controlling a four-road intersection, and this necessitated alteration of the overhead. Thereafter, trolleybus services terminating at the Central Station turned around this roundabout instead of using the square of streets surrounding St. Mary's Roman Catholic Cathedral.

The total number of trolleybuses in the fleet had fallen to 192 by 31st March 1954, twelve vehicles having been disposed of in the previous year. Only six of the older vehicles were left in stock, but probably not in service. Mr. J. Petrie remembers seeing one of the wartime utility trolleybuses being towed westwards over Byker Bridge at this time for scrap.

During the nineteen fifties Melbourne Street had been first disconnected, and then reconnected to the overhead line. Certainly it was reconnected by the summer of 1962.

The City obtained another local Act in 1954, and one clause in this restricted the number of standing passengers to eight on the trolleybuses instead of ten as previously. This brought them into line with the motorbuses. A disc was affixed to the window of the rear platform bulkhead of each vehicle giving the revised figure.

In order to obviate the necessity for conductors to leave the vehicle to operate manual frogs at busy road junctions, electric frogs were installed in the overhead at certain places about 1954. This was presumably regarded as an experiment, for only three such frogs were installed, these being at Haymarket (northbound), Great North Road (at Grandstand Road junction), and Market Street (junction with New Bridge Street westbound). Those at the Haymarket were introduced as from 6th May 1954. There may have been another set at the foot of Denton Bank, at the Denton Road turn-off, but confirmation is required. Prior to this, in 'pre-war days, frogs had been positioned at the very turn of the road junctions at which they were located. This caused traffic congestion as trolleybuses had to stop right on the turn for the conductor to alight from the vehicle to "pull the lever". On the suggestion of the crews themselves, the frogs were moved back from the corners, to the nearest stop if possible.

On 1st August 1955, service 34 was revised to become DENTON SQUARE —WALLSEND PARK ROAD or WALKER (CHURCH STREET), operating daily. Additional journeys were also operated FOX-&-HOUNDS—WALKER (CHURCH STREET) or ST. NICHOLAS' CATHEDRAL numbered 34A and 34B on Mondays to Saturdays, and on Sundays additional journeys were operated ST. NICHOLAS' CATHEDRAL—WALKER (CHURCH STREET). This arrangement remained virtually unaltered until the conversion of the route to motorbuses in 1963.

On 14th December 1955, the only known complete power breakdown to affect Newcastle's trolleybuses took place. This happened as a result of a failure in a switch compartment at Stella South Power Station, which, together with its companion on the north bank of the Tyne, Stella North, at Lemington, had recently been completed by the Central Electricity Generating Board. At 8.36 a.m., power was cut off automatically and much of Tyneside was without electricity, as were large parts of Northumberland and County Durham. British Railways' North and South Tyneside electric trains to the coast and South Shields were unable to move, and neither were South Shields' trolleybuses. Most of Newcastle's trolleybuses managed to come to rest at the nearest stop, except two at the junction of Westgate Road and Grainger Street which presumably used their traction batteries. Some power was restored at 11.35 a.m., but went off again two minutes later. The first trolleybuses were able to resume their journeys at 1.30 p.m., but it was "some time before full services were running". One of the authors well remembers the day—it was foggy and cold—seeing trolleybuses stranded on Fenham Hall Drive, looming out of the mist like darkened yellow houses on his way to school, and they were still there, the crews eating their "bait", on his way home at midday.

In the mid-fifties, possibly about 1956, a slight diversion of service 37 took place when westbound vehicles began to operate via Market Street instead of via Blackett Street. The exact date is unknown to the authors and information would be welcomed.

It had been possible to recommence work on Slatyford Depot in April 1953, and the task proceeded in four 9-monthly cycles of construction, regulated by the Ministry of Transport. At this period, and until about 1960, the depot was known officially as Slatyford Lane Depot and was shown as such on destination indicators (see Appendix E). Later it became known simply as Slatyford Depot.

Since the completion date of the new depot could now be estimated more accurately, firm plans were made to carry out the associated work of improving Silver Lonnen. On 2nd February 1955, a report was presented to the Council on the improvement of this road. It set out the following points:—

1. The road is at present 20 feet wide. It is inadequate and it is necessary to widen and strengthen it.

2. The Transport and Electricity Committee's new Slatyford Lane Depot will be in operation "in the next twelve months", and they need the road improvement "as an essential link between the depot and the West Road", for the "efficient and economic operation of their vehicles".

This was really the crux of the matter. Newcastle Transport had to have Silver Lonnen as a link. This way, to get a trolleybus to Denton Square ready to enter service from the depot, would involve a run of about $1\frac{1}{4}$ miles. Without Silver Lonnen, a run of between $4\frac{3}{4}$ and 5 miles was necessary, via Fenham Hall Drive, Stanhope Street and the West Road. Dead mileage from Wingrove Depot had been no real problem. Trolleybuses entering service in the morning simply had to turn up West Road to, say, Denton Square, or down Stanhope Street and via a left-hand connection up Barrack Road to Fenham terminus.

On 16th February 1955, Stage 1 of the Improvement was agreed and a sum of £16,000 was allocated to widen Silver Lonnen to 30 feet between Stamfordham Road and Lanercost Drive. Two months later, on 20th April 1955, Stage 2, involving the section between Lanercost Drive and West Road, was presented for approval. Sanction was obtained on 4th May 1955 at a cost of £23,000. As early as September 1954 Newcastle Transport had agreed to pay part of the costs of improving Slatyford Lane from the Depot to Silver Lonnen. Slatyford Lane was at this time a cul-de-sac approached from the West Road. After the depot was opened it became a through route to Silver Lonnen. On 1st February 1956, the Council was told that due to the Ministry of Transport raising the standards for major roads, Stage 2 of Silver Lonnen had now to be constructed to a minimum width of 33 feet, and that this modification would cost an extra £1,600. Although Slatyford Lane Depot was officially opened by the then Minister of Transport, Mr. Harold Watkinson, on 10th July 1956, the above modification to the roadway specification at such a late stage may have been the reason why Slatyford Lane and Silver Lonnen were not opened for traffic until 21st October 1956. Thus, electric traction returned to Silver Lonnen after 26 years.

The final cost of Slatyford Lane Depot was £186,500. It accommodated 120 vehicles—60 trolleybuses and 60 motorbuses. The layout consisted of offices, canteens, etc., at the west end, maintenance and washing bays, six motorbus parking bays, and six trolleybus parking bays at the east end. One "road" of trolleybus wiring ran through the maintenance bays. To enter the depot, trolleybuses ran down a service road on the west side parallel to Slatyford Lane to a yard at the south end. A controller sitting in a cabin selected which of the six parking bays the vehicle was to take, and pressed a button which preset the correct overhead frog. At the same time, an illuminated number corresponding to that of the "road" selected appeared on a large board thus informing the trolleybus driver, who then drove his vehicle into the appropriate bay. This arrangement was devised by a senior member of staff.

To supply Silver Lonnen and the Depot with power, a 600Kw mercury-arc rectifier was provided at the depot. The overhead at the depot was supplied by B.I.C.C., and span-wire construction and austere traction poles were a feature of Silver Lonnen.

It would be as well to mention at this point something about the street lighting arrangements on trolleybus routes. Experiments had been carried out with fluorescent lighting in Northumberland Street in 1948, but in 1956 most roads still had incandescent bulbs backed by mosaic reflectors. These were mounted on traction poles about 18 feet above ground level. Street lighting cables were carried from traction pole to traction pole about 3 feet from the top. On all routes outside the City boundary, where lighting was the responsibility of the relevant local authority, separate lighting standards were provided. The only roads having such an arrangement in the City were Netherby Drive and Silver Lonnen, together with the South Gosforth—Benton Park Road route from the North Road to Benton Four Lane Ends. By about 1960, most roads over which trolleybuses ran had been converted to sodium vapour lighting, and those in the central area to mercury vapour. The new lighting units were positioned at the very tops of traction poles, and many are still in place today.

To return to the opening of Silver Lonnen: the traffic potential of the area was good, there being new houses lining the road, so the opportunity was taken to develop fresh route patterns and services. Basically, an extension of service 36 beyond the foot of Netherby Drive was introduced numbered 44, but with some confusing ramifications. Commencing on 21st October 1956, the new service ran as follows:—

CENTRAL STATION (departures showing "44—FENHAM")—Neville Street—Grainger Street West—Grainger Street—Blackett Street—Gallowgate—Barrack Road—Ponteland Road—Fenham Hall Drive—Netherby Drive (destination then changed to "33—OSBORNE ROAD")—Silver Lonnen—Denton Road—Whickham View—Benwell Lane—Adelaide Terrace—Elswick Road—Westgate Road—Grainger Street—Market Street —Pilgrim Street—Northumberland Street—Barras Bridge—Jesmond Road —Osborne Road (turning via loop of Tavistock Road, Lonsdale Terrace and OSBORNE ROAD). Returning vehicles then showed "43—DENTON ROAD TERMINUS" as far as Delaval Road/Whickham View when destination blinds were turned to show "36—CENTRAL STATION". The service operated daily. Additional journeys (in effect short-workings of the above), numbered 33, operated DENTON ROAD TERMINUS— OSBORNE ROAD and others numbered 36 operated CENTRAL STATION—FENHAM.

As a result, route mileage increased to approximately 36.40 miles. It can be seen that the Elswick Road 33 group of services were integrated with the Fenham service (in effect a circular service with short-workings), and a very complicated route schedule evolved, similar to former tram services 00 and 10 to Gosforth. Service 44 remained the highest service number used by Newcastle's trolleybuses.

The ribbed concrete road surface, wide grass verges, and post-war semi-detached houses on Silver Lonnen, provided a very different landscape to Newcastle's earlier trolleybus routes with their cobbled roads and pre-1914 terraced houses.

As Denton Road and Silver Lonnen were not exactly aligned with each other at their junction with the West Road, a rather awkward reverse curve was described at this crossing. A diagram exists showing a more direct path, but this alternative was never adopted.

The opening of the new Slatyford Depot premises coincided with the closure of the old and faithful Wingrove Sheds. Right up to the end the date of construction, 1903, and the proud title "Newcastle Corporation Tramways" could be discerned as marks on the concrete frontage, although the metal letters which made the marks had long since been removed. On its closure, the building was leased to a motor dealer, and is today virtually intact. Only the forecourt, with its tramway scissors crossover and cobbled paving, which trolleybuses entering the depot used to rattle and pitch over before disappearing into the building, has been altered beyond recognition. The tracks are still inside and the inspection pits are covered with sleepers. The trolleybus exit wiring through the yard at the north end into Agricola Road and down Wingrove Road was removed. Two traction poles in Wingrove Road remain as lighting standards. The way the trolleybuses used to poke their noses out of Agricola Road into Wingrove Road, and slowly, almost ashamedly, glide along the single-road wiring to Westgate Road, is still a pleasant memory.

To go back in time a short while: on 1st June 1956, five trolleybus and nineteen motorbus stops in the City centre were repositioned (for example, in Westgate Road) to alleviate traffic congestion, and finding their new locations confused many passengers.

On 16th June 1956, two trolleybuses, one bound for Elswick Road, the other for Westgate Road, caught fire at the Big Lamp during the midday peak due to their resistances overheating and setting light to the floor whilst they had been following a heavy lorry crawling up Westgate Hill. Two fire appliances attended, and the passengers, including the father of one of the authors, were evacuated to await the next service trolleybus.

At some time between December 1956 and October 1957, service 31B was revised from Central Station—Grange Estate to Central Station—Polwarth Drive, still via Percy Street except on Saturdays when it was operated via Northumberland Street. There was still no Sunday service 31B operated.

At or about this time, Hollywood Avenue ceased to be used as an all-day terminus, although it continued to be used for Race Specials. Also about this time, only the 186 post-war trolleybuses were in service.

Still worsening motor traffic in the nineteen fifties had necessitated the alteration of several major road junctions. One of the first affecting trolleybuses was Chillingham Road Ends. It was agreed in November 1956 to construct a traffic roundabout here, at the junction of Stephenson Road, Benton Road and Chillingham Road, for a sum of £9,470 including £1,800 for the alteration of trolleybus overhead wiring. It is believed that the modifications were carried out during the summer of 1957.

Presumably to facilitate the running of school services, a left-hand trailing connection was put in from Fox-and-Hounds Lane westwards to the West Road during the summer of 1957, although it was seldom seen to be used.

At the Council meeting held on 4th May 1955, a report was presented by the Parliamentary and General Purposes Committee regarding the Heaton Works Light Railway over Shields Road. C. & A. Parsons and Co., the internationally-known turbine, generating, and electrical equipment manufacturers, have large premises known collectively as Heaton Works on both sides of Shields Road east of Byker Depot on what was the service 32 trolleybus route. In order to transport

101

large pieces of machinery from the premises on the north side of the road to those on the south, the firm wished to lay a railway line across Shields Road to connect with their existing internal railway system. To do this they intended to take out a Parliamentary Order.

Councillors, on receiving the Committee's report, expressed fears as to the traffic congestion that would result if huge loads were being moved over the railway. They were told that the Order would:—

1. Exclude movement between 8 a.m.-10 a.m., 11.30 a.m.-2 p.m., and 4.30 p.m.-6.30 p.m.
2. Restrict to not more than six, any closures within any 24 hour period, not more than one to be between 6 a.m. and 10 p.m.

Objections were invited to be presented to the Ministry of Transport by 31st May 1955, and all Committees were asked to give their observations. On 25th May 1955, the Town Clerk reported to the Parliamentary and General Purposes Committee giving the views of the various Committees. The Town Improvement and Streets Committee recommended the rails for the railway to be B.S.12—Dock Rail, weighing 126 lbs. per yard, set in 8 inches of concrete, topped with 2 inches of asphalt to the rail heads, with tarmac topping in Bethel Avenue (a side street to the south of Shields Road).

The Transport and Electricity Committee put forward the following points:—
1. Any alteration of the Undertaking's installations in Shields Road to be carried out at the company's expense.
2. A diversionary trolley vehicle route to be provided along the Fossway at the company's expense.
3. Any delay to services due to the construction, repair, or operation of the railway to be paid for by the company.

The Transport and Electricity Committee further suggested that the following Special Clauses be included in the Proposed Order:—

1. Any works passing over, under, or interfering with the poles and equipment of Newcastle Corporation Transport and Electricity Undertaking, including overhead electric street lighting cables, and also conduit carrying electric cables under the carriageway, the company shall give one month's notice of, and all works to be with the approval of the Corporation.
2. For the protection of the undertaking, and to prevent injury or impediment to the Undertaking's installations, or for the prevention of interruption to trolleybus services, the Undertaking may carry out works or temporary works necessary, including the alteration or resiting of equipment, new installations and the provision and equipment of a diversionary trolleybus route, commencing in the Fossway at its junction with Shields Road, along the Fossway to its junction with Coutts Road, and along Coutts Road to its junction with Shields Road (or any other diversionary route agreed with the Company) and the costs to be repaid by the company to the Corporation.
3. One month's notice of the necessity of altering trolleybus services to be given and the expense of any diversion to be borne by the company.

In July 1955, the Company agreed to the above, and the Corporation therefore did not object to the Order as so amended.

The Order became the Heaton Works Light Railway Order 1956, and the Company having paid the cost of the Fossway diversion, reputed to be £20,000, the new wiring was erected during the summer of 1957 on double bracket arms, mounted on poles set on the south kerb of the Fossway, between Byker Depot and Roman Avenue, and on the north kerb between Roman Avenue and Coutts Road. It was little used but its construction increased route mileage to 37.079 miles. When Parson's locomotive was working over Shields Road, tower wagons were used to jack up the Shields Road overhead to allow outsized pieces of machinery to pass beneath.

On 30th December 1957, only 14 months after Slatyford Lane Depot had replaced Wingrove Sheds in the west end, Newcastle Transport closed another former tram depot, that at Haymarket in the City centre. The University of Newcastle upon Tyne (King's College of Durham University as it was then), required part of the area west of Percy Street for expansion. The depot was, therefore, completely demolished and the University's multi-storey physics block now covers the site. One solitary traction pole was left in the entrance lane for years afterwards.

To replace Haymarket Depot a site in Morden Street, again off Percy Street, was chosen after much difficulty in deciding on a suitable site in or near the City centre. Previously, the Morden Street site was used as a commercial vehicle and car park, and a new "depot" was created by erecting overhead up Morden Street and onto the top end of the car park which had nothing more than a clinker surface. Two roads of wiring were provided, and the total sum expended on overhead was £4,000. Accommodation was provided for twelve motorbuses in addition to eighteen trolleybuses.

There is one problem. According to records the new depot (officially known as Handysides) did not come into use until April 1958. The question arises as to where the thirty vehicles were stabled in the intervening three months—at Byker?

During the financial year 1957-8, the section of the North Road from Three Mile Bridge northwards to a point 600 yards south of Gosforth Park terminus was reconstructed as dual-carriageway. This was necessary as this road, as its name implies, is the A1 trunk road to Edinburgh, and traffic had increased dramatically during the nineteen fifties.

The reconstruction ranged from laying a narrow concrete central island on the Three Mile Bridge—Broadway West section, to a 50 ft. wide tree and bush planted reservation north of the junction with Broadway West. This northern section of dual-carriageway was created by cutting an entirely new southbound carriageway 50ft. to the east of the existing roadway, which then became the northbound carriageway.

The trolleybus overhead wiring thus required considerable modification—in fact, completely new overhead construction was needed. As the two carriageways were so far apart span wires were out of the question, so each had its own line of wiring hung from bracket arms. (See Illustration.) V-shaped laybys were provided at many stops, often with a traction pole at the point of the V.

Since this section of the route was outside the City Boundary, the cost of alteration to the overhead was borne by Northumberland County Council, presumably aided by a grant from the Ministry of Transport.

103

CHAPTER TEN

THE END IS NIGH (1959-1966)

A spate of accidents, two of which resulted in serious vehicle damage, unfortunately begin this Chapter.

On Friday 13th February 1959, (yes!) a driver had just set off from Delaval Road, Benwell, terminus in charge of BUT three-axle vehicle No. 612 when the vehicle went out of control, and after ramming a traction pole, overturned onto its off-side in Benwell Lane. Six passengers were hurt. As illustrated, the overhead wiring was severed. 612 received extensive damage which was subsequently repaired at Byker and it was returned to traffic, but could be distinguished afterwards by its short metal maroon front wings and lack of ventilation slots over the front cab windscreens. The metal wings were themselves replaced by normal pattern deeper rubber ones in 1964.

Not long after this, on 12th May 1959, another B.U.T. three-axle, 591, was involved in an accident in the City centre. Having turned from Westgate Road into Grainger Street, the driver collapsed and died at the wheel, and 591 ran backwards out of control across the road into a car which was waiting at the traffic signals at St. John's Church. 591 escaped serious damage.

Another overturning accident took place on 30th September 1960, when 546, a Sunbeam/NCB two-axle vehicle travelling northbound in Northumberland Street on route 41, (the Heaton Road Circle), mounted a pile of gravel near roadworks, struck the canopy of Fenwick's Department Store and came to rest in the doorway of the delicatessen department on its off-side! Nine people were hurt. Although 546's bodywork appeared to be quite badly damaged, the vehicle was repaired and put back into service, not being withdrawn until February 1964.

The A69 West Road was suffering from increased traffic as was everywhere else at this time, and coupled with the fact that Denton Road/Silver Lonnen was becoming used as a western ring road, a roundabout was urgently required at the junction of West Road with Silver Lonnen and Denton Road, at the foot of Denton Bank. This alteration of the junction was debated in the Council as early as the summer of 1958, but construction was not sanctioned until April 1959 when it was expected to cost £13,000, including £2,600 for the alteration of the trolleybus overhead (for which no Ministry of Transport grant was available). The work was not put in hand immediately; it is believed that the roundabout was not completed until late 1961. As it transpired, the wiring alteration cost only £2,100, although, as can be seen from the maps, it was the most complex overhead junction in Newcastle, featuring (in best railway track parlance) "an aerial scissors crossover, an outside slip, and an inside slip"! One strange omission was a connection to allow westbound trolleybuses to turn right from Denton Bank to Silver Lonnen for Slatyford Depot. A journey to Denton Square to turn was therefore necessary.

About this period the remaining sub-stations still equipped with rotary convertors were modernised by substituting mercury-arc rectifiers. Certainly Westgate sub-station was converted at this time, and presumably Byker (in the depot) was, too. Manors remained a rotary convertor, however, and functioned as a control

104

point for the "slave" stations situated in the suburbs. So ended the comforting sensation when passing Westgate, particularly at night, and hearing the steady workmanlike whine of the converters in action, this being replaced by the ghoulish cold light of the mercury-arc shining through the windows.

One of the last major alterations to the overhead was the relocation of Denton Road Terminus. The turning at the junction of Denton Road and Whickham View had been awkward, and indeed dangerous, due to heavy motor traffic. An alteration in the late nineteen fifties which gave standing trolleybuses a layby in front of some shops at the north-east corner of the junction was not sufficient, so it was decided to move the whole terminus some distance farther west into Castlenook Place. To achieve this, Castlenook Place, which was formerly a cul-de-sac off Broadwood Road, was made a through road to Denton Road over the Denton Burn itself. The new turning circle, to the south of Castlenook Place, was actually built on top of the stream, which was culverted. The Council approved the construction work for the new terminus in April 1961 at an estimated cost of £12,770, including £4,348 for the extension of the overhead lines, and it was opened in the early summer of 1962, slightly increasing route mileage to 37.187 miles, the maximum it was to reach. The turning circle was arranged anti-clockwise and trolleybuses continued to use it as such until the last services using it, 33/43, were converted to motorbus operation in May 1965. After this date the motorbuses, which had been obliged to turn anti-clockwise like the trolleybuses for safety reasons, began to use the circle in the opposite direction. They still do.

An idea of the density of services on the system can be gained by quoting the flow of vehicles in Grainger Street as at January 1962. This street was the busiest point on the network, with an impressive total of 168 trolleybuses per hour at peak times (84 in each direction), made up service by service as follows:—

31:—6	33:—6	36:—6	39:—4	42:—4
31A:—6	33A:—12	37:—4	40:—4	43:—6
31B:—6	35C:—6	38:—4	41:—4	44:—6

A re-routing of the circular trolleybus routes took place on Sunday 1st April 1962. Services 39 and 40 both ceased to work from Central Station. Instead, their City centre terminal point became Newgate Street, which was carried on destination indicators. These services now entered the City centre via Percy Street and Newgate Street, and left by Newgate Street, Grainger Street, Northumberland Street, and Barras Bridge. Apparently, the change was made to reduce congestion in Northumberland Street, although more cynical observers said that it was an attempt to kill the 39's and 40's. Services 41 and 42 were altered to work IN-WARD journeys via Percy Street and Newgate Street, but outward journeys were still routed by way of Grainger Street, Market Street and Northumberland Street. Their City centre terminal points, therefore, became alternately Newgate Street and Central Station on each journey. To enable the revised services now operating from Newgate Street/Clayton Street junction and along Newgate Street to turn left at Grainger Street, a new length of eastbound wiring was erected in Newgate Street between these points. It was in fact the last new addition to the overhead layout in the central area.

At the commencement of the new decade the future of Newcastle's trolley-buses seemed to the layman to be assured. They were to be found in nearly all parts of the City working the most heavily-trafficked routes on the major arteries, and showing their excellent hill-climbing ability on such gradients as Westgate Hill. Their dominance is best illustrated by the situation which used to impress the authors, where for nearly $3\frac{1}{2}$ miles, on the whole length of Westgate Road/ West Road from the City centre to Denton Square, trolleybuses reigned supreme. The only Newcastle Transport motorbuses which dared to venture onto this road were those on Service 8 Circle in the Wingrove area, and Service 1 at Denton Burn. Both were for short distances only, a few yards in each case, as they passed along from one side road to another. All the City seemed to be given over to the trolleybus and drivers under training could be seen piloting their vehicles (generally NCB-bodied Sunbeam F4's or B.U.T. 9611T's) along the West Road. Let us attempt to see the system as it was . . .

CHAPTER ELEVEN

BENEATH TEN MILES OF TROLLEYBUS WIRES

In order to appreciate the system in its heyday, let us relive a journey on route 43/44, from the Central Station. This service was Newcastle's longest worked by trolleybuses, being 9.8 miles in length and taking 53 minutes to traverse.

Transferring to the present tense, let us assume that it is an early Summer's day in May 1963. We are in the City centre, in Neville Street. Facing us is the magnificent portico of Dobson's Central Station commanding the eighty-feet wide sweep of Neville Street which is divided by a central reservation constructed in 1955. Walking eastwards on the north side of the street towards the traffic round-about controlling a four road junction, we approach St. Mary's Roman Catholic Cathedral. On our side of the road, facing eastwards, stands the trolleybus which will carry us on our journey. It is most probably a B.U.T. 6-wheeler with a Metro-Cammell body dating from 1950.

Immediately in front of it is a trolleybus on the 31 group of services serving Gosforth Park. If we were familiar with the London Transport Q1 class vehicles of 1948 and 1952 we would find this Newcastle trolleybus strangely similar. It is, in fact, a London Q1 which never went to the Capital but found itself in New-castle Transport livery instead! The indicator layout is as required for London service except that Newcastle has painted the glass black to allow only one line to show. Even the indicator winders are stamped "L.P.T.B."! The Newcastle crews nickname them "the Gosforth 'buses" since they opened this route in April 1948. The indicator of the 1948 B.U.T. in front of our six-wheeler shows "31, Gosforth Park", but ours is of a later batch otherwise similar (apart from the destination layout and opening windows) which shows "44, Fenham", "via Barrack Rd. & Fenham", since an intermediate destination screen is also pro-vided. Standing behind the 44 is inevitably a 42, on one of the Heaton Road circular services, the vehicle most probably working this route being a B.U.T. 4-wheeler of 1948. There are two roads of wiring here in the shadow of the Cathedral and the 44 is standing with booms on the inner road, nearest the kerb. Behind it is a scissors crossover with a double slip. Immediately ahead the two roads become single then double again. The 31 in front of us stands with poles on the inner road.

The route 43/44 on which we are about to travel covers quite a large part of the City: Central Station—Fenham—Denton—Benwell—Elswick—City—Jesmond and reverse. There is a ten-minute service and it is not long before we move off, at slow speed at first, our booms transferring themselves to the outside road in order to pass the stationary Gosforth trolleybus ahead. We pass under a set of wires, running up Bewick Street along the side of the Cathedral to Clayton Street West, which were formerly used by services terminating at the Central Station before the roundabout was installed. Now all regular services simply turn around the roundabout. Bewick Street is still used by certain early morning services and in emergencies.

The wires turn left into Grainger Street West. A pause at the traffic signals and we cross the wires of the original route of 1935 in Westgate Road. The road is clear and we accelerate smartly up Grainger Street and draw up at the stop

107

opposite the Northern Gas Board premises. A set of wires bears left a little farther on into Newgate Street and another set turns out to join our line. This latter set was only inserted in 1962 for the alteration of the terminus of the 39 and 40 services from Central Station to Newgate Street, to enable them to work up Grainger Street and out of the central area via Northumberland Street. Although the Corporation had powers to erect wires to cross over this street junction, none do so, even though tram standards in the Bigg Market and past the Old Town Hall are still in place to receive them.

At the junction with Market Street, the frog is preset for that street and since we have to go straight on, our conductor jumps off to pull the lever. We crawl under the frog and the conductor jumps back on board, banging the side of the bus with his hand in so doing to inform the driver that he has reboarded. He remains on the platform, however, for the wires divide again as we approach Grey's Monument, a 130-foot high column. One set of wires turns right, towards Northumberland Street. We, however, take the inner set as the conductor again jumps aboard having "pulled the frog". The wiring arrangement is very complicated at the Monument and the criss-cross of overhead hangs heavily in the sky. After turning left into Blackett Street, we coast over the single road wiring emerging from Clayton Street, which is one way northwards, with our power off.

After the Newgate Street/Percy Street junction, we leave the City centre and our driver accelerates up Gallowgate, which is narrow at first, then becomes wider in a series of reverse curves. Near the point where the central reservation begins dividing the road into dual carriageway, we see Heber Street, small and narrow, where it was intended the Elswick Road trolleybuses would emerge onto Barrack Road. Also starting here is the elongated loop built to serve the Newcastle United football ground at St. James' Park. Trolleybuses from the east end of the City serving the ground are intended to take the siding which diverges just past Heber Street. The siding then enters a service road, parallel to Barrack Road and separated from it by a tree-planted island on which are mounted the traction poles supporting both siding and main line wires. We continue along the main road, however, past St. James' Park, pulling steadily up the incline.

Ahead, a quarter mile from the start of the loop, are the junctions at the foot of Stanhope Street. Our driver slows down here for the stop just before the junction. This gives us a chance to examine the wiring from our vantage point at the front of the upper deck. Immediately in front the roads divide, one set of wires going up Stanhope Street into the Arthur's Hill area, while the other carries straight on up Barrack Road. The wiring coming down Stanhope Street cuts across the Barrack Road wires farther ahead, and joins into the City-bound wires on the other side of the road. The head of the siding comes out of the service road on our left and sweeps in an arc right across the junction, crossing the City-bound wires and continuing as a long siding on their inside, down Barrack Road to a point about opposite its beginning where it rejoins the main wires.

On receiving the starting signal, the driver accelerates smoothly for about his own 'bus length, then cuts off power as the Stanhope Street frog must be coasted under to avoid arcing. A buzzer sounds in the cab to inform the driver as he negotiates the insulated sections that his trolleyheads are over the frog, and he reapplies power. Most drivers know by the position of the vehicle when they are under the frogs. "Whump, Whump," from the booms as we pass under first the head of the St. James' Park loop and then the Stanhope Street City-bound wires, and we are accelerating again. Coming in on our left is a connection from Stanhope Street, formerly used by trolleybuses coming on duty from Wingrove Depot in order to reach the Fenham terminus before Slatyford Depot was opened and Silver Lonnen was wired up in 1956. Its copper wires are green and tarnished through lack of regular use, although certain school services from Benwell to Fenham via West Road still use it. Some drivers cut off power for this connection, although it is not really necessary.

This is the last wiring junction before the Fenham terminus at Bingfield Gardens, just over two miles farther on. Although the road is still about 40 feet wide, the dual carriageway section has ended. We are still well within the City boundary but the number of houses is decreasing rapidly, for we are skirting the 900 acre Town Moor, completely ringed by the built-up area of the suburbs. Trolleybus stops are spaced every 8 or 10 poles, but as it is mid-morning we do not stop at any. As Fenham Barracks, which give Barrack Road its name, come into view on the right, the gradient we have climbed from the City centre eases, and the whine of our 120 h.p. motor rises as the driver builds up speed, taking advantage of the light traffic. This is one of the "racing stretches" of the system, others being the West Road, between Benwell High Reservoir and the Milvain Ballroom, and Silver Lonnen.

Apart from tyre noise, a muffled "whump" as the trolleyheads pass under each spacer, and a slight hum from the motor, our progress is silent. As we pass the Brighton Grove/Hunter's Road junction, tram standards can be seen standing in the latter road, although trams last ran in 1936. Our trolleybus is now moving at about 40 miles an hour as the road begins to rise again. We spy a City-bound B.U.T. 6-wheeler approaching us in the opposite direction. The B.U.T.s are amongst the fastest on the system and it flashes by travelling at what must be over 40 m.p.h., taking advantage of the falling gradient. Our dash is over now, and we begin slowing for the turn into Fenham Hall Drive. Turning into this road, which is, as its name might suggest, a former private drive to a mansion, we might notice the line of the proposed extension up Ponteland Road to Cowgate and ultimately to Kenton Bank Foot. Also of interest is the fact that the poles at the road junction, on the far side of Ponteland Road, are stayed back to two trees.

The speed on Fenham Hall Drive is much slower as the surface is poor. The shoulders of the road are concrete and tarmacadam and on the crown, the stone setts in which the tram tracks were laid are visible through the asphalt in places. We are entering the suburb of Fenham now, half-a-mile past the Ponteland Road junction. Some way on, at the Convent Road stop, near the Convent of the Sacred Heart, the driver and the conductor change the indicators, as is usual at this point, although the Fenham terminus is the official place for this procedure. We set off again, our indicators now reading "33A", "Osborne Rd.", "via Elswick Rd." Well into Fenham, we pause at Two Ball Lonnen junction, and cross the line of yet another proposed route extension. In Netherby Drive we are on a section of former tramway that was reserved track—part of the Westerhope Tramroad.

The first street we pass on the left is Ovington Grove, into which trolleybuses reversed from 1938 until November 1941. On the latter date, the terminus was moved to the foot of Netherby Drive and a new reverser constructed in Bingfield Gardens, at which point we now are. This is the terminus of the 32 and

36 routes, and we will probably see a Sunbeam S7 6-wheeler with locally-built Northern Coachbuilders' body ready to set out for Wallsend Boundary on the far side of the City.

Before 1956, we would now have arrived at a dead-end as far as the wiring was concerned. In that year, however, the Slatyford Depot and Silver Lonnen wiring was opened. We wait here for a few minutes, having passed under the reverser.

As we edge round the tight corner into Silver Lonnen, (and, incidentally, are treated to an example of rear bogie scrub), the bulk of Slatyford Depot is seen above the houses on the other side of the road, with the depot exit wiring emerging from Slatyford Lane onto Silver Lonnen. Picking up speed, we proceed smoothly along the concrete surface of the Lonnen until, a mile later, we reach the West Road, at the foot of Denton Bank. Prior to 1961, this was an ordinary junction, but in that year a roundabout was constructed and the overhead altered to suit. There are many connections which allow trolleybuses to make a variety of movements. Here we pass onto the line of the original 1935 Denton Loop in Denton Road. To the right, as we negotiate the roundabout and cross the A69 trunk road, is the overhead to Denton Square, a third of a mile away. To the left, three miles away, is the City centre. Having entered Denton Road, the overhead has changed from span wire to bracket arm suspension.

Speed is again low due to the indifferent road surface. Soon we are at the junction with Whickham View, where we turn sharp left and begin to run back towards the City centre. Before 1962, this very wide road junction formed the turning circle of Denton Road terminus, but after this a new turning-circle was opened in Castlenook Place, astride Denton Burn. This turning-circle is unusual in that it is anti-clockwise.

Travelling eastwards along Whickham View on a steadily rising gradient, we see that the overhead is supported on double-bracket arms, with the poles on the south kerb. The road is narrow, only about 20-22 feet in width, although the front garden walls of the houses are set back about another 20 feet from the edges of the road.

At the junction of Whickham View with Ferguson's Lane, we leave the original overhead of 1935 and pass onto the section erected in 1944 to connect Elswick Road with the Denton Loop. On this part of Whickham View, the road surface is very poor and this, coupled with a steep camber towards the south, restricts our speed to about 20 mph. Past the Workshops for the Blind the road narrows again and double bracket arms reappear until Delaval Road sub-terminus is reached. This was the ultimate tram terminus of the Elswick cars, the route being extended from the foot of Condercum Road in 1923. A reverser with a short siding now constitutes the trolleybus terminus. To turn round, trolleybuses proceed past Delaval Road on the south side of Benwell Lane (as Whickham View has now become) and reverse into Delaval Road, which has a steep down gradient. They then draw forward out of that street, over Benwell Lane, and into a short siding on its north side so that they now face the City centre.

We cross over these junctions, and pass a Sunbeam S7 which has just carried out the manoeuvre described.

We are now on the ex-tram route. A half-mile farther on, amongst older housing, we find the Benwell Church sub-terminus at Nichol Street. This reverser, generally only used at rush-hours, is somewhat unusual in that trolleybuses from the City have to cross over to the wrong (north) side of Adelaide Terrace, as the main road is called at this point, before reversing into Nichol Street. St. James' Parish Church, Benwell, from which the terminal point takes its name, is in fact 200 yards back to the west. Our journey continues along Elswick Road through the older suburbs of Benwell and Elswick. Stops are frequent, and traffic, both motor and pedestrian, is heavy, so it is some time before we reach the Big Lamp junction at the top of Westgate Hill. The junction takes its name from a large multi-globed gas lamp that used to illuminate the area in the 1880's.

Here we join the wires of the Westgate Road route which we last crossed three miles to the west at Denton Burn roundabout. As we pause at the top of the hill, we note Buckingham Street on the left, where it was intended the Elswick Road trolleybuses would go in order to reach Barrack Road. Dropping down Westgate Hill, we re-enter the City centre. (It was on this hill when mixed diesel and trolleybus operation was instituted after June 1963, that the electric vehicles showed their superior climbing ability. The former would be grinding up the gradient in bottom gear, at perhaps 10 mph., while the trolleybuses could hold 20-25 mph. with a full load, providing only one vehicle was on the section.)

Near the foot of the hill, at Blenheim Street, a long siding to a left turn into Clayton Street begins. Although at this period it was seldom used, it had been intended to allow what might be termed "parallel working" (i.e. a trolleybus on this siding could be passed by one intending to continue down Westgate Road). This part of the road is quite narrow, and since it is the A69 trunk road, traffic is heavy and our speed consequently low.

The wiring at Clayton Street junction is a simple right-angled double crossing with the left-hand connection mentioned. At Cowen's Monument our road of wiring splits again and the outer set of wires, nearly over the centre of the road, leads straight on down Westgate Road. The set we have taken forks left up Grainger Street.

We again proceed along this thoroughfare, but this time we turn right into Market Street and "down the dip" to Grey Street junction. Here the wires split into two roads once more, our trolleybooms taking the inner one over the preset frogs. A notice on one of the poles states "ALL TROLLEYBUS SERVICES TURN LEFT". The outer set of wires is very rarely used. As we creep round the tight curve into Pilgrim Street and the A1, the short section of tram overhead, its single traction wires looking out of place, is noticeable in the lower part of Pilgrim Street leading to the Tyne Bridge. This overhead is retained for feeder purposes from a section box situated on its length. (On abandonment of the trolleybus system in October 1966, this overhead was to be ruthlessly cut down along with the trolleybus overhead. It is unfortunate that it was not allowed to remain as a small memorial to the trams.)

There are three roads of wiring in Pilgrim Street, the northbound road we are on, and two southbound roads on the other side of the street. The inner of these forms part of the turning square for rush-hour use from the east end. We will probably see a "43" trolleybus working the other way round the route we are on, travelling close to the centre of the wide road, preparatory to turning right into Market Street, its booms at their maximum deflection, since the overhead is close to the east kerb.

After we pass under the wires used by trolleybuses on the Benton, Walker, and Wallsend Boundary services at Blackett Street junction, we travel up Northumberland Street, one of the main shopping streets in the City. Emerging at the Haymarket, we see the 12-storey tower of the Civic Centre rising over the area. We note a single set of wires diverging left across the Haymarket to the south of the Boer War Memorial. These make a trailing connection with the southbound wires in Percy Street. Prior to the closing of the Haymarket Depot in December 1957, these led to that depot.

Crossing over the busy junction we encounter the automatic frog, inserted in 1954, where the Jesmond Road and North Road services divide. Taking the outer road, our vehicle moves to the centre of the road and sweeps up to the Jesmond Road junction. This "parallel working" proves to be of value, for a Gosforth trolleybus passes on our inside before we finally turn into Jesmond Road.

We run along the good surface of the latter, leaving the Central area behind and moving into Jesmond. As we move over the red asphalt, we reflect that the tram rails are still buried beneath its surface. The surrounding buildings were once large villas, the homes of well-to-do Victorian families, but now most are used as offices, showrooms, hotels or college premises.

Soon we are at the turn to Osborne Road. Just before it we cross a railway bridge at Jesmond Station. Running alongside us are the tracks of another form of electric traction—the North Tyneside trains. This loop line from Newcastle to the coast was electrified in 1904 to counteract tram competition, but, alas, this too was to succumb to the all-conquering diesel in 1967. As we accelerate up Osborne Road we are entering the Jesmond area proper. In this select part of the City most of the property is owner-occupied unlike Jesmond Road. Many are shaded by mature trees.

Prior to 1948, the Osborne Road trolleybus route was the only one in the north-eastern part of the City, having been converted to trolleybus operation in 1938. The trams had terminated at St. George's Church at the north end of Osborne Road, but after we alight our trolleybus continues another fifty yards to perform its rather long terminal movement. Like Brighton Grove, this consists of a square of streets—Osborne Road, Lonsdale Terrace, Tavistock Road and back into Osborne Road.

If we walk round following the trolleybus overhead, we will see the traction poles positioned to connect Osborne Road with Jesmond Dene Road, but although only a short distance away, no wiring was ever erected. The poles are topped with finials and these contrast with the more austere flat-capped poles in Jesmond Dene Road.

To regain the City centre we need but board the trolleybus again. It will now carry on its destination indicators "Denton Road Terminus" "via Elswick Road" "43", and will unwind its course back to Central Station.

We have thus seen on our journey the majority of the west end routes, and most of the central area wiring, together with part of the routes serving the north-eastern suburbs, and have been under wiring dating from as early as 1935 and as late as 1956.

CHAPTER TWELVE

ABANDONED IN HASTE

The *Evening Chronicle* for Wednesday 19th December 1962 brought news "out of the blue" of a decision of the Transport and Electricity Committee to abandon the City's trolleybuses. This had been made following receipt of a report by the General Manager, Mr. F. S. Taylor. It came as a devastating bombshell, for in the back of one's mind there had been the pleasant anticipation of an announcement in the near future of orders for a new trolleybus fleet to replace the oldest of the existing vehicles. Knowing of Bournemouth's then recent delivery of modern Sunbeam MF2B's there had been enthralling thoughts of such vehicles running in the streets of Newcastle . . . perhaps by 1963?! But it was not to be.

The Committee Report was the first official policy statement on the suitability of trolleybuses for Newcastle. Presented to the Council in January 1963, it was entitled "Report of the Committee on the Central Area Redevelopment and Future Policy on Trolleybuses", and made the following points:—

(1)   The City Redevelopment Plan 1963, means the closing of roads which have formerly been through routes. Considerable work and expenditure will have to be incurred if trolleybus services are to continue. The City centre would still be left with a forest of poles and wires.

(2)   There are eighteen major trolleybus operators in the U.K. Twelve are abandoning or have abandoned their systems.

(3)   It is necessary to replace trolleybuses because:—

(a)   Due to lack of mobility, if new roads are constructed and one-way streets introduced, they cannot be switched to use them without large capital expenditure.

(b)   An integrated transport system, with one type of vehicle, would effect economies.

(c)   Motorbuses are cheaper to operate, costing 6½d. per mile less than trolleybuses.

(d)   Planning authorities, police, etc. are in favour of motorbuses. Trolleybuses cannot overtake and are slow at junctions, etc.

(e)   All trolleybuses are at a standstill if there is a power failure.

(f)   Overhead is unsightly.

(g)   Trolleybuses can be constructed to special order only.

(4)   Trolleybuses have "had their day".

(5)   The Pilgrim Street Roundabout works are to start early in 1963. Service 34 is to be converted by June 1963 and the remainder of the conversions to be phased 1963/4 and 1967/8.

It is not the place here to go into the pros and cons of the trolleybus as a means of transport, save only to say that point 3(g) above, was refuted by the manufacturers and points 3(f) and 4 were wide open to criticism of their validity and sense, as was 3(d). 3(e) had only happened once in Newcastle (see Chapter

113

9). The five points were in fact very similar to those advanced by London Transport for its trolleybus abandonment scheme, and subsequently used by many of the remaining trolleybus undertakings.

The Council was very reluctant to sanction the scheme, but finally agreed and passed the report. A considerable press correspondence controversy followed, but the Undertaking was not to be diverted or retarded in its plans.

There had been intermittent ill-informed criticism of trolleybuses in the local press previously. In September 1962, one correspondent claimed that three-axle trolleybuses were a danger when negotiating the S-bend of Mosley Street, Pilgrim Street, and City Road. This was counteracted by one of the authors mentioning the not inconsiderable front overhang on Leyland "Atlantean" motorbuses when turning corners.

On Whit Sunday, 2nd June 1963, Leyland "Atlantean" motorbuses (which were used to replace all of the City's trolleybuses) took over on service 34. It was indeed strange to see Newcastle Transport motorbuses working along the West Road. 594 had been the last trolleybus from Denton Square to Wallsend the previous evening. Some weeks before, white motorbus stop signs had appeared on traction poles at some trolleybus stops and were covered over with hessian sacking. Posters giving notice of the conversion had been exhibited in trolleybuses operating on the route together with the timetable to which the replacement motorbuses were to operate. Ten minutes were scheduled to be cut from the 8.3 mile journey which had a trolleybus journey time of 45 minutes. This was achieved by cutting out a large number of stops, top of Denton Bank and Two Ball Lonnen being two which spring to mind. The trolleybuses could no doubt have covered the route in a similar time had the timetables been drawn up to take full advantage of the accelerative powers available.

Older motorbuses used at rush-hours made VERY heavy weather of Westgate Hill compared with that which had gone before; 8-ft. wide AEC "Regent III's" fitted with new destination blinds reading "Denton Square" or "Condercum Road", laden with stoical commuters and looking so alien, ground their way up Westgate Hill at 8-10 mph, in bottom gear.

The conversion of this route caused the Sunbeam F4 Metro-Cammell two-axle vehicles to be withdrawn, together with some of the Sunbeam F4 NCB two-axle stock.

Originally, it was intended to turn motorbuses at the *Fox & Hounds* in the same way as the trolleybuses had, but since permission was refused to reverse out onto the West Road, a turning loop via Westacres Crescent was envisaged. Local residents objected. In effect, motorbuses resorted to the old Condercum Road tram terminus at rush-hours, but although they carried "Condercum Road" on their blinds, they actually turned in Baxter Avenue/Hoyle Avenue beside the Milvain Ballroom about a hundred yards short of Condercum Road. At Denton Square, part of the grass island in the centre of the turning circle was cut away to allow double standing of motorbuses and trolleybuses, motorbuses standing on the inside of the circle.

One hardship which the conversion to motorbuses of the trolleybus services caused with the withdrawal of the facility for Old Age Pensioners' Concessionary Fare Passes (at a flat fare of 1d.). The Undertaking was only allowed to give this facility on trolleybuses. As the conversion scheme progressed this featured hotly in the local press both in correspondence and editorials. Eventually the regulations were changed to allow Newcastle Transport to offer the concession on motorbuses also.

The necessity of starting work on the giant Pilgrim Street underpass and elevated roundabout (readers from the south who have passed through Tyneside and Newcastle on their way to Scotland will know this large development as it is now) was given as the reason for the conversion of service 34. Roadworks did not start to affect traction poles until early 1964 but the overhead wires were removed in a matter of weeks after conversion. (See complete list of wiring removals, Appendix L.) Since Westgate Road/West Road was still used by trolleybus services 35, 37, and 38, overhead was only removed eastward of St. Nicholas' Street to Church Street junction on Walker Road. From there to the eastern terminus at Park Road, Wallsend, the wires were left up for use by workmen's services to Park Road via Welbeck Road from the west end, which continued to run until 30th May 1965.

The situation which had existed in the winter of 1935/6, when motorbuses were run as peak-hour extras to trolleybuses, was reversed after June 1963 when motorbuses on service 34 sometimes had trolleybuses running as extras at peak times from Denton Square and *Fox & Hounds* to St. Nicholas' Cathedral turning loop. This continued until at least the late spring of 1965. The loop was still used by Elswick Road trolleybuses, mainly on service 35C, until its removal on 19th December 1965.

Opposition to the Council's policy of abandonment of trolleybuses was not yet stifled. A Mr. A. J. Wickens of Jesmond mounted a "Trolleybus Retention Campaign" in October 1963 and distributed some well-argued leaflets and other publicity material. No official reaction was forthcoming, however, and the effort collapsed in the vacuum.

Alteration to the overhead was still taking place. October/November 1963 saw the overhead wiring in Whickham View being modified due to the construction of lay-bys at certain stops. This involved the removal of several double bracket arms and the wiring became supported on newly-erected poles and span wires.

The next stage of the abandonment took effect from 1st February 1964, when trolleybuses on services 31, 31A, and 31B (the Central Station—North Road —Gosforth services), 37, 38, (Benton Road—Denton Road Terminus services via Heaton Road and Jesmond Road respectively) and 39 and 40 (Central Station—Benton Park Road Circles) all ran for the last time. The next day, Sunday 2nd February 1964, the 39 and 40 circular services no longer existed. Instead a motorbus operated service 38 was routed via the North Road and South Gosforth to terminate at Benton Park Road in front of the Ministry of Pensions and National Insurance (as it was then) and Leyland "Atlantean" motorbuses on service 37 were extended from Swarland Avenue to meet it from an easterly direction. A 38, on reaching "the Ministry" at Benton Park Road, became a 37 to Denton Road Terminus, and in the opposite direction, a 37 became a 38 at the same point. Swarland Avenue then became used as the terminus of some Gateshead joint services such as 68 and 70, thus recalling the pre-1948 pattern of through tram workings from Heworth to Chillingham Road which had brought Gateshead balcony trams into north-east Newcastle.

115

The 31 group of services was renumbered 45, 46, and 47 on the same date, the reason being that the newest "Atlanteans" had two track route number indicators and thus did not have a track for showing suffixes such as A, B, etc. Service 46 to Polwarth Drive was extended into Brunton Park Estate as mentioned earlier in the text.

Motorbuses on services 37 and 38 now showed "Whickham View" as their destination on westbound journeys, not "Denton Road Terminus" and they operated via Pease Avenue, Pendower (in both directions) instead of via the narrow Fox-and-Hounds Lane. Trolleybuses operating at rush-hours as extras to the diesel 'buses (from St. Nicholas' Cathedral) naturally still used the latter road. This peak-hour working continued at least as long as the similar 34 working. The westbound frogs at the Big Lamp were set for Elswick Road, since most trolleybuses arriving at the junction now turned along that road, and it now was necessary to "Pull Lever for Westgate Road". Power was cut off from the North Road section at Jesmond Road junction on the first day of diesel 'bus operation. By the autumn, all overhead and traction poles outside the City boundary had been removed—which included the 5½-year-old overhead on the widened sections of North Road. One pole on the curve in Haddrick's Mill Road, South Gosforth, was removed during the summer to allow an entrance to a plant-hire firm's premises to be widened leaving the overhead hanging dangerously low for several weeks from the pole on the opposite side of the road!

In spite of the fact that their bodywork was in better condition, this second conversion to motorbuses led to the withdrawal of the remainder of the Sunbeam and BUT/NCB-bodied two-axle vehicles instead of the Sunbeam S7's, thus leaving only high-capacity three-axle vehicles of Sunbeam and BUT manufacture in stock. As a result of the Stage Two abandonments, the overhead in the two most westerly bays in Slatyford Depot was removed and route mileage was reduced to 25.725 as at 31st March 1964.

It could be seen that there was no hope for Newcastle's trolleybuses now, but it was not until some 15 months later that the next stage took place. The date had been advanced, for it will be remembered that, according to the original schedule, no more abandonments should have taken place until 1967/8. Visitors to the City were being advised to "have a last ride on a Newcastle trolleybus". Just before the conversion, two poles at the junction of Fenham Hall Drive and Wingrove Road were replaced since the existing ones had rusted through.

When Sunday 30th May 1965 dawned, half the trolleybus system that had been operating the night before had disappeared. Only 14.925 route miles were left after Stage Three of the conversion. Trolleybuses on services 32, 33, 33A, 33B, 36, 41, 42, 43, and 44 were withdrawn, together with through workmen's services from the west end to Wallsend Boundary (via Shields Road) and Wallsend Park Road (via Welbeck Road). This left only the 35 group of routes, including 35C to Delaval Road, worked by trolleybuses.

Rationalisation of the rather complex trolleybus service numbers on the converted routes took place, probably for the same reason as the 31 group were renumbered. Services 33, 33A, 33B, and 43 (Osborne Road to Delaval Road, Denton Road Terminus, and Fenham, via Elswick Road) were renumbered simply 33 and in the reverse direction, the 36 and 44 service became just 36. Westbound 33's from Osborne Road now showed "Fenham" over the whole route to Denton Road Terminus, where they changed to "Central Station—36". (This indication of "Fenham" is rather misleading to strangers, since although it does EVENT-UALLY get to Fenham, it gives the passenger a grand tour of the west end first! There are much more direct services.) The Heaton Road circular services, 41 and 42, were altered to terminate on all journeys at Central Station. Frequencies were reduced to 20 minutes in the evenings in many cases.

Trolleybuses left Slatyford and Handysides depots for good as a result of the Stage Three conversion, all remaining services being worked from Byker until final abandonment in October 1966, and with the exception of 501, all the Sunbeam S7's were withdrawn for scrap. 501 was preserved by the Corporation, for eventual inclusion in a new Science and Technology wing of the Laing Art Gallery. It was temporarily stored in the paintshop at Byker Depot, where it remained for some years.

Following the Stage Three conversion, no time was lost in removing the overhead. Bingfield Gardens reverser at Fenham terminus was removed on the night of 8/9th June 1965, only one week after it was last used. Thereafter, removal proceeded steadily throughout the late summer and into the winter. Memories are still vivid of seeing overhead gangs cutting down running wires, cutting span wires, and taking out frogs on such places as Barrack Road, Fenham Hall Drive and Silver Lonnen, late in the cold, dark winter nights of 1965. How strange Fenham Hall Drive looks without trolleybus wires!

The removal of the overhead wiring was executed from east-end to City to west-end (in general), and by October 1965 the absence of running wires in Fox-and-Hounds Lane definitely prevented the operation of trolleybuses as rush-hour extras on services 37 and 38. By April 1966, as in tram days, Delaval Road again became the absolute terminus, as by this date the overhead in Whickham View had gone.

Strangely, two miles of wiring were retained along Elswick Road from the Big Lamp to Delaval Road, solely for the service 35C which ran only inter-mittently on weekdays and all day on Saturdays as from 1st June 1965, instead of daily as formerly.

Delivery of further Leyland "Atlanteans" had caused the withdrawal of all the famous 1948 batch of BUT three-axle vehicles—the "Gosforth buses"—together with 11 of the more modern 1950 vehicles, leaving only 39 trolleybuses in stock—33 in service and 6 as spares. In November 1965, 615 was withdrawn after an accident, and 597 reinstated. Indeed, a winter 1935/6 situation developed with "Atlanteans" augmented by older motorbuses running as rush-hour extras to the trolleybuses up Stanhope Street.

While all the redundant wiring was being torn down, the overhead on Westgate Road was being altered at the Wingrove. This stretch of Westgate Road between Grainger Park Road and Keldane Gardens was noticeably narrower than the standard 40ft. width of Westgate Road/West Road westwards from Brighton Grove junction, and a short length west from Grainger Park Road actually had gantry construction. The south kerb was moved back 6-8 feet at this time, and the traction poles repositioned to which new span wires were attached. Some new poles were also erected on the north side of Westgate Road, to accommodate the altered overhead construction. On could easily tell that this part of the road had been widened since the westbound road of wiring was not moved correspondingly and thus became nearer the new centre of the road as a result.

117

Further substantial overhead alterations had been carried out in Walker soon after the May 1965 conversions. Church Street, along which trolleybuses had run since 1937, was to be closed for redevelopment and building of the Church Walk Centre, and new junctions were therefore put in to enable service 35 trolleybuses to turn right from Welbeck Street to White Street (a continuation of Walker Road), in order to be extended to the foot of Church Street via Walker Road and Procter Street. At the junction of Procter Street and Church Street a new reverser was installed. The turning-circle at the east end of Welbeck Road was retained.

As from Sunday 22nd August 1965 service 35 was thus extended and service 35A, which formerly ran down Church Street to its junction with Walker Road, now stopped short at the 35C terminal point at Westbourne Avenue. Service 35B was withdrawn. Trolleybuses now used the head of the former wiring in Church Street, which was cut off a few yards into that street as a reverser. A new short siding was inserted on the south side of Welbeck Road, just west of Church Street, as a standing point.

Also in 1965, the laying of pads for traffic signals at the Brighton Grove/Westgate Road junction ("*the Brighton*") meant that inspectors had to be stationed in Brighton Grove for a few days to dewire the westbound trolleybuses on services 35, for these had to crawl past the roadworks on the wrong side of the road using their traction batteries.

All through the last 16 months of operation it was galling (and still somehow unreal) to see trolleybuses hustled at stops on the West Road by the growling, jerking "Atlanteans" which were beginning to dominate the motorbus fleet. Properly driven, the remaining trolleybuses could still show a clean pair of heels when climbing Denton Bank.

Right up to the late summer of 1966 the exact date of the final conversion was still unknown. Only about a month beforehand the date of final abandonment was announced as 1st October. Enthusiasts began arriving in the City in not inconsiderable numbers, to record on film and on tape recorders, the sights and sounds of Newcastle's trolleybuses.

The writer was equally busy in the last fortnight, thankfully blessed with sunny weather, although this lasted only until Friday 30th September.

Saturday, 1st October dawned. It was pouring with rain. That sums it up. All day it teemed down and visibility was almost nil. It was as if the heavens were weeping in sympathy. We know this was said at the Sheffield and Glasgow tram closures—but it has happened at a number of other tram and trolleybus last days—or else they were freezing cold! It was not a lashing rain, but the type which insidiously soaks everything, gently persistent. Many enthusiasts, including the writer, spent most of the day riding on the vehicles and smiling wryly at the antics of hopeful ciné enthusiasts wielding their dripping cameras. At about five o'clock there was a change, and a strong wind blew up and drove the clouds away, but the sun was too low for photography by then.

Strangely—one might say typically—Newcastle had made no formal requiem arrangements for its departing electric traction. Stories are told that a very senior official was embarrassed and somewhat annoyed when 200 or so people turned up to see the last trolleybuses enter Byker Depot sometime after midnight.

Mr. John Petrie remembers that there was no ceremony whatsoever. Enthusiasts simply gathered in the Depot yard, the night being fine and mild, and watched the vehicles run into the building; saw the last one (599) perform the same manoeuvre; the doors close—and that was that: the end of one of the largest trolleybus systems in the United Kingdom.

The last service 35 right through to Walker (Church Street) was scheduled to depart from Denton Square at 10.51 p.m. and arrived at its east end terminus at 11.35 p.m. The very last trolleybus from Denton Square was scheduled to leave there at 11.24 p.m. to arrive at Potts Street, Byker (for Byker Depot) at 11.55 p.m., and this was No. 599.

The final service 35C over the whole route from Delaval Road to Westbourne Avenue was also scheduled to depart at 10.51 p.m. arriving at Walker at 11.22 p.m. The last depot working was at 11.23 p.m. from Delaval Road, to arrive at Potts Street at 11.47 p.m. and was fittingly worked by 628, Newcastle's highest-numbered trolleybus, thus numerically the last. The writer is ashamed to say that, due to a stupid mistake on his part, he DID NOT SEE the very last service 35 from Denton Square! He was stationed, with a friend, on the West Road at the Milvain Ballroom about 11.20 p.m. Soon, over the brow of the hill at Benwell High Reservoir, from the west, came the shape of a brightly-illuminated trolleybus gliding down to the City centre. It carried placards and was full of enthusiasts, some riding in the cab—it was 583. As it passed—at the time scheduled for the very last journey from Denton Square to pass the Milvain—the writer assumed it was the last Newcastle trolleybus and as it disappeared down the West Road, growing smaller in the distance, he turned sadly for home. How vexing (and embarrassing!) to find, on telephoning Newcastle Transport on the following Monday morning, that 599, passing the Milvain some 5-7 minutes later, had been the final trolleybus. It had been delayed at Denton Square by enthusiasts taking photographs! And so a fine British trolleybus system died, 31 years to the day since inauguration.

The local press covered the closure without giving it undue prominence, and on Sunday, 2nd October 1966, the local BBC News Studio televised a half hour film on trams, which also included a few minutes of Newcastle trolleybuses shot in the last few weeks and gave some mention of trolleybus enthusiasts from the Huddersfield Trolleybus Preservation Society.

As can be gathered from Appendix L, wiring removals began almost immediately following the final abandonment, the overhead in the eastern end of Welbeck Road and round to the foot of Church Street going on the night of 14/15th October 1966. Again, the gangs worked from east to west, and they had cleared the central area by early December 1966. Westgate Road/West Road was the last to be cleared, fittingly perhaps, as it had been the first to be erected in 1935. The eastbound wires from Denton Square to the Big Lamp, including those from Brighton Grove to the Big Lamp which had not seen regular working for over a year, were amongst the last to be removed during the periods 29th January to 4th February and 6th to 8th February 1967. The very last lengths of wiring to be removed were the remaining eastbound wires from the Big Lamp into the City centre at Stephenson's Monument, where in the earliest days photographs of the original vehicles were posed. This was cut down after four days work on 8th to 11th February 1967.

The last vehicles went to their death at Autospares' yard on the edge of the bleak moor above Bingley, Yorks. 628 had a chance last-minute reprieve and instead of going for scrap she was purchased for preservation by the London Trolleybus Preservation Society and was towed south. As far as Yorkshire she was in company with one of her sisters on suspended tow—destined for scrap.

In 1974, Newcastle Transport no longer exists. On 1st January 1970, the Tyneside Passenger Transport Executive took over the municipal 'bus fleets of Newcastle and South Shields. Today, Leyland "Atlanteans" predominate in Newcastle, but a rapid-transit system is now under construction. This should be in operation by 1979, whereafter Tyneside will have its "Tyneside Tube" burrowing below the central area of the City. Through electric services to Gateshead are once again envisaged!

The new Tyneside Passenger Transport Executive began to reshuffle services immediately after taking over, and, for example, service 38 partially follows the old trolleybus route again along Jesmond Road before turning up Osborne Road along the former service 14 motorbus route, and on to Benton Park Road. Service 37 today runs over the path of the former service 20 motorbus route through High Heaton to Benton Park Road also. Services 41 and 42 (Heaton Road Circular) are integrated with Circular Service 8 describing a figure-of-eight. Service 32 now runs from Central Station, the cross-City link to Wallsend being broken, although it is now extended beyond Bingfield Gardens. It now crosses over Stamfordham Road to Cowgate but it still shows "Fenham" as a destination!

Very quickly after abandonment of the trolleybus system, in May 1967, many streets in the central area of Newcastle were made one-way. They are now part of a complex system covering all the City centre. A new street, known as John Dobson Street, has been constructed to take the A1 traffic away from Northumberland Street, which is now virtually a pedestrian-only precinct. On the east side of Newcastle, Chillingham Road Ends is the first underpass on the Coast Road motorway.

Luckily, two Newcastle trolleybuses have been saved for future generations to see. As mentioned earlier, a 1948 Sunbeam S7 with Northern Coachbuilders' body, 501 (LTN 501) is owned by the City's Laing Art Gallery, but is at present stored at the North East Open Air Museum at Beamish, Co. Durham, whilst a BUT 9641T with Metro-Cammell body, 628 (NBB 628) is owned by the London Trolleybus Preservation Society and is at their museum at Carlton Colville, near Lowestoft, Suffolk. Some reminders of trolleybus operation still exist. The L.T.P.S. has several Stop signs, and at least two of the section breaker signs (a red spot on a white background), which used to be mounted on the traction poles, still survive. In addition, there are the electrical sub-stations, several of which remain, together with section and feeder boxes at the roadside.

As can be seen from Appendix L, many traction poles have been uprooted and replaced by tubular steel lighting standards, though large numbers can still be seen in the City. There is still a sign at the new Denton Road Terminus, warning motorists not to park as this is a trolleybus turning circle!

Fox-and-Hounds Lane, now partially blocked off at its junction with Pease Avenue, is a quiet backwater, and it is difficult to appreciate that 10-ton three-axle trolleybuses ran up and down it at intervals of a few minutes over 30 years. *Sic transit gloria mundi* . . .

CHAPTER THIRTEEN

UNFULFILLED PLANS AND EARLY DAYS

In opening this section of "The Trolleybuses of Newcastle upon Tyne", we must turn our attention to the early years of the 20th century, over twenty five years before trolleybus services actually commenced in the City. During the first decade of this century, electric tramways flourished throughout the United Kingdom. However there were many routes on the outskirts of cities and towns which did not have the traffic potential to support a tram service, or on which some physical consideration prevented the laying of tramways.

To serve this type of route, both Leeds and Bradford introduced "trackless trolleys"—or trolleybuses in modern parlance—in 1911. "Trackless trolleys" offered the advantages of utilising the electric power distribution network already created to serve the trams, but not requiring the expensive laying of rails in the roadway.

Even at this early date, Newcastle Corporation saw the possibilities of this form of electric street traction, for they attempted to obtain powers through their Corporation Parliamentary Bill of 1911. On 28th April 1910, the "Trackless Trolley System Subcommittee" of the Tramways Committee had been formed to deal with the detail of the proposed system which was "for the purpose of linking up Newburn with the City". By the 13th October 1910, the committee's scope had been widened to embrace discussion of proposed routes to Westerhope and Whorlton Church, and from Scotswood to Blaydon. The intended powers were set out as follows: the Corporation asked to operate trolley vehicles ("mechanically propelled vehicles ... moved by electric power ... transmitted ... from some external source") but not to manufacture them. Such vehicles would form part of the tramway undertaking, be to Board of Trade approved construction and dimensions, and not exceed 5 tons in weight, including load. Furthermore, the Corporation requested powers to run trolley vehicles, subject to Board of Trade approval, on any other route in the City which they might apply for, by means of a Provisional Order.

Two routes were initially proposed in the Bill; one to Blaydon, in County Durham, one to Westerhope. The intended routes were described thus:—

Route 1. (1 mile 560 yards approximately) The Blaydon Route.
Situated partly in the City and partly in the Urban District of Blaydon in the County of Durham, extending from the existing tramway terminus in Scotswood Road to the corner of Wesley Place and Tyne Street in Blaydon, by way of Scotswood Road, Scotswood Suspension Bridge, Scotswood Bridge Road, Tyne Street, Church Street and Wesley Place.

Route 2. (2 miles, 1000 yards approximately) The Westerhope Route.
Situated partly in the City and partly in the Urban District of Newburn and the Rural District of Castle Ward in the County of Northumberland, extending from the junction of Fenham Hall Drive with

Ponteland Road, by way of Ponteland Road and Stamfordham Road to the junction of that road and the road leading to Newbiggin Hall.

These would have resulted in a system with a total route mileage of 3 miles 1560 yards.

Newcastle Corporation Tramways had made an earlier attempt, in 1904, to serve Blaydon when it was intended to extend the Scotswood Road trams south over Scotswood Bridge. This scheme was abandoned due to the existence of the North Eastern Railway's excellent local train service and the presence of weight restrictions on Scotswood Bridge. The 1911 Bill trolleybus proposals envisaged a self-contained route with vehicles shuttling between Scotswood and Blaydon, acting as feeders to the trams on the Scotswood Road trunk route. As can be seen from Route 1 of the Bill, the "trackless trams" would have looped round streets in Blaydon town centre, with a terminus close to Blaydon railway station in Tyne Street. Since the trolleybus route was to be isolated, about $3\frac{1}{2}$ miles of "boom and trailing skate" working along Scotswood Road tram tracks would have been necessary for the "trackless" to reach the nearest depot at Haymarket in the City centre. The only alternative would have been the construction of a special small depot at Scotswood to house the trolleybuses.

The Westerhope route was also intended to be a tramway feeder service. The Fenham tram route, opened in 1907, turned into Fenham Hall Drive off Ponteland Road, and the "trackless trolley" route was envisaged as starting at this point and running northwards along Ponteland Road to Cowgate then in a general westerly direction on Stamfordham Road to Westerhope, where it would terminate at the western end of the then village. As with the Blaydon proposals, the route presumably anticipated a self-contained entity, not continuing into the City centre; lengthy "boom and trailing skate" would have been necessary to and from Wingrove or Haymarket depots.

However, the Corporation's trolleybus proposals encountered objections that were many and varied. Although Newburn U.D.C. supported Newcastle in principle with its scheme, it pointed out that a regular service of trolleybuses would cause "congestion", and such heavy traffic would soon break up the road surface. Additionally, they considered the intended route inconvenient in that it terminated at Westerhope: extension to a colliery at North Walbottle, where miners living in Westerhope worked, would be far better. Furthermore, they considered the proposed fares excessive. Northumberland County Council's objections centred on the fact that the Newcastle powers were to apply outside the City boundary, that the form of traction was experimental, and that it would damage the roads. The North Eastern Railway's objection was to the competitive nature of the route to its services at Coxlodge Station, two miles to the north east.

The Blaydon route had to meet objections from Durham County Council regarding possible damage to road surfaces, and worries as to the effect on Scotswood Bridge (built in 1831) of the weight of poles, wires etc., as well as of the 5 ton trolleybuses: the maximum permitted weight on the bridge was 6 tons—on reflection, careful selection of a suitable trolleybus design would have been necessary to achieve the stipulated weight limit. For instance, Bradford's contemporary single-deckers had an unladen weight of 3 tons 12 cwt; with 28 passengers and a driver, they would have exceeded 5 tons in weight.

In the event, the Parliamentary Committee who considered the Bill took the view that "owing to the fact that it is a new method of traction, more should be known before general powers are granted" and struck out the relevant sections.

So Newcastle was denied the honour of being one of the earliest trolleybus operators in this country, and had to wait another 24 years before its system was inaugurated. As recounted earlier, the City provided Westerhope with transport in 1912 in the form of motorbuses, and later, trams. The subsequent attempts to get trolleybuses to the area have been described in the main part of this volume.

Moving forward twenty years to 1931 and the depths of the Great Depression, we next consider the thwarted initial trolleybus proposals for Osborne Road, Jesmond. In April 1931, the Transport and Electricity Committee considered the future policy of the Undertaking and debated the possibility of "trackless trolleys" (as they were still described), authorising the Chairman and Vice-Chairman to accompany the General Manager to visit existing trolleybus systems.

At their June meeting, the Committee received a report from the City Engineer expressing concern over the state of the tram tracks on the Westgate Road route. This track had been in poor condition after 1918, so the section on Westgate Hill had been relaid; additionally, many rail-joints had been welded. However, it appears from the City Engineer's report that the conditions of the permanent way had again deteriorated. Also at this meeting, the development of the Jesmond Towers Estate, off Matthew Bank, north of the existing Osborne Road tram terminus, was reported, and its transport needs considered. It was suggested the tracks be extended northwards, but the Committee also expressed concern over the condition of the existing track, and asked for a report on this topic.

At the next meeting on 29th July, the costs of renewing Westgate Hill and Osborne Road tracks were given, but authority for renewals was delayed until a further requested report on the probable life of the whole of the track on the Westgate Road route, and estimated cost of repairs, was ready. By October, the report on the Osborne Road track and on the general condition of the system's tracks was ready. Figures were given on the cost of substituting trolleybuses for trams on the Osborne Road route; it was estimated that ten vehicles would cost £2,000 each, and overhead wiring alterations £2,850. Information from the deputation which had visited other trolleybus systems was given. After much discussion, it was agreed to present a report to the City Council recommending that motorbuses be substituted for the Osborne Road trams, and they be extended to Matthew Bank Estate. As was described earlier in this work, the Council rejected this plan, so the track was repaired. This still left Matthew Bank Estate without a transport link, so in February 1932, the General Manager was authorised to introduce a motorbus service to this area, running mainly along Osborne Road to reach the estate. To protect the tram service, a higher fare was to be charged on the motorbuses.

Nothing was heard of trolleybuses for almost exactly one year until, on 28th March 1933, a City Engineer's report on the condition of the Westgate Road route tracks was presented to the Transport and Electricity Committee. The Committee then asked the General Manager to prepare a report on the estimated costs of working the Westgate Road—Wallsend route by each of three modes of transport: trams, motorbuses, and "trackless trolleys". This he did, and this report formed the basis of the later report to the City Council, presented in May 1934 and detailed earlier. There was, in the meantime, uncertainty as to whether the City already had legal powers to run trolleybuses; the Town Clerk, in September 1933, stated that the Corporation had no powers to work "trackless trolleys" on the Westgate Road—Wallsend route, or elsewhere in the City, and it would be necessary to obtain powers to run such vehicles. Nevertheless, the General Manager was instructed by the Committee the following month to proceed with the preparation of a scheme for an "experimental" trolleybus route for the Westgate Road-Wallsend tram service.

On 1st May 1934 authority was given to go ahead with the Parliamentary Bill for trolleybus powers, subject to Council approval. This, as we know, was given on 8th May. All was set to tender for the vehicles and the overhead wiring conversion for the route.

The inspiration for the front-exit, rear entrance layout of Newcastle's prewar trolleybus fleet has already been stated as the City's extensive front-exit tram fleet, but an additional impetus for the folding front-exit door arrangement was given by the department's solitary A.E.C.Q.-type motorbus. This was No. 156 (ABB 449) delivered in 1933 and had an entrance/exit with folding doors ahead of the front axle. In the preparatory work for the trolleybus fleet, a folding door test rig was made at Byker Depot, and various door actuating methods investigated. The information gained from these tests proved useful in subsequent design work for trolleybus front-exit doors.

Visitors to the area today often comment on the bright and cheerful yellow livery of Tyne & Wear P.T.E. motorbuses and Metro cars, and it is worth remembering that this owes its origins to the livery adopted for the City's trolleybuses in 1935. The General Manager showed "silhouettes" (presumably small wood cut-out side elevations) of various proposed painting styles for the trolleybuses to the Transport & Electricity Committee on 26th March 1935. It was agreed to adopt "a modified tramway colouring, the whole of the tops to be one colour" (possibly referring to the cream roofs).

As work progressed on both the conversion of the overhead wiring and the manufacture of the trolleybuses intended for the City, naturally some problems occurred. It was reported in June 1935 that the General manager, Mr. Easton, and the Chairman had visited Guy Motors factory (which was building 10 BTX chassis later to become fleet Nos. 30-39) to hear the manufacturer's explanation for production delays. Guy's progress was running three weeks behind the other two chassis manufacturers, A.E.C. and Karrier. The Newcastle delegation were told the chassis should be complete by the end of August. As it turned out, the completed vehicles were delivered during the second half of September.

The incident of a runaway traction engine demolishing a new traction pole on Denton Bank in the summer of 1935 has been referred earlier, and more detail can now be given. A report in the "Newcastle Daily Journal" for Thursday 11th

July featured a photograph taken at dusk on the previous evening. This showed the traction engine on its right side in the roadway, its nearside front wheel beside it, and the trolleybus traction pole it had uprooted lying beside the engine. The caption mentioned that the steam engine weighed 12 tons and had been hauling three trailers; little wonder the traction pole was bowled over!

By the late summer, the Undertaking had decided on an opening date for the system. On the day the first test run took place over the whole length of the wiring, 17th September, it was stated that 17 trolleybuses had been delivered from the manufacturers. The General Manager therefore suggested 1st October 1935 as a suitable date, and this was adhered to. The gratifying upsurge in traffic following the conversion left Newcastle Transport with a very small reserve of trolley vehicles. With the expected extra traffic for Christmas 1935 imminent, and several electric vehicles off the road due to "the recent bad weather, and the dangerous state of the roads causing accidents", the General Manager arranged with Metro-Cammell to hire a trolleybus. This vehicle, it was stated "had been on show", and became No. 40 (CVK 52). He therefore requested, and gained, authorisation to purchase this trolleybus for £2,322.19s.6d., at the Transport and Electricity Committee's meeting at 30th January 1936. This information solves the mystery of the authorisation for No 40's purchase.

By the time the authorisation was given, in September 1936, for the conversion of the Brighton Grove—Welbeck Road tram route to trolleybuses the Department had experienced nearly twelve months operation of trolleybuses under the overhead wiring erected by the contractors, Clough-Smith, on the Denton Burn-Wallsend route. This experience had not been entirely satisfactory. Numerous dewirements in early days had been put down to the fault of the drivers, but it became clear that badly positioned overhead was the primary cause. The testimony of former staff members confirms this. Therefore it is not surprising to find that the Undertaking resolved to carry out the overhead conversion of the Brighton Grove—Welbeck Road route themselves. Clough-Smith made an approach in November 1937 offering to "co-operate" with future overhead work, but it was resolved that all future work would be carried out by the Department's own overhead gangs.

In October 1936, the General manager reported on the performance of the initial trolleybus fleet after a year's experience in traffic. He summarised each type in turn: the Karriers had suffered a number of broken road springs, as had the A.E.C.s; in the latter, the springs had been replaced by a heavier type. The Guys had experienced an ingress of mud into the rear bogie wheel bearings; consequently, the vehicles' mud shields had to be redesigned. As with the other types of trolleybus chassis, the Guy's road springs were considered by the General Manager to be too light for the loads imposed on them. Turning to the bodywork, Mr. Easton unreservedly praised Metro-Cammell's workmanship, design, and materials on their twenty bodies. The five English Electric bodies he found satisfactory, but the general finish and workmanship were not to a high standard. He next considered the five Brush bodies; these he felt were not satisfactory at all; design was weak, and the front end framework not strong enough. This lead to the bodywork "working" in traffic. This had necessitated the Department rebuilding the bodies twice in twelve months. He therefore recommended that further chassis of the same three types be purchased in future, but that no more Brush bodies be obtained. The English Electric bodies were satisfactory, and he concluded by saying that the best type were the Metro-Cammell bodies (as had been found with the motorbus fleet). Also in this month, authority was given to accept for trial the Daimler CTM6 that later become No. 112 (DHP 112), though the vehicle did not arrive in the City until 1938.

The Undertaking's plan to convert the entire tramway system to trolleybus operation were, as recounted earlier, not announced until 1939, but plans existed some two years earlier. In April 1937, Mr. Easton gave costings to the Transport and Electricity Committee: to change over all routes (except the Gosforth Park Light Railway and the Gateshead joint routes) to trolleybuses was estimated to cost £661,000, whilst the vehicles to equip the services would cost £272,000. The latter figures included reserve vehicles for race traffic. By June, Mr. Easton recommended the substitution of trolleybuses on the Central Station—Fenham, Pilgrim Street—Wallsend Boundary, and, interestingly, the Denton Burn—Armstrong Road—Westmorland Road—Osborne Road route. The reason for the Armstrong Road—Westmorland Road powers, granted in the 1938 Provisional Order, is now clear. It appears a through trolleybus service, replacing the motor-bus/tram route on Armstrong Road and Westmorland Road, and the separate Osborne Road tram route, was envisaged. Only the Osborne Road route was converted to trolleybus operation, as it happened.

When the Westgate Road—Wallsend tram route had been converted to trolleybuses in October 1935, the new electric vehicles had followed the route of the trams under the railway at the Carville boundary (Fisher Street hill, Walker). When the City's tramways had met the Tyneside Tramways and Tramroads Company's lines from Wallsend at this point, in 1903, it had been necessary to construct a private underbridge at the point where the railway crossed over the tramway. This private underbridge was separate from the public road underbridge slightly to the west. The tramway underbridge, although rather narrow, had a double line of unpaved track (a crossover was inserted at a later date). It was the narrowness of this bridge which gave rise to the Ministry of Transport trolleybus regulations given on p.23, as it was not safe for two trolleybuses to pass under the bridge. In November 1937 it was reported to the Transport and Electricity Committee that confusion and danger was being caused by motor and other traffic using the private underbridge, which had been paved for the trolleybuses. It was therefore resolved to dedicate it as a public road and make it one-way westbound. Consequently, a new line of wiring was to be constructed through the public underbridge, which would become one-way eastbound. This intention was carried out, and trolleybuses subsequently used this arrangement until they ceased to operate workman's services on this route in 1965. The authors are indebted to Mr. G. S. Hearse for providing information on the tramway layout at Carville.

In preparation for the opening, on 24th April 1938, of the extension from Denton Burn to Denton Square in the west end of the City, a "temporary" reverser had been constructed at Denton Square to turn trolleybuses. However, on 5th April, the Transport and Electricity Committee were told that, in view of the impending widening of the West Road between Slatyford Lane junction and Denton Square, it was proposed to construct a turning circle at the latter point, at a cost of £1,280. This turning circle was subsequently used until 1966 by trolleybuses, and is still used by motorbuses. On the other side of the City, at Walkerville, Newcastle Transport originally intended to construct a turning loop at Wallsend Boundary terminus, via Lilac Road and Rowantree Road. An objection not previously recorded in these pages was received in January 1938 from the Tyneside Tramways and Tramroads Company. The Company possibly felt that the intended trolleybus route might adversely effect their motorbus services in the area. In view of the Company's objection, Newcastle Transport resolved to compromise by erecting a reverser in Oaktree Avenue, Walkerville, right on the boundary between the City and Wallsend.

When the Central Station—Osborne Road (Jesmond) trolleybus route (service 9) commenced in September 1938, the vehicles operating it were housed in the Haymarket Depot in the northern part of the City centre. The cramped nature of the depot has already been described, and it is therefore not surprising to find the General Manager, in the April, taking his Committee to inspect it. He was concerned at its restricted site, and felt it unsuitable for trolleybuses. The Committee also inspected an alternative site, at Dinsdale Place. In spite of this, trolleybuses did use Haymarket until 1957, when it was replaced by an open-air site in Morden Street, close by.

It has always been thought that the automatic frogs (or points) in the system's overhead wiring were first installed in the 1950s (then there were only four of them) but it is evident that proposals were made for such devices as early as 1939. Allowances were made in the 1939/40 Financial Year estimates—in February 1939—for four Forest City automatic frogs, at a total cost of £112. Initially, one only was to be purchased at £28. If it proved satisfactory, three more were to be acquired. It is possible that the outbreak of World War II prevented this plan being implemented; information from readers on this topic would be welcomed. Another consequences of increasing road traffic was the fitting of direction indicators to trolleybuses, from 1939. In January 1939, the fitting of such devices was approved, each costing £3.7s.6d. (£3.37$\frac{1}{2}$) per vehicle. They took the form of illuminated directional arrows placed on the rear panel. It is not known which vehicles of the prewar fleet were so fitted.

The advent of the Second World War, in September 1939, brought many hardships and restrictions: one was the imposition of blackout. Immediately, Newcastle Transport decided to adopt London Transport's method of window masking on all vehicles, to prevent light being seen from outside the vehicle. This masking took the form of anti-shatter netting. By April 1940, the Ministry of Transport had restricted the number of standing passengers on trolleybuses from ten to eight. After the cessation of hostilities in 1945, the original figure was restored, only to be reduced again in 1954 (see p.97).

In view of the vartime shortage of new vehicles, it seemed very likely that the Elswick Road conversion, planned in September 1939 (p.51/2) would be delayed and the City Engineer was asked to continue maintaining the tracks on the road at least for another three years. He estimated the cost of this work would be only

£750, as the track was in such good condition. Even as early as May 1940 (the route was not converted until 1944), the Department was resigned to abandoning the Buckingham Street/Heber Street part of the proposals. As described on p.65, the Ministry of Transport objected to operating trolleybuses on such narrow roadways, and Transport and Electricity Committee was told there was little likelihood of widening either "for some time". Therefore it was decided not to proceed with this part of the proposed route.

The West Road air-raid incident mentioned in Chapter 6 (p.54) is now known to have taken place during the night of 29th/30th July 1940. There was a Transport and Electricity Committee meeting on the 30th, and members were informed that trolleybus feeder cables had been damaged, though not cut. One of the German bombs, falling in the West Road opposite Ellesmere Road, Benwell, had cratered the road and disturbed cables. The foresight of the Undertaking in installing a new high-tension feeder on Westmorland Road was proved, as supplies were continued by means of this cable.

By the early summer of 1941, Newcastle Transport was feeling the burden of increased traffic from Stamfordham Road Estate (near the present Slatyford Depot) on its motorbus service on Stamfordham Road (operating from Westerhope to the City via Cowgate). The General Manager studied the problem, and stated that the motorbuses could better serve the area by a diversion through the estate along Druridge Drive, but this would require precious fuel and the reconstruction of the roadway. Instead, he recommended the extension of the Fenham trolleybus route (service 6) from its Two Ball Lonnen terminus some 570 yards along Netherby Drive to Bingfield Gardens. This extension to the wiring, costing £775, and using materials from stock, opened in November 1941.

The withdrawal of a trolleybus service was proposed in May 1941, when it was intended that the Denton Loop services via Whickham View would only operate to the junction of Whickham View and Denton Road (the future Denton Road Terminus), and be split off from the 4B's running via West Road and Denton Bank to Denton Square. This would leave Denton Road without any trolleybus service, and was intended to save electricity and vehicle wear and tear. Intending passengers, it was reasoned, would only have to walk a maximum distance of 400 yards to either Denton Road Terminus, or the foot of Denton Bank. It was also proposed to extend service 12 (Central Station—Wallsend Boundary) via Westgate Road and Denton Bank to Denton Square. New wiring connections at the junction of Grainger Street and Westgate Road, in the City centre, would be necessary to enable vehicles to turn west into Westgate Road and vice versa. This rather drastic proposal to cease serving Denton Road was not implemented, and as recounted on p.54 service 12 was extended to the newly constructed Denton Road Terminus turning circle on 30th June 1941.

Wartime conditions were still causing traffic on Newcastle Transport's vehicles to increase at this period. Consequently, the Department was forced to cast around for more trolleybuses to augment its overstretched fleet. It has been rumoured that the City investigated the possibility of obtaining trolleybuses similar to the South African ones diverted to London, and this can now be confirmed. At the end of November 1941, enquiries were made to the Ministry of

Transport as to the availability of "trolleybuses manufactured for service abroad" (which were unable to be exported due to shipping restrictions). The Ministry replied the following month, stating that, unfortunately, all such vehicles had now been allocated to operators in the U.K. Thus thwarted, the Undertaking turned to other transport departments in this country for trolley vehicles. Mr. Godsmark, the new General Manager, stated he had made enquiries regarding the hire of trolleybuses from Brighton, but he did not recommend this course of action, as the hire charges demanded were expensive. No other source must have been immediately available however, for we next hear him, in March 1942, informing his Committee of these proposed hire charges. The conditions asked by Brighton were as follows: for five vehicles: £1 per day per vehicle, plus $1\frac{1}{4}$d ($\frac{1}{2}$p) per mile run; Newcastle Transport to be responsible for towing to and from Brighton, and for all insurance on the vehicles. As described on p.55, those three-year-old trolleybuses arrived in Newcastle in May 1942, but left the City as quickly as September and October of the same year. In the interim, the Department was still pursuing various avenues in an attempt to obtain further trolleybuses.

The vehicle shortage was worsened in July 1942 by an alteration of shift-changeover hours for workmen employed in the vital Walker shipyards in the east end of the City. A very heavy burden was stated to have been placed on trolleybus services by this changeover, and insufficient vehicles were available to meet the demand. The trolleybuses on order (the 20 Karrier E6A's intended for the Elswick Road conversion—which vehicles were destined never to arrive) were not expected before May of the next year, so Mr. Godsmark contacted Bradford City Transport, who offered to hire six 3-axle trolleybuses, dating from 1930, to Newcastle. Newcastle's General Manager was not very enthusiastic about these vehicles, and now contacted Mr. T. E. Thomas of the London Passenger Transport Board, asking if it was possible to hire any of the capital's more modern trolleybuses. Newcastle, at this period, still intended to hire the Bradford vehicles if the London approach failed.

By the September, it was possible to start returning the expensive Brighton 2-axle trolleys, as arrangements had been concluded with London Transport to obtain nine trolleybuses. These nine were not native London vehicles, but half of the eighteen Bournemouth trolleybuses which had been running in the capital, and these 3-axle vehicles arrived in the City during that month. The hire charges were less demanding than Brighton's: £25 per month per vehicle, plus a tyre mileage rate. It is intriguing to speculate which of London Transport's own trolleybuses might have found their way north to Newcastle if the Bournemouth vehicles had been unavailable. The most likely candidates were the A.E.C. Classes C1, C2, and C3 of 1935/6: these had very similar English Electric electrical equipment to that installed in many of the City's own trolleybuses. Additionally, many featured Metro-Cammell bodies, also common on Newcastle's electric vehicles. The red livery of these London trolleybuses would have been a very noticeable contrast to the yellow livery of Newcastle's own trolleybuses. It was obviously felt that still more vehicles were required, for there was a recommendation in September 1942 that either six or ten of the Bradford trolleybuses be purchased, and of course ten of these elderly vehicles were delivered to Newcastle in the December.

Wartime conditions additionally imposed requirements of economy in both staff time and materials; in March 1942 the Undertaking resolved to paint, initially, the expected new utility-bodied motorbuses and trolleybuses in what was officially termed "RAF blue/grey". Two months later, reluctant approval was given to extend this economy measure to embrace all vehicles—trams, trolleybuses, and motorbuses, on the request of the Government Regional Transport Commissioner. However, as Mr. J. Ring, a retired coachpainter at Byker Depot, recollects, vehicles were fully repainted in wartime grey only if absolutely necessary. More normal practice was to "touch-up" the existing prewar livery as required. The only large areas repainted on prewar liveried vehicles were the lower panels, as these suffered from stone-chipping. Cadmium yellow paint was prized as supplies were almost impossible to obtain. Similarly, postwar livery was only applied in accordance with the normal programmed cycle of vehicle repainting.

The dramatic incident of the runaway trolleybus on Westgate Road on 8th June 1942 has been described in Chapter 6 (p.56), and more technical details are now available about the origin of the incident. The vehicle, AEC 664T No. 69 of 1937, had just pulled away from Northcote Street stop on Arthur's Hill at 2.36 p.m., when it was obliged to draw up in order to lower its booms to pass a damaged section of overhead. A tower wagon was repairing a damaged line hanger affected by the dewirement of a previous trolleybus. Driver Walton, instead of pulling on the handbrake to hold 69 on the gradient until it was possible to pass the tower wagon, kept his foot on the air-brake pedal. This exhausted the air-brake reservoir tank, as it was not being recharged due to the vehicle being disconnected from the overhead lines. After passing the damaged section of overhead Walton found that the air-brake was inoperative, and attempted to stop No. 69—now running at 5/6 m.p.h.—on the handbrake. With 74 passengers on board (an indication of wartime overloading) this was insufficiently powerful and the vehicle continued to gather speed. Subsequent events are described on p.56.

By the summer of 1942, steps had been taken to recover the equipment from the Westerhope Tramroad, unused since 1938, when trolleybuses took over the Fenham route. Traction poles, bracket arms and other overhead fittings were to be stored for future trolleybus installations (were they perhaps used to equip Whickham View between Delaval Road and Ferguson's Lane junctions when the Elswick Road service was converted in June 1944?). The rails and sleepers were to be put into the City Engineer's stock for future track renewals.

The unfulfilled schemes to operate trolleybuses in Gateshead had been discussed in detail on earlier pages, and Newcastle Transport's 1945 Provisional Order (p.68) was a significant event, giving legal powers to operate trolleybuses over both Tyne and High Level bridges. This Order specified three official routes: proposals, in October 1943, though, detailed four official routes, as follows:—

Route 1. (3 furlongs, 5.5 chains)
        Commencing in Pilgrim Street at its junction with Mosley Street, by a junction with Trolley Vehicle Route 1 of 1935, and Route 14 of 1938, and proceeding in a southerly direction along Pilgrim Street onto New Tyne Bridge, and terminating in the County Borough of Gateshead at the tramway junction opposite the north east corner of Hills Street.

Route 2. (2 chains)
Commencing in High Street by a junction with Route 1 of this Order, at a point 1.25 chains north west of the junction of High Street with Hills Street, and passing into, and along, Hills Street, and terminating with the junction of the existing tramways 1.25 chains south west of the junction of Hills Street with High Street.

Route 3. (2 furlongs, 6.83 chains)
Commencing in St. Nicholas Street, 0.9 chains north west of the junction with Westgate Road, by a junction with Route 2 of 1935, and passing in a southerly direction by way of the High Level Bridge, and into and along Wellington Street in the County Borough of Gateshead, and terminating, by a junction with the existing tramway, 0.8 chains south east of the junction of Wellington Street, with Hudson Street.

Route 4. (4 furlongs, 7.86 chains)
Commencing in Percy Street, at the junction with St. Thomas Street, by a junction with Route 16 of the Order of 1938, and passing along Percy Street, Newgate Street, Bigg Market and Groat Market and St. Nicholas Street, and terminating in that street 1.13 chains south of the junction with Collingwood Street by a junction with Route 2 of the Act of 1935.

Route 2 of this Order is something of a puzzle: at first glance it seems to indicate a link along Hills Street between the projected trolleybus wires over the Tyne and High Level bridges. When it is read more closely, though, it is seen to merely give power to erect wiring over 44 yards of roadway at the junction of Hills Street and High Street at the south end of the Tyne Bridge. It is possible that a turning circle was contemplated at this point, and readers' comments and suggestions would be welcomed. Route 2 was dropped from the Order as granted in 1945.

The traction or running wire to equip the overhead for the Elswick Road route conversion of June 1944 was ordered in the previous September. A tender from Thos. Bolton and Sons for 15 miles of trolley wire at £1,847.10s.8d. (£1,847.53½) was accepted. It was stated that only 8 miles were required for the new route, but the remainder was to be held in stock. The equipment for the electrical sub-station projected in Northbourne Street, Elswick, for the route, was obtained from London Transport as, it was stated, had been the equipment for the Walker Road sub-station brought into service in December 1942. Perhaps readers could be of assistance in pinpointing the precise origins of this electrical equipment: was it redundant to London Transport's requirements following prewar tram abandonments?

CHAPTER FOURTEEN

THE POSTWAR VEHICLE CRISIS AND THE 1948 "Q1's"

The Corporation's 1946 Act of Parliament (detailed in Chapter 8) had intended to include two further routes which were not finally incorporated. This pair of routes, first mentioned in October 1944, were:—

Route 14a. (1 furlong, 5 chains) Stotts Road—Fossway—Neptune Road (Wallsend).

Route 17. (3 furlongs, 3.4 chains) Gosforth Park (West Gates)—Great North Road—Hazelrigg Road Ends (Wideopen).

The first would have provided a link between the Shields Road trolleybus route in Walkergate and the eastern end of the Fossway close to the riverside boundary with Wallsend; it might possibly have been used to institute a circular trolleybus service. The second route, nearly half a mile in length, would have revived a tramway proposal (originally planned by the Tyneside Tramways and Tramroads Company early this century) to extend north to the Wideopen area from Gosforth Park. By December 1944, it had been realised that, for legal reasons, the intended Wideopen route could not be incorporated in the Bill, as it was currently phrased. As an alternative it was hoped to include a $5\frac{1}{2}$ furlong route from Gosforth Park Gates northwards to the colliery railway level crossing in the heart of Wideopen. Two months later, however, on the advice of the Town Clerk, the provision was withdrawn from the Corporation's Bill. In substitution, he asserted he could get powers to run trolleybuses on Benton Park Road incorporated by means of a Late Bill (see Route 16 of the 1946 Act). Only in recent years have P.T.E. motorbuses been extended from Gosforth Park West Gates north to serve this part of outer north Newcastle.

Just over three years later, in January 1948, the City's Town Clerk enquired if the Transport Department wanted any trolleybus routes inserted in the Corporation's forthcoming Parliamentary Bill, and the General Manager replied with the following suggestions. Extend Route 4 of the 1946 Act along the Coast Road to the City boundary (see. p.83); extend Route 12 to Beaumont Terrace, Westerhope; and the extension of the Great North Road route along Broadway West to Grange Estate, Gosforth. As has been described, the Grange Estate extension was opened in 1951, and although the Westerhope extension was incorporated in the 1952 Act, it was never acted on (p.87-88). This leaves the question of the Coast Road plans. Even though this route appears never to have been incorporated in any legal powers, Newcastle Transport's plans for this area must have been more than tentative, as the destination was shown on indicator blinds. There would have been adequate room for trolleybuses to turn at the "Coast Road" terminus, under the large railway bridge forming the City boundary at this point, for the Coast Road was single-carriageway at this period, with a wide grass verge.

There were persistent rumours in the air at this period of another possible extension. Coach Lane, Benton, runs north as an extension of Red Hall Drive in Cochrane Park Estate. Together, these two streets connect the Coast Road (at the south end) near the City boundary mentioned above, and (at the north end) Front Street, Benton. At this time Coach Lane was a narrow unmade track, totally unsuitable for heavy P.S.V.'s such as trolleybuses. However, c.1948-49, a partial reconstruction of the road took place. A concrete road surface with laybys at intervals, and properly kerbed and cambered on the west side, was constructed on the northern half of Coach Lane's length, almost to Front Street, Benton. The work appeared to have been only partially completed, however, as the road was surfaced only on its western half. The local rumours that trolleybuses were to be introduced along Coach Lane lingered for some years, but such vehicles never operated along this road. The authors acknowledge N. Pollard for information on this "might have been" trolleybus route.

If the mileages of the City's unused trolleybus powers, plus possible routes like Coach Lane are added to the actual maximum route mileage of 37.184, we arrive at a very imposing total of approximately $64\frac{3}{4}$ route miles. Should we add the $18\frac{3}{4}$ miles of the intended extended Gateshead system of 1937, a grand total of $83\frac{1}{4}$ is reached. Had such a system actually been constructed, the Newcastle and Gateshead trolleybus system would have been the second largest in the U.K. outside London.

Even though all of the proposals were not implemented, Newcastle Transport still required a great quantity of overhead fittings and line to equip its intended routes under the 1946 Act. In addition to the traction poles etc. ordered in 1947 (p.75) 280 such poles (235 medium, 45 heavy), 100 B.I.C.C. 16-foot bracket arms and 16 miles of trolley wire were ordered in July 1945, and a further 15 miles of wire in October 1946. Information has been given on p.79 on the new Karrier CK3 tower wagons ordered in 1946 to cope with the massive overhead conversion, but two similar vehicles were bought earlier, in October 1945. These were Civil Defence surplus trucks, JL 6287, a 3-ton Bedford costing £195, and JX 7971, a 3-ton Austin costing £240, both manufactured in 1939. They become fleet numbers 901 and 902 respectively. In January 1946 it was agreed to buy two tower wagon bodies to fit these vehicles, from S. Rawlinson Ltd., at a total of £648. However, in official lists, they are simply described as "general haulage wagons". Additionally, four Leyland Lynx wagons were delivered in 1948, at a cost of £450 each.

For many years the origins of the famous Newcastle Transport 1948 BUT 9641T trolleybuses—the "Gosforth Buses"—with London Transport Q1 Class style bodywork has been obscure, and the circumstances of their diversion from the capital unclear. We hope now to give full details of how Newcastle obtained these twenty fine vehicles.

To appreciate the background, it is necessary to go back to 1945 and examine the City's plans for its postwar trolleybus fleet. The wartime 2-axle utility vehicles could only be considered as a stop-gap, although of recent delivery, and the entire prewar fleet was becoming prematurely life-expired due to the heavy burden placed on it by wartime conditions. Furthermore, much of the tram track was in very poor condition (as we shall see) as were the trams themselves, and the Undertaking was committed to a policy of replacing them by trolleybuses. The Department was therefore disappointed to hear in the July of 1945 that the

Ministry of War Transport allocated only ten of the thirty-six trolleybuses requested. The figure of thirty-six presumably refers to the Sunbeam F4/Metro-Cammell vehicles (ordered as Karriers) actually ordered in February 1946. In the previous December, there had been discussion by the Department as to the type of vehicle to be ordered for the postwar fleet. Thirty-six vehicles would be required to convert the Central Station—Gosforth Park (with its extension to Wideopen) tram route, and the Gosforth—Low Fell, Heworth, and Wrekenton joint tram services. The relative merits of 2-axle and 3-axle trolleybuses were considered. It was felt there would be restrictions imposed by the Ministry of Transport on the use of front-exits, though the reasoning behind this argument was not revealed. If this was to be the case, future vehicles would have to abandon the standard body of the prewar fleet. After consideration, it was decided to order thirty-six 64-seat 3-axle vehicles without front-exits, though as we know, they arrived in Newcastle as 56-seat 2-axle 'buses (Nos. 443-478) in 1948/9.

The Ministry further stated that the ten trolleys could not be delivered "until the end of 1946", at the earliest. Much concerned, the General Manager and the Chairman of his Committee travelled to London to petition Whitehall to release the required trolley vehicles to the City, in view of the deteriorating condition of the North Road track, especially north of Henry Street, Gosforth. Little seems to have resulted from this London trip, for we next hear, in November 1945, that following the 1945-6 allocation of trolleybus chassis by the Government, Newcastle Transport and the manufacturers were left to discuss between themselves the delivery of the remaining twenty-six chassis of the City's order. The initial ten were not now expected until late 1947, although Metro-Cammell Weymann had now accepted the order for the bodies.

The serious tramway accident at Gosforth in July 1946 was really the catalyst for the eventual arrival of the 1948 BUT 3-axle vehicles. At about 3.15 p.m. on the 8th of July, two B Class trams, No. 276 northbound, and No. 300 southbound, collided head-on on the Great North Road between Broadway West and Park Avenue. 276 had derailed into the path of the other car, fatally injuring one passenger and less seriously injuring 15 other persons. No. 276's leading end was severely damaged, and 300 was similarly affected (both cars were subsequently scrapped). The poor condition of the Great North Road track was blamed as the primary cause of the derailment. It was felt vital, therefore, to hasten plans to operate trolleybuses over the route, providing the necessary vehicles were forthcoming. In October 1946 two different routes through the City centre were planned for the Gosforth trolleybuses. One service was to terminate at the Central Station (approaching it via Grainger Street), whilst the other was to use a loop: Percy Street—Newgate Street—Grainger Street— Neville Street—Westgate Road—St. Nicholas Street—Bigg Market—Newgate Street, and out of the City centre.

Had this latter proposal been followed, it would have seen several wiring connections at street junctions, which were never actually constructed (e.g. a right-hand curve from Newgate Street south into Grainger Street). The second route, however, received objections from the Chief Constable, who suggested using Clayton Street and Westgate Road instead of Neville Street and Westgate Road. An earlier plan had been to use Castle Garth, near the High Level Bridge, as a terminal point for the second route. When they began to operate in April 1948, service 31B trolleybuses used Grainger Street—Newgate Street—Percy Street as their outward route from the Central Station, and returned southbound via Percy Street—Newgate Street—Clayton Street—Clayton Street West.

In the November of 1946, Councillors were told that the Transport Department was legally committed to introduce trolleybuses on certain routes, but "the type of vehicle to be used in substitution for tramcars on other routes would be a matter for discussion as the time of conversion approached". A hint of a retreat from total commitment to a "trolleybuses for trams" replacement policy? At this Transport and Electricity Committee meeting on 20th November 1946, the twenty BUT 3-axle vehicles were first specified as part of the future fleet, and placed on order. In the first month of the new year, it was stated that these vehicles could not be expected in the City before "the autumn of 1947".

Newcastle Transport's acute shortage of trolleybuses, and the immediate postwar passenger boom, was being keenly felt, for in April 1947 it was announced that there was the possibility of acquiring six double-deck trolleybuses on order for Darlington Corporation. Authority to purchase these vehicles was given to the City's General Manager by his Committee, should they become available. However this plan suffered a reverse, as the Darlington General Manager next said he could not transfer the order for these BUT 9611T 2-axle trolleybuses with East Lancashire bodies, until he was assured of a supply of motorbuses in substitute. This interesting transfer plan was finally smothered in the September, when Darlington announced they could not proceed with the substitution of motorbuses for trolleybuses, and therefore could not release the six electric vehicles to Newcastle.

The Great North Road tram tracks had seen another year of pounding since the fatal accident of July 1946, when Sir A. Mount, the Ministry of Transport's Chief Inspecting Officer, was prevailed upon to inspect them. His opinion was that they were in a "terrible" state of disrepair, and promised to expedite the delivery of twenty of the trolleybuses on order from Metro-Cammell Weymann, stating that Newcastle should have them "by autumn 1947". The manufacturers immediately refuted this, claiming that "the end of 1947" was the very earliest they could promise delivery.

That is was still the intention of the Undertaking to use the February 1946 order of 36 Sunbeam 2-axle trolleybuses to convert the Great North Road tram service was borne out by a request to the Ministry of Transport Inspecting Officer in July 1947 to relax restrictions on operating these 8-feet wide vehicles on the Barras Bridge—Central Station portion of the intended route through the City centre. Permission had already been given in 1946 for 8-feet wide trolleybuses on the Great North Road, with provision they were not to operate on portions of the route still with trams running. Also in July 1947, the General Manager suggested the later accepted route of the future service 31B's through the City centre. It was also proposed to link the Osborne Road (service 9) and Benwell (service 3) routes, saving a Central area terminus and two vehicles. The northern terminus of the Osborne Road service, it was intended, should be extended to serve Matthew Bank Estate (shades of 1931!), and poling and wiring was reported to be underway on this section, as described on p.72. This short wiring link was, for some reason, never completed.

The Transport and Electricity Committee meeting in September 1947 heard from their General Manager a resumé of the expected delivery dates of the 86 trolleybuses and 80 motorbuses on order for the Undertaking. He informed the Committee that of the 36 trolleybuses on order from Metro-Cammell since 1946, twenty were promised by the November, and these would be used for the Gosforth service conversion. He had asked the Metro-Cammell company for assurances on their ability to confirm delivery dates. If this was not forthcoming, he intended to ask the company's Managing Director to attend the Committee meeting scheduled for 30th September, to give an explanation. Obviously such assurances were not given by Metro-Cammell, for both English Electric (who were supplying motors and electrical equipment) and Metro-Cammell representatives were obliged to attend on the 30th.

At this tense meeting, the English Electric representative stated that, if Newcastle were prepared to accept "certain variations in specification", the company could commence delivery of the electrical equipment and motors for the twenty 3-axle trolleybuses on order by the second week in November. Mr. Cheseley, the Production Manager for Metro-Cammell, explained that steel supplies had deteriorated in quantity and this had led to receding vehicle delivery dates. In compensation, he offered to accelerate the delivery of the order for the twenty 3-axle trolleybuses, rather than the 36 2-axle vehicles. This would be possibly ONLY if Newcastle was prepared to take the standard L.P.T.B. body design, rather than the City's own specified design. He further stated that if the BUT 9641T chassis were delivered to Metro-Cammell's works promptly, he could promise to commence delivery of the complete vehicles by January 1948, and supply the whole twenty by March 1948. This offer was immediately accepted by the Undertaking. (London Transport had ordered 77 BUT 9641T/MCW vehicles, to become its Class Q1, early in 1946, but with postwar production delays, these were not delivered to the capital until early 1948). This then was the event which led directly to the diversion of the twenty London bodies to Newcastle.

Physical alterations to the Gosforth tram route were necessary if trolleybuses were to operate the service. In October 1946, authorisation had been given to set back the gates and wall at the West Gates entrance to the Gosforth Park Light Railway, to allow the construction of a trolleybus turning circle. The High Gosforth Park Company asked, in September 1947, if trolleybuses could be extended into the park to serve the racecourse, as the trams had done, and Newcastle Transport agreed to consider the request. By the November it had been agreed that the section of track at West Gates be removed to allow the trolleybus turning circle to be constructed, although this would prevent trams running into the park from the Great North Road. The setting back of the wall and gates was complete by the end of the December.

As described earlier, the 1946 Act gave powers to operate trolleybuses along the whole course of the Gosforth Park Light Railway, and to run Race Specials via Benton and West Moor through the East Gates entrance to the park. In December 1947, however, we hear that the Park Company had asked for trolleybuses to run into the park over the western half of the light railway only, as far as the Grandstand Tramway Station. This partial conversion, the General Manager estimated, would cost £12,000, in addition to £2,000 for the erection of a turning circle at the Tramway Station. This sum of money would provide an 18-foot wide roadway on the trackbed of the double line light railway. The General Manager felt this was an insufficient width for 8-feet wide trolleybuses, especially on the section of tramway on an embankment. He considered a 22-feet wide roadway was the minimum necessary, and as the tramway varied from 20ft. 6ins. to 23-feet wide over this section, considerable expense would be necessary to widen the embankment sufficiently. Two-way trolleybus traffic would not be possible on an 18-foot roadway, and one-way traffic would not be practicable. Therefore the Park Company's suggestion was not accepted. The alternative was to make a 10-foot footpath along the tramway right-of-way, at a cost of £2,000, but the General Manager felt this path would be little used if it were constructed. Neither this partial conversion scheme, nor the full light railway conversion, were ever implemented.

As the new year, 1948, began the City Engineer presented a very disturbing report on the condition of remaining tramway track. This he described as "very bad": tram wheels were running, in many places, on their flanges in the rail groove. In some places this groove was itself worn through, and the wheel flanges were running directly on the concrete trackbed! This situation applied especially on the ex-Tyneside Tramways and Tramroads Company's track on the Great North Road north of Henry Street, Gosforth. The City Engineer further reported that no new rails had been laid since the outbreak of war in 1939.

It was vitally important to abandon the remaining tram routes and replace them with trolleybuses, and a meeting with local Members of Parliament on 29th December 1947 had resulted in a statement by the General Manager confidently expecting delivery of 86 of the 96 trolleybuses anticipated in 1948. The condition of the tramcars themselves was a cause of concern: of the 139 in service, at least 71 were 22-26 years old. The existing trolleybus fleet also came under scrutiny; it was revealed that of the 137 vehicles in stock, 6 were 17 years old, 101 were 10/12 years old, and 30 were between 3 and 8 years of age. Great maintenance difficulties, the General Manager reported, had been encountered—in many cases complete bodies had to be rebuilt to extend vehicle lives. To replace the above vehicles, 136 trolleybuses were now on order. Of the 96 scheduled to be delivered in 1948, 20 were now expected in January-March, 36 April-June, 20 April-June, 10 July-September, and 10 October-December. Representation had been made to the Ministry of Transport about Newcastle's serious position, and "sympathetic consideration" was promised. Of the twenty BUT 3-axle vehicles on order, Metro-Cammell promised in December 1947 that delivery would be as follows: 4 in January 1948; 8 in February 1948; 8 in March 1948. As can be realised from reading p.76-7, this schedule was not adhered to.

An indication that all tram routes might not be converted to trolleybus operation was given in a report by the General Manager to Committee in February 1948. He argued that in view of the very bad state of the tram track and the necessity of best utilising the limited supply of new vehicles expected in 1948, it would be necessary to introduce a combination of motorbus and trolleybus services which would enable "as much tramway as possible to be abandoned". Therefore he proposed to implement trolleybus Routes 4 (Jesmond Road—Benton Bank), 7 (Chillingham Road—Benton—West Moor), 15 (South Gosforth— Matthew Bank), and 16 (Newton Road—High Heaton—Benton Lane Ends) of the 1946 Act. These proposals were not adhered to in this form.

As the reader will already know, the first of the Newcastle BUT "Q.1's", believed to be number 482, was delivered to Byker Depot on 17th February 1948 (all new trolleybuses, from 1935 on, had always been delivered to Byker from the manufacturers, irrespective of their subsequent depot allocation). London Transport had taken delivery to Fulwell Depot of its first Q1 (No. 1776?) on 31st January 1948. They placed this vehicle and No. 1768 in service on 20th February, whilst Newcastle Transport placed 482 into revenue earning service on 1st March. According to "A Trolley Retrieved" (Trolleybooks, 1978), output from Metro-Cammell's coachworks of "Q1" bodies at this time was shared on the basis of one body for London and one for Newcastle, thus effectively doubling the initial production run to 40 vehicles.

At this period, Newcastle Transport always used paint from two Ripon paint manufacturers, and sufficient quantity of such paint was sent down to Birmingham by the Undertaking for Metro-Cammell to finish the twenty bodies in Newcastle livery. A similar arrangement also applied to the paint supplies for other bodybuilders. On the arrival of the twenty BUT's in Newcastle, there were still a number of small jobs to be completed before the vehicles could enter service. Mr. J. Ring remembers the awkward task of blanking off the London-style large destination indicators with black paint, so as to only leave one line showing for the more compressed Newcastle displays. At a later date, Mr. Ring was allocated to the task of painting the trolleybuses decorated for the Coronation in 1953. They were spray-painted with gold paint—a very difficult finish to remove when the vehicles were restored to normal livery at the end of the festivities, he recalls!

We shall now move nearly forty years forward from 1948, to the present day, and the changes that have taken place in Newcastle's transport since the first edition of this book was published in 1974. The most significant event has been the opening of the Tyne and Wear Metro rapid transit system in stages from August 1980. This "super tram" system has revolutionised transport patterns on Tyneside, and is conveying more traffic than expected. Many bus services feed into Metro stations, and more stations are being constructed. All the trolleybus replacement Leyland Atlantean motorbuses have been withdrawn and replaced by later vehicles. Many former trolleybus traction poles still remain in Newcastle's streets, but are now painted in either light green, with dark green bases, or in beige with dark brown bases—and very smart they look. Other traction poles are again supporting overhead wires—on certain parts of the Metro, replanted alongside the tracks.

The two preserved Newcastle trolleybuses, Sunbeam S7 501 of 1948, and BUT 9641T 628 of 1950, still exist. 501 is kept at Beamish Open Air Museum, County Durham, and has been undergroing extensive body panel renewal work over the last few years. It is still capable of running over the short section of trolleybus overhead at the museum: both the authors rode on it in 1979! 628, at the East Anglia Transport Museum at Carlton Colville, Lowestoft, Suffolk, is by contrast, in pristine condition. It has been well restored in appearance, but its brakes are causing trouble at the moment. There are no plans to return either vehicle to Newcastle in the forseeable future.

In the City itself, Morden Street car park (Handysides Depot) appears to no longer be used for stabling P.T.E. 'buses. Fewer roadside section and feeder boxes now survive—for instance the one at Two Ball Lonnen, illustrated in this book, has been removed. West Moor and Barrack Road sub-stations have been demolished, though Westgate sub-station is in use as a school annexe. The Manors generating station building still stands, proudly displaying the City coat-of-arms, and the lettering "Tramways", writ large in stone over the entrance. *Ad finum fidelis.*

CHAPTER FIFTEEN

FROM EAST TO NORTH

In the chapter 'Beneath Ten Miles of Trolleybus Wires' we saw most of the trolleybus routes in the west end of the City. Let us now redress the balance and look at the busy Wallsend Boundary route in the east end, and also take a ride on the Gosforth Park service up the Great North Road. So the reader may get the 'feel' of the ride better, we shall again take the present tense.

It is the glorious summer of 1959, the last week of June to be precise. We are standing on the south side of Shields Road at Wallsend Boundary terminus of route 32 to Fenham awaiting the arrival of a trolleybus to take us three miles west into the City centre. It is just approaching mid-day when our vehicle a 1948, 3-axle Sunbeam S7 with Northern Coachbuilders bodywork, registration number LTN 514, arrives. We watch it perform its terminating movement. There is a reverser in Oaktree Avenue opposite, and the Sunbeam draws past this almost to the limit of the eastbound wires and to the very boundary of the City with Wallsend, before reversing and then drawing out onto Shields Road again, but facing west. Wallsend Boundary had been the junction of Newcastle Corporation Tramways and the Tyneside Tramways & Tramroads Company's lines until 1930.

We board our trolleybus, admiring its smart NCB bodywork, very similar to that on the 2-axle trolleybuses delivered to South Shields and Maidstone, and take our seats at the front of the upper deck. The indicators have first been changed to 'FENHAM' via 'SHIELDS ROAD'. All the sliding ventilators are fully open in view of the hot weather. Soon we are off, noticing the span wires supporting the overhead, and the street lights on curved brackets on alternative traction poles. After a quarter of a mile we slide under Skew Bridge, Walkerville which carries the electric trains of British Railways between Newcastle Central Station and the Coast, and enter the suburb of Walkergate. The railway is high up on an embankment to our right as we approach Walkergate Station and the overhead wiring junctions at Coutts Road. These connections to and from the left were only inserted two years ago as part of the diversionary route constructed along the Fossway, necessitated by the laying of railway lines across Shields Road to connect the internal railway systems of C.A. Parsons engineering works. Our trolleybus passes under these overhead junctions and we hum along, the noise of the trolleyheads passing under each span wire, more noticeable with our NCB body than on the Metro-Cammell vehicles of the fleet. As we continue our gradual climb up Shields Road we are now overshadowed by the high buildings of C.A. Parsons Heaton Works as we bump over the rails of the Heaton Works light railway as they cross the roadway. When abnormal loads are being worked over this railway, trolleybuses are diverted along the Fossway, and the overhead on Shields Road is jacked up by tower wagons to ensure sufficient headroom. A 1950 BUT No. 613, passes us at speed en route for Wallsend, having picked up workmen from C.A. Parsons main factory going home for lunch.

The next point of interest is Byker Depot, coming up on our left as we leave

Heaton Works behind. Byker is known to Newcastle Transport staff as 'The Car Sheds' from its tramcar origins and is the largest depot on the system. The original part of the complex was opened in 1901 to house 80 trams of the then new electric fleet. Subsequently, many extensions and additions have been made and the depot currently stables 100 trolleybuses. Additionally, there is extensive motorbus garaging and facilities for heavy mechanical, electrical, and coachwork repairs and maintenance. Our trolleybus slows for the overhead junctions forming the entrance wiring for the depot, and we see a short siding take off left immediately in front of us before it turns into the depot approaches, joining with another connection cutting across our main wires from the eastbound Shields Road wires.

We cannot see much of the trolleybuses in the depot—the corrugated iron former tram erecting shop blocks our view, but we spy another Sunbeam S7 moving along the main line of wires which run right through the depot yard from Shields Road to the Fossway, bypassing the depot building. There are two or three BUT 9641Ts glimpsed beside the Central Workshops. The gradient steepens slightly as we now turn on a fairly sharp lefthand curve. Just before this we see the redundant tram traction poles in Chillingham Road to our right. Further up Chillingham Road, they still carry tram traction wires (unused since 1949) retained as electrical feeders to the trolleybus overhead in the parallel Heaton Road.

We begin to turn to the right slightly and a complicated mass of overhead wiring comes into view at the junctions of Shields Road, the Fossway and Union Road. Again, the reduction in speed of our vehicle enables us to digest the details. First we pass under wires enabling trolleybuses to divert from Shields Road along the Fossway, whilst immediately after is a link from the westbound wires in the Fossway to the eastbound wires in Shields Road. We pass under these, the vibration from the trolleyheads through the trolleybridge on the roof causing the roof panels to buzz and resonate. Next comes a lefthand trailing connection from the Fossway's westbound wires to Shields Road's westbound wires, followed by a long arc of wiring which sweeps across the wide junction of Union Road and Shields Road. This single line links the Union Road westbound wires with eastbound ones in Shields Road, and enables trolleybuses coming off duty from the Walker termini to gain access to the wires for Byker Depot. Finally our trolleybooms negotiate the crossing of the eastbound wires from Shields Road to Union Road and pass under the trailing frogs where westbound Union Road and Shields Road wires join. We are now running west on Shields Road and descending towards the City centre, $1\frac{1}{2}$ miles away; we have entered the busy shopping area of Shields Road. There is a wide variety of shops, from department stores to corner premises, serving the City's east end, and motor and pedestrian traffic is heavy. We soon arrive at Heaton Road Junction where we are stopped by the traffic duty policeman. This allows us to observe the double wiring junctions connecting the Shields Road overhead with that in Heaton Road. A BUT 6-wheeler emerges from the latter street and turns west ahead of us, on route 37. He is correctly carrying "Denton Road Terminus" on his rear destination screen, but the conductress leans out unconcernedly from the rear platform as she winds on the side screen to the correct indication. She has obviously omitted to do this task at Swarland Avenue terminus.

The traffic policeman now waves us on and narrow Raby Street is glimpsed on our left, its tram traction standards unused for 11 years. We pull into the kerb behind the route 37 6-wheeler at the stop beside Parrish's department store. As we draw up to within 6 inches of the preceding vehicle we see its fleet number "583" on the lower deck cant rail above the rear platform window, and are able to observe the grease and rain streaks from the trolleyheads on the rear roof dome. 583 has obviously loaded his passengers, for he swiftly draws away from the stop, his booms setting the overhead bouncing ahead of us. Very soon afterwards we set off to follow him through the congested shopping area. Still on a descending gradient, we pass Albion Row on our left, where the wartime emergency wiring linking Shields Road and Walker Road stood, unused to 1956. Ahead of us is Byker Bridge and its elaborate overhead wiring. The traction poles are joined across the road by gantries, whilst bracket arms lower down the outer sides of the poles are held by staywires to the bridge deck. Additionally, the traction wires are supported by intermediate span wires between each pair of gantries, these span wires being braced to the traction poles. The whole forms a very rigid arrangement. We enter the bridge and pass the sign attached to the first traction pole on the left, stating "WARNING: Speed of double deck vehicles on this bridge not to exceed 20 M.P.H." However No. 583's driver is obviously interpreting this rather liberally, as the BUT is drawing rapidly away from us. On our right is British Railway's Ouseburn Viaduct, with an express for Scotland running over it, headed by an A3 class locomotive. To the left is the deep Ouseburn valley leading to the River Tyne and Gateshead beyond. We hum steadily over the bridge, climb a slight rise, and pass St. Dominic's Priory to our left, noticing the section box emblazoned "Corporation Tramways, 1925" near the corner of Crawhall Road.

Having left the stop at St. Dominic's, we next negotiate the frogs for Melbourne Street wiring. This road was wired up during the war as an emergency measure. The stone setts showing the marks where the tram rails have been removed are still in situ, turning off down Melbourne Street. We, however, continue along the smooth surface of New Bridge Street, pass over the East Coast Main Railway Line at Red Barns and after a short steep incline and slight curve to the right, see the battered remains of New Bridge Street Goods Station. It looks very woebegone since its bombing in 1941 but is still busy with freight traffic, and there are many railway wagons loading and unloading.

There is trouble ahead though, for our impatient friend, the driver of BUT 583 on route 37, has managed to dewire his trolleybooms on the automatic points where New Bridge Street and Market Street wires diverge ahead. Other road traffic is gingerly passing round the stranded trolleybus but our driver must wait until the overhead is clear before proceeding. 583's negative (lefthand) boom has become tangled in the lighting wires, so the crew hook down the positive boom whilst they tackle the other. Efforts with the bamboo pole every trolleybus carries fail, and the driver is obliged to open the rear emergency window in order to climb onto the vehicle roof to get at the boom. An inspector now appears on the scene, and as the overhead is now clear, and a Brighton Grove route 35 trolleybus has drawn up behind us, the inspector waves us forward to pass the stationary BUT 9641T. We cautiously overtake, our power on to operate the solenoids in the overhead in accordance with the instructions on the sign suspended from the overhead before the automatic frogs. As the solenoid is energised by our trolleyheads we see the point tongues ahead slam over successfully. We accelerate smartly to pass through the green traffic lights before cutting off power to pass under the eastbound wires emerging from Market Street on our left. As we are about to alight now, we begin to make our way downstairs as our Sunbeam S7 passes the B.B.C. Broadcasting House. As we stand on the rear platform we see a Tyneside Tramways green and cream Leyland PD2/3 motorbus at its terminal point in Croft Street. Our trolleybus slows down to allow the booms to take the inside road of wiring; the outer line is the beginning of the Pilgrim Street terminal loop. This is used by trolleybuses from the east end on rush hour shortworkings of route 32 and the 35 group of routes.

We get off opposite the Central Library and begin to walk westward to Pilgrim Street to catch our 31 for Gosforth Park. Over the entrance to the Dex Garage in New Bridge Street, the two roads of wiring just mentioned cross in a scissors crossover, so we see our 6-wheeler's trolley poles transferring themselves to the outer road, which leads over Pilgrim Street junction into Blackett Street. The purpose of this wiring arrangement is to enable trolleybuses terminating at Pilgrim Street to pass other trolleybuses standing at our alighting stop.

We now walk round the corner to Pilgrim Street and cross to the west side to await our next trolleybus, noticing that there are three roads of wiring in this street; one northbound and two southbound. The inner set of southbound wires form part of the Pilgrim Street turning square. Soon a BUT 9641T with Metro-Cammell body appears, turning the tight corner from Market Street into Pilgrim Street. It is LTN 482, one of the famous Gosforth Buses delivered in 1948 and has bodywork to London Transport design. Its indicators are showing "31" "Gosforth Park", and we board, making our way to the upper deck front seats, noticing the unusual (for Newcastle) half droplights with their winding handles and notices cautioning against leaning out. The front drop screens are fixed shut, however.

Soon we are on our way, passing under the wiring our previous vehicle has used to cross from New Bridge Street to Blackett Street, and we enter Northumberland Street, the City's prime shopping street. After many stops we emerge at the Haymarket, pass the overhead junctions for Percy Street on our left, and take another automatic frog where the Great North Road and Jesmond Road wires diverge in Barras Bridge. We obey the white metal sign suspended from a bracket arm; "Power off for Gosforth", and see its companion "Power on for Jesmond Road". Noise from the trolleybooms is noticeably quieter than on our previous vehicle. We are checked by the heavy traffic, but as the outer lane is clearer we are passed by a 1950 BUT 9641T on route 38 to Benton Road (Swarland Avenue), sweeping along to turn off at Jesmond Road.

Shortly, we are on the open stretch of the Great North Road with the Town Moor on our left, and the houses of Jesmond half seen through the trees to our right. The overhead here is supported on bracket arms over the 50 feet wide road. Our speed rises to approximately 40 m.p.h.; this is one of the "racing stretches" of the system. Just over a mile further on we notice the amusements and sideshows of the Town Moor Temperance Festival, or "The Hoppings" as it is more usually known. This fair always visits the City this week of the year. Once more,

143

automatic frogs appear in the overhead in front of us, where the Jesmond Dene Road wiring to South Gosforth turns off right. Immediately after are the lefthand facing frogs of the Town Moor turning circle in Grandstand Road, built to serve "The Hoppings" crowds, and we see two NCB bodied 2-axle vehicles standing on the railed in turning circle, disgorging fairgoers.

A further mile sees us threading the busy High Street through Gosforth, outside the City boundary, but still in the built-up area of Newcastle. At Henry Street, a former tram sub-terminus, the central reservation dividing the road begins, and we will be on dual carriageway almost to Gosforth Park terminus. The special wiring provision at Gosforth Greyhound Stadium—a two road standing in Hollywood Avenue—is seen on our right as we speed north. All the overhead we are now using is barely a year old—it was erected when this section of the A1 trunk road was reconstructed completely in 1958. A flash of yellow over to the right is revealed to be a southbound "31" travelling on the opposite carriageway 50 feet away through the trees. The extension to Grange Estate, constructed in 1951, is passed to the left, its traction poles and span wires marching away over the concrete surface of Broadway West. Next we see another BUT 6-wheeler standing on the turning circle at Polwarth Drive, but we continue on. The road reverts to single carriageway as we run alongside the west side of Gosforth Park, Newcastle's racecourse. We alight as our trolleybus turns at West Gates turning circle, the gateway to the former Gosforth Park Light Railway behind it, and prepares to return to the Central Station five miles away.

In our travels we have seen the Undertaking's largest depot, some of the central area wiring, three of the four automatic frogs, the famous Town Moor turning circle, and new overhead on the Great North Road—all in 8 miles of riding.

A dramatic night photograph of Benton Road, Swarland Avenue terminus, c.1951. The Sunbeam S7 No. 507 is ready to depart on service 37 to Denton Road Terminus on the opposite side of the City.   I. C. Gumm

Homebuilt for Newcastle—bodywork being constructed on ten of the batch of thirty Sunbeam S7 chassis at the Claremont Road works of Northern Coachbuilders Ltd. in 1948.   Newcastle Chronicle & Journal

Close to Northern Coachbuilders factory in Claremont Road, Newcastle, stands newly built Sunbeam S7 No. 499. This trolleybus was numerically the first of a batch of thirty built at the NCB factory in 1948.   Tyne & Wear P.T.E.

A fine example of overhead wiring construction frames Sunbeam S7 No. 513 as it turns from Welbeck Road into Church Street at Westbourne Avenue, Walker terminus. Note the trolleybus stop sign, "X&F" sign, feeder cables and gantry construction.

M. J. C. Dare

A view showing the devastation caused to the bodywork of Sunbeam F4/NCB No. 546, as it overturned outside Fenwicks department store, Northumberland Street, 30th September 1960.   Newcastle Chronicle & Journal

At the end of the line: Sunbeam F4 No. 538 stands in High Street West, Wallsend, at the very limit of the eastbound overhead at Wallsend Boundary terminus, prior to reversing before setting out for Fenham on service 32. 29th January 1964.   T. Steele

A rare view of the Wingrove Depot exit wiring in Wingrove Road. This pre-1956 photograph shows Sunbeam S7 No. 523 about to turn left in Westgate Road to take service on 35a to Church Street. The stop sign on the pole proves it was possible for passengers to board a trolleybus in Wingrove Road!   R. F. Mack

After the Benton Park Road circular services (39/40) had been introduced, BUT 9611T/NCB, No. 569 pauses for the official photographer. The scene is near the junction of Jesmond Dene Road and Great North Road in winter 1949/50.   Tyne & Wear P.T.E.

A wet day in Neville Street, at the Central Station. This point was the terminus of several trolleybus routes. BUT 9611T with NCB bodywork, No. 571 is nearest the camera.

C. Carter

The neat lines of the Northern Coachbuilders 56-seat bodies mounted on Sunbeam F4 chassis are well shown in this view of No. 544. The location is the Bewick Street stand of service 40, c. 1950/51.

C. Carter

The junction of Grainger Street and Westgate Road in the City centre in the mid 1950s. The rear of a 1948 BUT 9641T is seen on the left followed by Sunbeam F4 No. 553 on route 41, a Gateshead Guy motorbus, and another Newcastle Transport 2-axle trolleybus.
R. F. Mack

A general view of Slatyford Depot, taken shortly after the opening in 1956, showing the neat finished appearance of the building, which was originally an RAF hanger in Westmorland. The 600Kw sub-station can be seen on the extreme right. Note the long span wires across the forecourt.
Tyne & Wear P.T.E.

c.9.00 a.m., 5th July 1956. Rush hour traffic southbound in Northumberland Street includes a 1948 BUT 9641T trolleybus, a Newcastle Transport double deck motorbus, and two Gateshead motorbuses. Had the Gateshead proposals been implemented, the two Gateshead motorbuses in this photograph would have in fact been trolleybuses.

Newcastle City Libraries

About to set off on the newly introduced 31A service to Grange Estate, Gosforth, BUT 9641T No. 625 waits at the Central Station terminus in Neville Street.   C. Carter

151

The railway bridge at the Manors on City Road frames No. 585, a BUT 9641T of the 1950 batch, in August 1962. Newcastle Transport Head Office is off to the right. The little used Melbourne Street wires can just be discerned above the vehicle's roof.   N. Hanson

BUT 9641T No. 591 leads a line of traffic west down Benton Bank. This post-April 1962 view was taken on the 42 circular service. Benton Bank was drastically reconstructed for the trams early this century.   A. N. Other

TROLLEYBUS ROLLING STOCK LIST

In presenting the Rolling Stock List and Disposals of Rolling Stock the authors would like to acknowledge with thanks the considerable help received from the staff at Byker Depot, Mr. F. P. Groves, Mr. M. H. Heard and the P.S.V. Circle, in providing the finer details. There are still some gaps left, however, and the authors invite any comments, corrections, and additional information which readers may have so that correct records may be maintained in the future. The compilation of these records and of Class Details has been undertaken by Mr. J. R. Whitehead, to whom we also extend our grateful thanks.

I—NEWCASTLE UPON TYNE CORPORATION TRANSPORT
TROLLEYBUS FLEET

Fleet No.	Reg. No.	Chassis Make and Type	No.	Elec. Equip and motor	Builder	Body Seating	Date deliv.	Into serv.	Wdn
10	BVK800	A.E.C. 664T	664T.001	E.E.C.	E.E.C.	H33/27D	12. 9.35	1.10.35	31. 5.49
11	BVK801	A.E.C. 664T	664T.003	E.E.C.	E.E.C.	H33/27D	22. 9.35	10.35	.50
12	BVK802	A.E.C. 664T	664T.007	E.E.C.	E.E.C.	H33/27D	26. 9.35	10.35	31. 5.49
13	BVK803	A.E.C. 664T	664T.006	E.E.C.	E.E.C.	H33/27D	29. 9.35	10.35	.50
14	BVK804	A.E.C. 664T	664T.008	E.E.C.	E.E.C.	H33/27D	3.10.35	10.35	31. 5.49
15	BVK805	A.E.C. 664T	664T.002	E.E.C.	Brush	H33/27D	24. 7.35	10.35	29. 2.48
16	BVK806	A.E.C. 664T	664T.004	E.E.C.	Brush	H33/27D	28. 7.35	10.35	31. 5.49
17	BVK807	A.E.C. 664T	664T.009	E.E.C.	Brush	H33/27D	3. 8.35	10.35	31.10.48
18	BVK808	A.E.C. 664T	664T.010	E.E.C.	Brush	H33/27D	22. 8.35	10.35	.50
19	BVK809	A.E.C. 664T	664T.005	E.E.C.	Brush	H33/27D	25. 8.35	1.10.35	30. 4.49
20	BVK810	Karrier E6A	54116	MV	M.C.C.W.	H33/27D	28. 7.35	10.35	24. 3.49
21	BVK811	Karrier E6A	54117	MV	M.C.C.W.	H33/27D	7. 8.35	10.35	.50
22	BVK812	Karrier E6A	54113	MV	M.C.C.W.	H33/27D	11. 8.35	10.35	.49
23	BVK813	Karrier E6A	54122	MV	M.C.C.W.	H33/27D	15. 8.35	10.35	.50
24	BVK814	Karrier E6A	54121	MV	M.C.C.W.	H33/27D	18. 8.35	10.35	.50
25	BVK815	Karrier E6A	54118	MV	M.C.C.W.	H33/27D	22. 8.35	10.35	.50
26	BVK816	Karrier E6A	54114	MV	M.C.C.W.	H33/27D	29. 8.35	10.35	28. 2.49
27	BVK817	Karrier E6A	54120	MV	M.C.C.W.	H33/27D	1. 9.35	10.35	.50
28	BVK818	Karrier E6A	54115	MV	M.C.C.W.	H33/27D	4. 9.35	10.35	.50
29	BVK819	Karrier E6A	54119	MV	M.C.C.W.	H33/27D	9. 9.35	10.35	28. 2.49
30	BVK820	Guy BTX	24090	B.T-H.	M.C.C.W.	H33/27D	19. 9.35	10.35	28. 2.49
31	BVK821	Guy BTX	24089	B.T-H.	M.C.C.W.	H33/27D	18. 9.35	10.35	28. 8.49
32	BVK822	Guy BTX	24092	B.T-H.	M.C.C.W.	H33/27D	20. 9.35	10.35	.49
33	BVK823	Guy BTX	24091	B.T-H.	M.C.C.W.	H33/27D	23. 9.35	10.35	.49
34	BVK824	Guy BTX	24093	B.T-H.	M.C.C.W.	H33/27D	23. 9.35	10.35	.49
35	BVK825	Guy BTX	24099	B.T-H.	M.C.C.W.	H33/27D	23. 9.35	10.35	.49
36	BVK826	Guy BTX	24098	B.T-H.	M.C.C.W.	H33/27D	25. 9.35	10.35	.49
37	BVK827	Guy BTX	24100	B.T-H.	M.C.C.W.	H33/27D	29. 9.35	10.35	.49
38	BVK828	Guy BTX	24102	B.T-H.	M.C.C.W.	H33/27D	29. 9.35	10.35	.49
39	BVK829	Guy BTX	24101	B.T-H.	M.C.C.W.	H33/27D	30. 9.35	10.35	.49
40	CVK52	Karrier E6A	54125	MV	M.C.C.W.	H33/27D	21.12.35	12.35	.50

Fleet No.	Reg. No.	Chassis Make and type	No.	Elec. Equip. and motor	Builder	Body Seating	Date deliv.	Into serv.	Wdn
41	DTN141	Karrier E6A	31002	MV	M.C.C.W.	H33/27D	28.11.36	12.36	.50
42	DTN142	Karrier E6A	31001	MV	M.C.C.W.	H33/27D	4.12.36	12.36	.50
43	DTN143	Karrier E6A	54126	MV	M.C.C.W.	H33/27D	6.12.36	12.36	24. 3.49
44	DTN144	Guy BTX	24224	(a)	M.C.C.W.	H33/27D	6.12.36	12.36	28. 2.49
45	DTN145	Guy BTX	24205	(a)	M.C.C.W.	H33/27D	17.12.36	12.36	28. 2.49
46	DTN146	Guy BTX	24223	(a)	M.C.C.W.	H33/27D	7.12.36	12.36	28. 2.49
47	ETN47	Karrier E6A	31011	MV	M.C.C.W.	H33/27D	2. 7.37	9.37	.49
48	ETN48	Karrier E6A	31012	MV	M.C.C.W.	H33/27D	30. 6.37	9.37	24. 3.49
49	ETN49	Karrier E6A	31013	MV	M.C.C.W.	H33/27D	30. 6.37	9.37	.49
50	ETN50	Karrier E6A	31014	MV	M.C.C.W.	H33/27D	2. 7.37	9.37	.49
51	ETN51	Karrier E6A	31015	MV	M.C.C.W.	H33/27D	6. 7.37	9.37	.49
52	ETN52	Karrier E6A	31016	MV	M.C.C.W.	H33/27D	9. 7.37	9.37	.49
53	ETN53	Karrier E6A	31017	MV	M.C.C.W.	H33/27D	29. 7.37	9.37	.49
54	ETN54	Karrier E6A	31018	MV	M.C.C.W.	H33/27D	6. 8.37	9.37	.49
55	ETN55	Karrier E6A	31104	MV	M.C.C.W.	H33/27D	19. 9.37	9.37	.49
56	ETN56	Karrier E6A	31105	MV	M.C.C.W.	H33/27D	30.11.37	.37	.56
57	ETN57	Guy BTX	24438	(a)	M.C.C.W.	H33/27D	28. 8.37	19. 9.37	24. 3.49
58	ETN58	Guy BTX	24437	(a)	M.C.C.W.	H33/27D	25. 8.37	19. 9.37	.49
59	ETN59	Guy BTX	24439	(a)	M.C.C.W.	H33/27D	29. 8.37	19. 9.37	.49
60	ETN60	Guy BTX	24436	(a)	M.C.C.W.	H33/27D	25. 8.37	19. 9.37	31.12.48
61	ETN61	Guy BTX	24441	(a)	M.C.C.W.	H33/27D	30. 8.37	19. 9.37	30. 4.49
62	ETN62	Guy BTX	24440	(a)	M.C.C.W.	H33/27D	29. 8.37	19. 9.37	30. 4.49
63	ETN63	Guy BTX	24442	(a)	M.C.C.W.	H33/27D	3. 9.37	20. 9.37	.49
64	ETN64	Guy BTX	24444	(a)	M.C.C.W.	H33/27D	2. 9.37	19. 9.37	.49
65	ETN65	Guy BTX	24443	(a)	M.C.C.W.	H33/27D	2. 9.37	19. 9.37	.49
66	ETN66	Guy BTX	24445	(a)	M.C.C.W.	H33/27D	30. 8.37	19. 9.37	.49
67	ETN67	A.E.C. 664T	664T382	E.E.C.	M.C.C.W.	H33/27D	8. 9.37	19. 9.37	.50
68	ETN68	A.E.C. 664T	664T383	E.E.C.	M.C.C.W.	H33/27D	11. 9.37	19. 9.37	31. 1.49
69	ETN69	A.E.C. 664T	664T384	E.E.C.	M.C.C.W.	H33/27D	1. 9.37	19. 9.37	.50
70	ETN70	A.E.C. 664T	664T385	E.E.C.	M.C.C.W.	H33/27D	23. 8.37	13. 9.37	.49
71	ETN71	A.E.C. 664T	664T386	E.E.C.	M.C.C.W.	H33/27D	26. 8.37	19. 9.37	.49

Fleet No.	Reg. No.	Chassis Make and type	No.	Elec. Equip. and motor	Builder	Body Seating	Date deliv.	Into serv.	Wdn
72	ETN72	A.E.C. 664T	664T387	E.E.C.	M.C.C.W.	H33/27D	20. 8.37	12. 9.37	.50
73	ETN73	A.E.C. 664T	664T388	E.E.C.	M.C.C.W.	H33/27D	29. 8.37	19. 9.37	.50
74	ETN74	A.E.C. 664T	664T389	E.E.C.	M.C.C.W.	H33/27D	8. 9.37	19. 9.37	.50
75	ETN75	A.E.C. 664T	664T390	E.E.C.	M.C.C.W.	H33/27D	4. 9.37	19. 9.37	.50
76	ETN76	A.E.C. 664T	664T547	E.E.C.	M.C.C.W.	H33/27D	15. 9.37	19. 9.37	30. 4.49
77	ETN77	A.E.C. 664T	664T548	E.E.C.	M.C.C.W.	H33/27D	4. 9.37	19. 9.37	.50
78	FBB78	Guy BTX	24229	(a)	Roe (7215)	H34/26D	19.12.37	6. 1.38	30. 4.49
79	FVK79	A.E.C. 664T	664T553	E.E.C.	Roe (7328)	H34/26D	20. 6.38	3. 8.38	.50
80	FVK80	A.E.C. 664T	664T554	E.E.C.	Roe (7327)	H34/26D	23. 6.38	1. 8.38	.50
81	FVK81	A.E.C. 664T	664T555	E.E.C.	Roe (7332)	H34/26D	28. 6.38	1. 8.38	.50
82	FVK82	A.E.C. 664T	664T556	E.E.C.	Roe (7329)	H34/26D	30. 6.38	1. 8.38	.50
83	FVK83	A.E.C. 664T	664T557	E.E.C.	Roe (7331)	H34/26D	22. 6.38	1. 8.38	.50
84	FVK84	A.E.C.664T	664T558	E.E.C.	Roe (7330)	H34/26D	24. 6.38	2. 8.38	.50
85	FVK85	Karrier E6A	31126	MV	M.C.C.W.	H33/27D	16. 7.38	1. 8.38	.49
86	FVK86	Karrier E6A	31125	MV	M.C.C.W.	H33/27D	20. 7.38	1. 8.38	.49
87	FVK87	Karrier E6A	31123	MV	M.C.C.W.	H33/27D	23. 7.38	4. 8.38	.49
88	FVK88	Karrier E6A	31124	MV	M.C.C.W.	H33/27D	26. 7.38	6. 8.38	.49
89	FVK89	Karrier E6A	31117	MV	M.C.C.W.	H33/27D	26. 7.38	31. 7.38	.49
90	FVK90	Karrier E6A	31120	MV	M.C.C.W.	H33/27D	27. 7.38	31. 7.38	.49
91	FVK91	Karrier E6A	31115	MV	M.C.C.W.	H33/27D	30. 7.38	2. 9.38	.49
92	FVK92	Karrier E6A	31113	MV	M.C.C.W.	H33/27D	30. 7.38	2. 9.38	31. 1.49
93	FVK93	Karrier E6A	31114	MV	M.C.C.W.	H33/27D	30. 7.38	1. 9.38	31. 1.49
94	FVK94	Karrier E6A	31121	MV	M.C.C.W.	H33/27D	14. 8.38	2. 9.38	.49
95	FVK95	Karrier E6A	31122	MV	M.C.C.W.	H33/27D	14. 8.38	3. 9.38	.49
96	FVK96	Karrier E6A	31119	MV	M.C.C.W.	H33/27D	18. 8.38	2. 9.38	.49
97	FVK97	Karrier E6A	31118	MV	M.C.C.W.	H33/27D	18. 8.38	2. 9.38	.49
98	FVK98	Karrier E6A	31116	MV	M.C.C.W.	H33/27D	2. 9.38	6. 9.38	.49
99	FVK99	Guy BTX	24674	(a)	M.C.C.W.	H33/27D	20. 8.38	3. 9.38	.49
100	FVK100	Guy BTX	24668	(a)	M.C.C.W.	H33/27D	14. 8.38	2. 9.38	24. 3.49
101	FVK101	Guy BTX	24671	(a)	M.C.C.W.	H33/27D	21. 8.38	2. 9.38	.49
102	FVK102	Guy BTX	24673	(a)	M.C.C.W.	H33/27D	24. 8.38	1. 9.38	.49
103	FVK103	Guy BTX	24672	(a)	M.C.C.W.	H33/27D	25. 8.38	1. 9.38	.49

Fleet No.	Reg. No.	Chassis Make and type	No.	Elec. Equip. and motor	Body Builder	Seating	Date deliv.	Into serv.	Wdn
104	FVK104	Guy BTX	24230	(a)	M.C.C.W.	H33/27D	3. 9.38	8. 9.38	24. 3.49
105	FVK105	Guy BTX	24666	(a)	M.C.C.W.	H33/27D	2. 9.38	5. 9.38	.49
106	FVK106	Guy BTX	24669	(a)	M.C.C.W.	H33/27D	3. 9.38	5. 9.38	.49
107	FVK107	Guy BTX	24670	(a)	M.C.C.W.	H33/27D	2. 9.38	5. 9.38	.49
108	FVK108	Guy BTX	24675	(a)	M.C.C.W.	H33/27D	14. 9.38	16. 9.38	24. 3.49
109	FVK109	Guy BTX	24667	(a)	NCB	H33/27D	7.11.38	1.12.38	30. 4.49
112	DHP112	Daimler CTM6	21001	MV	M.C.C.W.	H33/27D	10. 3.38	14. 3.38	.50
113	HVK113	Karrier E6A	31163	MV	Roe (259)	H34/26D	19.12.39	27.12.39	.50
114	HVK114	Karrier E6A	31164	MV	Roe (260)	H34/26D	26. 2.40	4. 3.40	.50
115	HVK115	Karrier E6A	31165	MV	Roe (262)	H34/26D	28. 2.40	7. 3.40	.50
116	HVK116	Karrier E6A	31168	MV	Roe (263)	H34/26D	14.12.40	18.12.40	.50
117	HVK117	Karrier E6A	31169	MV	Roe (261)	H34/26D	1. 3.40	8. 3.40	.50
118	HVK118	Karrier E6A	31174	MV	Roe (258)	H34/26D	16.12.39	22.12.39	.50
119	HVK119	Karrier E6A	31172	MV	M.C.C.W.	H33/27D	20. 3.40	3. 7.40	.50
120	HVK120	Karrier E6A	31171	MV	M.C.C.W.	H33/27D	28. 3.40	6.12.40	.50
121	HVK121	Karrier E6A	31173	MV	M.C.C.W.	H33/27D	4. 4.40	2.10.40	.50
122	HVK122	Karrier E6A	31167	MV	M.C.C.W.	H33/27D	11. 4.40	6.12.40	.50
123	HVK123	Karrier E6A	31170	MV	M.C.C.W.	H33/27D	17. 4.40	6.12.40	.50
124	HVK124	Karrier E6A	31166	MV	M.C.C.W.	H33/27D	24. 4.40	6.12.40	.50
1	KW9461	E.E.C. E11	153	E.E.C. DK122	E.E.C.	H30/26R	30.11.42	11. 4.43	12.48
2	KW9463	E.E.C. E11	150	E.E.C. DK122	F.F.C.	H30/26R	4.12.42	5. 3.43	12.48
3	KW9453	E.E.C. E11	142	E.E.C. DK122	E.E.C.	H30/26R	11.12.42	9. 4.43	12.48
4	KW9454	E.E.C. E11	143	E.E.C. DK122	E.E.C.	H30/26R	8.12.42	6. 3.43	?
5	KW9455	E.E.C. E11	144	E.E.C. DK122	E.E.C.	H30/26R	10.12.42	4. 3.43	31.12.48
6	KW6063	E.E.C. E11	105	E.E.C. DK122	E.E.C.	H30/26R	19.12.42	(b)	(b)
7	KW9460	E.E.C. E11	151	E.E.C. DK122	E.E.C.	H30/26R	3.12.42	1. 3.43	31.12.48
8	KW6656	E.E.C. E11	104	E.E.C. DK122	E.E.C.	H30/26R	16.12.42	(b)	(b)
9	KW6655	E.E.C. E11	102	E.E.C. DK122	Park Royal	H30/26R	17.12.42	(b)	(b)
0	KW9464	E.E.C. E11	149	E.E.C. DK122	E.E.C.	H30/26R	2.12.42	(b)	(b)
125	JTN955	Karrier W4	50044	MV 207C1	E.E.C.	UH30/26R	2.12.43	11. 6.44	.53
126	JTN956	Karrier W4	50045	MV 207C1	Park Royal	UH30/26R	31.12.43	11. 6.44	.53

Fleet No.	Reg. No.	Chassis Make and type	No.	Elec. Equip. and motor	Builder	Body Seating	Date deliv.	Into serv.	Wdn
127	JTN957	Karrier W4	50046	MV 207C1	Park Royal	UH30/26R	12. 1.44	11. 6.44	.53
128	JTN958	Karrier W4	50047	MV 207C1	Park Royal	UH30/26R	26. 1.44	11. 6.44	.53
129	JTN959	Karrier W4	50048	MV 207C1	Park Royal	UH30/26R	10. 2.44	11. 6.44	.53
130	JTN960	Karrier W4	50049	MV 207C1	Park Royal	UH30/26R	15. 3.44	11. 6.44	.53
131	JTN961	Karrier W4	50050	MV 207C1	Park Royal	UH30/26R	28. 3.44	11. 6.44	.53
132	JTN962	Karrier W4	50051	MV 207C1	Park Royal	UH30/26R	31. 3.44	11. 6.44	.56
133	JTN963	Karrier W4	50052	MV 207C1	Park Royal	UH30/26R	14. 4.44	11. 6.44	.56
134	JTN964	Karrier W4	50053	MV 207C1	Park Royal	UH30/26R	21. 4.44	11. 6.44	.56
135	JTN965	Karrier W4	50054	MV 207C1	Park Royal	UH30/26R	28. 4.44	11. 6.44	.56
136	JTN966	Karrier W4	50055	MV 207C1	Park Royal	UH30/26R	22. 4.44	11. 6.44	.56
137	JVK277	Karrier W4	50121	MV 207C1	Weymann	UH30/26R	14. 3.45	1. 7.45	.53
138	JVK278	Karrier W4	50122	MV 207C1	Weymann	UH30/26R	12. 4.45	1. 7.45	.53
139	JVK279	Karrier W4	50119	MV 207C1	Park Royal	UH30/26R	8. 3.45	4. 5.45	.53
140	JVK280	Karrier W4	50120	MV 207C1	Park Royal	UH30/26R	21. 3.45	1. 6.45	.53
141	JVK281	Karrier W4	50123	MV 207C1	Park Royal	UH30/26R	2. 3.45	4. 5.45	.53
142	JVK282	Karrier W4	50124	MV 207C1	Park Royal	UH30/26R	8. 3.45	1. 6.45	.53
443	LBB43	Sunbeam F4	50475	MV 209	M.C.C.W.	H30/26R		1. 2.49	30. 5.63
444	LBB44	Sunbeam F4	50476	MV 209	M.C.C.W.	H30/26R		1. 3.49	1.62
445	LBB45	Sunbeam F4	50477	MV 209	M.C.C.W.	H30/26R		1. 3.49	12.61
446	LBB46	Sunbeam F4	50478	MV 209	M.C.C.W.	H30/26R		1. 3.49	12.61
447	LBB47	Sunbeam F4	50479	MV 209	M.C.C.W.	H30/26R		1. 3.49	1.62
448	LBB48	Sunbeam F4	50480	MV 209	M.C.C.W.	H30/26R		1. 1.49	30. 5.63
449	LBB49	Sunbeam F4	50481	MV 209	M.C.C.W.	H30/26R		1. 3.49	12.61
450	LBB50	Sunbeam F4	50482	MV 209	M.C.C.W.	H30/26R		10.11.48	30. 5.63
451	LBB51	Sunbeam F4	50483	MV 209	M.C.C.W.	H30/26R		1. 2.49	30. 5.63
452	LBB52	Sunbeam F4	50484	MV 209	M.C.C.W.	H30/26R		1. 1.49	12.61
453	LBB53	Sunbeam F4	50485	MV 209	M.C.C.W.	H30/26R		1.12.48	30. 5.63
454	LBB54	Sunbeam F4	50486	MV 209	M.C.C.W.	H30/26R		1. 1.49	30. 5.63
455	LBB55	Sunbeam F4	50487	MV 209	M.C.C.W.	H30/26R		1. 2.49	3.62
456	LBB56	Sunbeam F4	50488	MV 209	M.C.C.W.	H30/26R		1. 1.49	5.62
457	LBB57	Sunbeam F4	50489	MV 209	M.C.C.W.	H30/26R		1. 3.49	30. 5.63
458	LBB58	Sunbeam F4	50490	MV 209	M.C.C.W.	H30/26R		25. 3.49	30. 5.63

Fleet No.	Reg. No.	Chassis Make and type	No.	Elec. Equip. and motor	Body Builder	Body Seating	Date deliv.	Into serv.	Wdn
459	LBB59	Sunbeam F4	50491	MV 209	M.C.C.W.	H30/26R		1. 3.49	30. 5.63
460	LBB60	Sunbeam F4	50492	MV 209	M.C.C.W.	H30/26R		1. 2.49	9.62
461	LBB61	Sunbeam F4	50493	MV 209	M.C.C.W.	H30/26R		1. 2.49	30. 5.63
462	LBB62	Sunbeam F4	50494	MV 209	M.C.C.W.	H30/26R		1. 3.49	30. 5.63
463	LBB63	Sunbeam F4	50495	MV 209	M.C.C.W.	H30/26R		25. 3.49	30. 5.63
464	LBB64	Sunbeam F4	50496	MV 209	M.C.C.W.	H30/26R		1. 3.49	30. 5.63
465	LBB65	Sunbeam F4	50497	MV 209	M.C.C.W.	H30/26R		1. 1.49	30. 5.63
466	LBB66	Sunbeam F4	50498	MV 209	M.C.C.W.	H30/26R		25. 3.49	30. 5.63
467	LBB67	Sunbeam F4	50499	MV 209	M.C.C.W.	H30/26R		1. 3.49	30. 5.63
468	LBB68	Sunbeam F4	50500	MV 209	M.C.C.W.	H30/26R		16.11.48	30. 5.63
469	LBB69	Sunbeam F4	50501	MV 209	M.C.C.W.	H30/26R		16. 1.49	6.61
470	LBB70	Sunbeam F4	50502	MV 209	M.C.C.W.	H30/26R		1. 3.49	30. 5.63
471	LBB71	Sunbeam F4	50503	MV 209	M.C.C.W.	H30/26R		16. 1.49	30. 5.63
472	LBB72	Sunbeam F4	50504	MV 209	M.C.C.W.	H30/26R		25. 3.49	30. 5.63
473	LBB73	Sunbeam F4	50505	MV 209	M.C.C.W.	H30/26R		1. 1.49	10.62
474	LBB74	Sunbeam F4	50506	MV 209	M.C.C.W.	H30/26R		1.12.48	30. 5.63
475	LBB75	Sunbeam F4	50507	MV 209	M.C.C.W.	H30/26R		1. 3.49	30. 5.63
476	LBB76	Sunbeam F4	50508	MV 209	M.C.C.W.	H30/26R		25. 3.49	30. 5.63
477	LBB77	Sunbeam F4	50509	MV 209	M.C.C.W.	H30/26R		16.11.48	30. 5.63
478	LBB78	Sunbeam F4	50510	MV 209	M.C.C.W.	H30/26R		1. 2.49	12.61
479	LTN479	B.U.T. 9641T	9641T.257	E.E.C. 410	M.C.C.W.	H40/30R		15. 4.48	30. 5.65
480	LTN480	B.U.T. 9641T	9641T.258	E.E.C. 410	M.C.C.W.	H40/30R		15. 4.48	30. 5.65
481	LTN481	B.U.T. 9641T	9641T.259	E.E.C. 410	M.C.C.W.	H40/30R		15. 4.48	30. 5.65
482	LTN482	B.U.T. 9641T	9641T.260	E.E.C. 410	M.C.C.W.	H40/30R		1. 3.48	30. 5.65
483	LTN483	B.U.T. 9641T	9641T.261	E.E.C. 410	M.C.C.W.	H40/30R		15. 4.48	30. 5.65
484	LTN484	B.U.T. 9641T	9641T.262	E.E.C. 410	M.C.C.W.	H40/30R		15. 4.48	30. 5.65
485	LTN485	B.U.T. 9641T	9641T.263	E.E.C. 410	M.C.C.W.	H40/30R		15. 4.48	30. 5.65
486	LTN486	B.U.T. 9641T	9641T.264	E.E.C. 410	M.C.C.W.	H40/30R		15. 4.48	30. 5.65
487	LTN487	B.U.T. 9641T	9641T.265	E.E.C. 410	M.C.C.W.	H40/30R		15. 4.48	30. 5.65
488	LTN488	B.U.T. 9641T	9641T.266	F.F.C. 410	M.C.C.W.	H40/30R		15. 4.48	30. 5.65
489	LTN489	B.U.T. 9641T	9641T.267	E.E.C. 410	M.C.C.W.	H40/30R		15. 4.48	30. 5.65

Fleet No.	Reg. No.	Chassis Make and type	No.	Elec. Equip. and motor	Builder	Body Seating	Date deliv.	Into serv.	Wdn
490	LTN490	B.U.T. 9641T	9641T.268	E.E.C. 410	M.C.C.W.	H40/30R		15. 4.48	30. 5.65
491	LTN491	B.U.T. 9641T	9641T.269	E.E.C. 410	M.C.C.W.	H40/30R		15. 4.48	30. 5.65
492	LTN492	B.U.T. 9641T	9641T.270	E.E.C. 410	M.C.C.W.	H40/30R		15. 4.48	30. 5.65
493	LTN493	B.U.T. 9641T	9641T.271	E.E.C. 410	M.C.C.W.	H40/30R		15. 4.48	30. 5.65
494	LTN494	B.U.T. 9641T	9641T.272	E.E.C. 410	M.C.C.W.	H40/30R		15. 4.48	30. 5.65
495	LTN495	B.U.T. 9641T	9641T.273	E.E.C. 410	M.C.C.W.	H40/30R		15. 4.48	30.10.64
496	LTN496	B.U.T. 9641T	9641T.274	E.E.C. 410	M.C.C.W.	H40/30R		15. 4.48	30. 5.65
497	LTN497	B.U.T. 9641T	9641T.275	E.E.C. 410	M.C.C.W.	H40/30R		15. 4.48	30. 5.65
498	LTN498	B.U.T. 9641T	9641T.276	E.E.C. 410	M.C.C.W.	H40/30R		15. 4.48	30. 5.65
499	LTN499	Sunbeam S7	70001	MV 210AG20	NCB	H39/31R		1. 7.48	30.10.64
500	LTN500	Sunbeam S7	70002	MV 210AG20	NCB	H39/31R		1. 9.48	30.10.64
501	LTN501	Sunbeam S7	70003	MV 210AG20	NCB	H39/31R		1. 9.48	30. 5.65
502	LTN502	Sunbeam S7	70004	MV 210AG20	NCB	H39/31R		1. 9.48	30. 5.65
503	LTN503	Sunbeam S7	70005	MV 210AG20	NCB	H39/31R		1. 9.48	30. 5.65
504	LTN504	Sunbeam S7	70006	MV 210AG20	NCB	H39/31R		1.11.48	30. 5.65
505	LTN505	Sunbeam S7	70007	MV 210AG20	NCB	H39/31R		1.11.48	30. 5.65
506	LTN506	Sunbeam S7	70008	MV 210AG20	NCB	H39/31R		1.11.48	30.10.64
507	LTN507	Sunbeam S7	70009	MV 210AG20	NCB	H39/31R		1.11.48	30. 5.65
508	LTN508	Sunbeam S7	70010	MV 210AG20	NCB	H39/31R		1.11.48	30. 5.65
509	LTN509	Sunbeam S7	70011	MV 210AG20	NCB	H39/31R		1.11.48	30. 5.65
510	LTN510	Sunbeam S7	70012	MV 210AG20	NCB	H39/31R		1.11.48	30. 5.65
511	LTN511	Sunbeam S7	70013	MV 210AG20	NCB	H39/31R		1.11.48	30. 5.65
512	LTN512	Sunbeam S7	70014	MV 210AG20	NCB	H39/31R		1.11.48	30. 5.65
513	LTN513	Sunbeam S7	70015	MV 210AG20	NCB	H39/31R		1.11.48	30.10.64
514	LTN514	Sunbeam S7	70016	MV 210AG20	NCB	H39/31R		1.11.48	30. 5.65
515	LTN515	Sunbeam S7	70017	MV 210AG20	NCB	H39/31R		1.11.48	30. 5.65
516	LTN516	Sunbeam S7	70018	MV 210AG20	NCB	H39/31R		1.11.48	.63
517	LTN517	Sunbeam S7	70019	MV 210AG20	NCB	H39/31R		1.11.48	30. 5.65
518	LTN518	Sunbeam S7	70020	MV 210AG20	NCB	H39/31R		1.11.48	30. 5.65
519	LTN519	Sunbeam S7	70021	MV 210AG20	NCB	H39/31R		1.11.48	30. 5.65
520	LTN520	Sunbeam S7	70022	MV 210AG20	NCB	H39/31R		1.11.48	30. 5.65

Fleet No.	Reg. No.	Chassis Make and type	No.	Elec. Equip. and motor	Builder	Body Seating	Date deliv.	Into serv.	Wdn
521	LTN521	Sunbeam S7	70023	MV210AG20	NCB	H39/31R		1.11.48	30. 5.65
522	LTN522	Sunbeam S7	70024	MV 210AG20	NCB	H39/31R		1. 1.49	30. 5.65
523	LTN523	Sunbeam S7	70025	MV 210AG20	NCB	H39/31R		1.12.48	1.65
524	LTN524	Sunbeam S7	70026	MV 210AG20	NCB	H39/31R		11.11.48	30. 5.65
525	LTN525	Sunbeam S7	70027	MV 210AG20	NCB	H39/31R		1. 1.49	30. 5.65
526	LTN526	Sunbeam S7	70028	MV 210AG20	NCB	H39/31R		1. 1.49	3.65
527	LTN527	Sunbeam S7	70029	MV 210AG20	NCB	H39/31R		1. 1.49	30. 5.65
528	LTN528	Sunbeam S7	70030	MV 210AG20	NCB	H39/31R		16. 1.49	30. 5.65
529	LTN529	Sunbeam F4	50687	MV 209	NCB	H39/31R		1.12.49	2. 2.64
530	LTN530	Sunbeam F4	50688	MV 209	NCB	H30/26R		1.12.49	30. 5.63
531	LTN531	Sunbeam F4	50689	MV 209	NCB	H30/26R		1. 1.50	2. 2.64
532	LTN532	Sunbeam F4	50690	MV 209	NCB	H30/26R		1. 1.50	2. 2.64
533	LTN533	Sunbeam F4	50691	MV 209	NCB	H30/26R		1. 1.50	2. 2.64
534	LTN534	Sunbeam F4	50692	MV 209	NCB	H30/26R		1. 1.50	2. 2.64
535	LTN535	Sunbeam F4	50693	MV 209	NCB	H30/26R		1. 1.50	30. 5.63
536	LTN536	Sunbeam F4	50694	MV 209	NCB	H30/26R		1. 1.50	2. 2.64
537	LTN537	Sunbeam F4	50695	MV 209	NCB	H30/26R		1. 1.50	2. 2.64
538	LTN538	Sunbeam F4	50696	MV 209	NCB	H30/26R		1. 1.50	2. 2.64
539	LTN539	Sunbeam F4	50697	MV 209	NCB	H30/26R		1. 1.50	2. 2.64
540	LTN540	Sunbeam F4	50698	MV 209	NCB	H30/26R		1. 1.50	2. 2.64
541	LTN541	Sunbeam F4	50699	MV 209	NCB	H30/26R		1. 2.50	30. 5.63
542	LTN542	Sunbeam F4	50700	MV 209	NCB	H30/26R		1. 2.50	30. 5.63
543	LTN543	Sunbeam F4	50701	MV 209	NCB	H30/26R		1. 2.50	30. 5.63
544	LTN544	Sunbeam F4	50702	MV 209	NCB	H30/26R		1. 2.50	2. 2.64
545	LTN545	Sunbeam F4	50703	MV 209	NCB	H30/26R		1. 2.50	30. 5.63
546	LTN546	Sunbeam F4	50704	MV 209	NCB	H30/26R		1. 2.50	2. 2.64
547	LTN547	Sunbeam F4	50705	MV 209	NCB	H30/26R		1. 2.50	30. 5.63
548	LTN548	Sunbeam F4	50706	MV 209	NCB	H30/26R		1. 2.50	2. 2.64
549	LTN549	Sunbeam F4	50707	MV 209	NCB	H30/26R		1. 3.50	2. 2.64
550	LTN550	Sunbeam F4	50708	MV 209	NCB	H30/26R		1. 3.50	2. 2.64
551	LTN551	Sunbeam F4	50709	MV 209	NCB	H30/26R		1. 3.50	2. 2.64

Fleet No.	Reg. No.	Chassis Make and type	No.	Elec. Equip. and motor	Builder	Body Seating	Date deliv.	Into serv.	Wdn
552	LTN552	Sunbeam F4	50710	MV 209	NCB	H30/26R		1. 3.50	30. 5.63
553	LTN553	Sunbeam F4	50711	MV 209	NCB	H30/26R		1. 3.50	30. 5.63
554	LTN554	B.U.T. 9611T	9611T.083	E.E.C. 410	NCB	H30/26R		1. 5.49	2. 2.64
555	LTN555	B.U.T. 9611T	9611T.084	E.E.C. 410	NCB	H30/26R		1. 5.49	2. 2.64
556	LTN556	B.U.T. 9611T	9611T.085	E.E.C. 410	NCB	H30/26R		1. 5.49	2. 2.64
557	LTN557	B.U.T. 9611T	9611T.086	E.E.C. 410	NCB	H30/26R		1. 5.49	2. 2.64
558	LTN558	B.U.T. 9611T	9611T.087	E.E.C. 410	NCB	H30/26R		1. 5.49	2. 2.64
559	LTN559	B.U.T. 9611T	9611T.088	E.E.C. 410	NCB	H30/26R		1. 5.49	2. 2.64
560	LTN560	B.U.T. 9611T	9611T.089	E.E.C. 410	NCB	H30/26R		1. 5.49	2. 2.64
561	LTN561	B.U.T. 9611T	9611T.090	E.E.C. 410	NCB	H30/26R		1. 6.49	2. 2.64
562	LTN562	B.U.T. 9611T	9611T.091	E.E.C. 410	NCB	H30/26R		1. 6.49	2. 2.64
563	LTN563	B.U.T. 9611T	9611T.092	E.E.C. 410	NCB	H30/26R		1. 5.49	2. 2.64
564	LTN564	B.U.T. 9611T	9611T.093	E.E.C. 410	NCB	H30/26R		1. 6.49	2. 2.64
565	LTN565	B.U.T. 9611T	9611T.094	E.E.C. 410	NCB	H30/26R		1. 5.49	2. 2.64
566	LTN566	B.U.T. 9611T	9611T.095	E.E.C. 410	NCB	H30/26R		1. 6.49	2. 2.64
567	LTN567	B.U.T. 9611T	9611T.096	E.E.C. 410	NCB	H30/26R		1. 6.49	2. 2.64
568	LTN568	B.U.T. 9611T	9611T.097	E.E.C. 410	NCB	H30/26R		1. 6.49	2. 2.64
569	LTN569	B.U.T. 9611T	9611T.098	E.E.C. 410	NCB	H30/26R		1. 7.49	2. 2.64
570	LTN570	B.U.T. 9611T	9611T.099	E.E.C. 410	NCB	H30/26R		1. 7.49	2. 2.64
571	LTN571	B.U.T. 9611T	9611T.100	E.E.C. 410	NCB	H30/26R		1. 7.49	2. 2.64
572	LTN572	B.U.T. 9611T	9611T.101	E.E.C. 410	NCB	H30/26R		1. 7.49	2. 2.64
573	LTN573	B.U.T. 9611T	9611T.102	E.E.C. 410	NCB	H30/26R		1. 7.49	2. 2.64
574	LTN574	B.U.T. 9611T	9611T.103	E.E.C. 410	NCB	H30/26R		1. 7.49	2. 2.64
575	LTN575	B.U.T. 9611T	9611T.104	E.E.C. 410	NCB	H30/26R		1. 8.49	2. 2.64
576	LTN576	B.U.T. 9611T	9611T.105	E.E.C. 410	NCB	H30/26R		1. 8.49	2. 2.64
577	LTN577	B.U.T. 9611T	9611T.106	E.E.C. 410	NCB	H30/26R		1. 8.49	2. 2.64
578	LTN578	B.U.T. 9611T	9611T.107	E.E.C. 410	NCB	H30/26R		1. 8.49	2. 2.64
579	NBB579	B.U.T. 9641T	9641T.450	E.E.C. 410	M.C.C.W.	H40/30R		4. 5.50	5.65
580	NBB580	B.U.T. 9641T	9641T.451	E.E.C. 410	M.C.C.W.	H40/30R		1. 6.50	1.10.66
581	NBB581	B.U.T. 9641T	9641T.452	E.E.C. 410	M.C.C.W.	H40/30R		1. 5.50	5.65
582	NBB582	B.U.T. 9641T	9641T.453	E.E.C. 410	M.C.C.W.	H40/30R		4. 5.50	1.10.66

Fleet No.	Reg. No.	Chassis Make and type	No.	Elec. Equip. and motor	Builder	Body Seating	Date deliv.	Into serv.	Wdn
583	NBB583	B.U.T. 9641T	9641T.454	E.E.C. 410	M.C.C.W.	H40/30R		1. 6.50	1.10.66
584	NBB584	B.U.T. 9641T	9641T.455	E.E.C. 410	M.C.C.W.	H40/30R		1. 6.50	5.65
585	NBB585	B.U.T. 9641T	9641T.456	E.E.C. 410	M.C.C.W.	H40/30R		1. 5.50	1.10.66
586	NBB586	B.U.T. 9641T	9641T.457	E.E.C. 410	M.C.C.W.	H40/30R		1. 6.50	1.10.66
587	NBB587	B.U.T. 9641T	9641T.458	E.E.C. 410	M.C.C.W.	H40/30R		1. 6.50	1.10.66
588	NBB588	B.U.T. 9641T	9641T.459	E.E.C. 410	M.C.C.W.	H40/30R		1. 6.50	30. 5.65
589	NBB589	B.U.T. 9641T	9641T.460	E.E.C. 410	M.C.C.W.	H40/30R		1. 7.50	1.10.66
590	NBB590	B.U.T. 9641T	9641T.461	E.E.C. 410	M.C.C.W.	H40/30R		1. 7.50	1.10.66
591	NBB591	B.U.T. 9641T	9641T.462	E.E.C. 410	M.C.C.W.	H40/30R		1. 7.50	6.65
592	NBB592	B.U.T. 9641T	9641T.463	E.E.C. 410	M.C.C.W.	H40/30R		1. 7.50	30. 5.65
593	NBB593	B.U.T. 9641T	9641T.464	E.E.C. 410	M.C.C.W.	H40/30R		1. 7.50	31. 7.66
594	NBB594	B.U.T. 9641T	9641T.465	E.E.C. 410	M.C.C.W.	H40/30R		1. 7.50	1.10.66
595	NBB595	B.U.T. 9641T	9641T.466	E.E.C. 410	M.C.C.W.	H40/30R		1. 7.50	1.10.66
596	NBB596	B.U.T. 9641T	9641T.467	E.E.C. 410	M.C.C.W.	H40/30R		1. 7.50	1.10.66
597	NBB597	B.U.T. 9641T	9641T.468	E.E.C. 410	M.C.C.W.	H40/30R		1. 8.50	1.10.66
598	NBB598	B.U.T. 9641T	9641T.469	E.E.C. 410	M.C.C.W.	H40/30R		1. 8.50	30. 5.65
599	NBB599	B.U.T. 9641T	9641T.470	E.E.C. 410	M.C.C.W.	H40/30R		1. 8.50	1.10.66
600	NBB600	B.U.T. 9641T	9641T.471	E.E.C. 410	M.C.C.W.	H40/30R		1. 8.50	30. 5.65
601	NBB601	B.U.T. 9641T	9641T.472	E.E.C. 410	M.C.C.W.	H40/30R		1. 8.50	6.65
602	NBB602	B.U.T. 9641T	9641T.473	E.E.C. 410	M.C.C.W.	H40/30R		1. 8.50	6.65
603	NBB603	B.U.T. 9641T	9641T.474	E.E.C. 410	M.C.C.W.	H40/30R		1. 8.50	1.10.66
604	NBB604	B.U.T. 9641T	9641T.475	E.E.C. 410	M.C.C.W.	H40/30R		1. 8.50	1.10.66
605	NBB605	B.U.T. 9641T	9641T.476	E.E.C. 410	M.C.C.W.	H40/30R		1. 9.50	1.10.66
606	NBB606	B.U.T. 9641T	9641T.477	E.E.C. 410	M.C.C.W.	H40/30R		1. 9.50	1.10.66
607	NBB607	B.U.T. 9641T	9641T.478	E.E.C. 410	M.C.C.W.	H40/30R		1. 9.50	1.10.66
608	NBB608	B.U.T. 9641T	9641T.479	E.E.C. 410	M.C.C.W.	H40/30R		1. 9.50	30. 5.65
609	NBB609	B.U.T. 9641T	9641T.480	E.E.C. 410	M.C.C.W.	H40/30R		1. 9.50	1.10.66
610	NBB610	B.U.T. 9641T	9641T.481	E.E.C. 410	M.C.C.W.	H40/30R		1. 9.50	30. 5.65
611	NBB611	B.U.T. 9641T	9641T.482	E.E.C. 410	M.C.C.W.	H40/30R		1. 9.50	1.10.66
612	NBB612	B.U.T. 9641T	9641T.483	E.E.C. 410	M.C.C.W.	H40/30R		1. 9.50	1.10.66
613	NBB613	B.U.T. 9641T	9641T.484	E.E.C. 410	M.C.C.W.	H40/30R		1. 9.50	1.10.66

Fleet No.	Reg. No.	Chassis Make and type	No.	Elec. Equip. and motor	Builder	Body Seating	Date deliv.	Into serv.	Wdn
614	NBB614	B.U.T. 9641T	9641T.485	E.E.C. 410	M.C.C.W.	H40/30R		1. 9.50	1.10.66
615	NBB615	B.U.T. 9641T	9641T.486	E.E.C. 410	M.C.C.W.	H40/30R		1.10.50	10.65
616	NBB616	B.U.T. 9641T	9641T.487	E.E.C. 410	M.C.C.W.	H40/30R		1.10.50	6.65
617	NBB617	B.U.T. 9641T	9641T.488	E.E.C. 410	M.C.C.W.	H40/30R		1.10.50	1.10.66
618	NBB618	B.U.T. 9641T	9641T.489	E.E.C. 410	M.C.C.W.	H40/30R		1.i0.50	1.10.66
619	NBB619	B.U.T. 9641T	9641T.490	E.E.C. 410	M.C.C.W.	H40/30R		1.10.50	1.10.66
620	NBB620	B.U.T. 9641T	9641T.491	E.E.C. 410	M.C.C.W.	H40/30R		1.10.50	1.10.66
621	NBB621	B.U.T. 9641T	9641T.492	E.E.C. 410	M.C.C.W.	H40/30R		1.10.50	31. 8.66
622	NBB622	B.U.T. 9641T	9641T.493	E.E.C. 410	M.C.C.W.	H40/30R		1.11.50	1.10.66
623	NBB623	B.U.T. 9641T	9641T.494	E.E.C. 410	M.C.C.W.	H40/30R		1.10.50	1.10.66
624	NBB624	B.U.T. 9641T	9641T.495	E.E.C. 410	M.C.C.W.	H40/30R		1.11.50	1.10.66
625	NBB625	B.U.T. 9641T	9641T.496	E.E.C. 410	M.C.C.W.	H40/30R		1.11.50	1.10.66
626	NBB626	B.U.T. 9641T	9641T.497	E.E.C. 410	M.C.C.W.	H40/30R		1.11.50	1.10.66
627	NBB627	B.U.T. 9641T	9641T.498	E.E.C. 410	M.C.C.W.	H40/30R		1.11.50	5.65
628	NBB628	B.U.T. 9641T	9641T.499	E.E.C. 410	M.C.C.W.	H40/30R		1.11.50	1.10.66

(a) These vehicles were fitted with B.T-H. control equipment and E.E.C. motors.
(b) Nos. 6, 8, 9, 0 did not enter passenger carrying service.

NOTES
Nos. 1-5, 7, 10-142 were renumbered in 1946 by the addition of 300 to their existing fleet numbers, becoming 301-5, 307, 310-442.

Nos. 10-19 had regenerative motors, believed to be type 408.

Nos. 20-43, 47-56, 85-98 and 112-124 had MV or B.T-H. motors believed to have been type 202 (non-regenerative) or 206 (regenerative).

44-46, 57-84, 99-109 had non-regenerative motors, believed to be type 409.

The seating capacity 'code' is made up as follows: First letter(s)—H: highbridge layout (centre gangway in upper saloon). Prefix U indicates wartime 'utility' specification. Figures indicate number of seats in upper and lower saloons respectively. Final letter gives number and position of passenger doors — R: rear open platform. D: dual entrance/exit doors.

164

II—VEHICLES DEMONSTRATED TO THE UNDERTAKING

Fleet No.	Reg. No.	Chassis Make and type	No.	Elec. Equip. and motor	Body Builder	Seating	Date deliv.	Into serv.	Out of serv.
58	CNE474	Crossley TDD6	92301	MV206	Crossley	H38/30R	30. 6.36	6. 7.36	14. 7.36
		(Returned to Crossley Motors Ltd., 15.7.36)							
—	CWK67	Daimler CTM4	20001	MV	Willowbrook	H28/24R	13. 9.37	17. 9.37	17.11.37
		(Returned to Daimler Commercial Vehicles Ltd, 18.11.37)							

III—WARTIME LOANS OF TROLLEYBUSES TO THE UNDERTAKING

Fleet No.	Reg No.	Chassis Make and type	No.	Elec. Equip. and motor	Body Builder	Seating	Date deliv.	Into serv.	Out of serv.	Date left Newcastle
From BRIGHTON CORPORATION TRANSPORT										
11	FUF11	A.E.C. 661T	661T.303	C.P.A.W.(a)	Weymann (M1927)	H28/26R	8. 5.42	8. 6.42	25. 9.42	9.10.42(b)
12	FUF12	A.E.C. 661T	661T.304	C.P.A.W.(a)	Weymann (M1928)	H28/26R	15. 5.42	8. 6.42	13.10.42	23.10.42(b)
13	FUF13	A.E.C. 661T	661T.305	C.P.A.W.(a)	Weymann (M1929)	H28/26R	20. 5.42	8. 6.42	30. 9.42	10.10.42(b)
14	FUF14	A.E.C. 661T	661T.306	C.P.A.W.(a)	Weymann (M1930)	H28/26R	31. 5.42	4. 9.42	13.10.42	20.10.42(b)
15	FUF15	A.E.C. 661T	661T.307	C.P.A.W.(a)	Weymann (M1931)	H28/26R	7. 6.42	4. 9.42	30. 9.42	4.10.42(b)

(a) Crompton Parkinson motor type C400 B2; Allen West control equipment
(b) returned to Brighton Corporation Transport

Fleet No.	Reg No.	Chassis Make and type	No.	Elec. Equip. and motor	Body Builder	Seating	Date deliv.	Into serv.	Out of serv.	Date left Newcastle
From BOURNEMOUTH CORPORATION TRANSPORT										
72	AEL400	Sunbeam MS2	12031S	B.T-H. 201	Park Royal	H31/25D	11. 9.42	19.10.42	23. 5.45	29. 5.45(a)
73	AEL401	Sunbeam MS2	12032S	B.T-H. 201	Park Royal	H31/25D	12. 9.42	19.10.42	30. 4.45	30. 4.45(a)
77	AEL405	Sunbeam MS2	12037S	B.T-H. 201	Park Royal	H31/25D	17. 9.42	19.10.42	5. 2.43	25.10.43(a)
78	AEL406	Sunbeam MS2	12030S	B.T-H. 201	E.E.C.	H31/25D	28. 9.42	2.12.42	26. 2.43	2. 3.43(b)
79	AEL407	Sunbeam MS2	12033S	B.T-H. 201	E.E.C.	H31/25D	22. 9.42	19.10.42	26. 2.43	2. 3.43(b)
82	AEL410	Sunbeam MS2	12040S	B.T-H. 201	E.E.C.	H31/25D	3.10.42	4.12.42	12. 5.45	30. 4.45(a)
87	ALJ63	Sunbeam MS2	12050S	B.T-H. 201	Park Royal	H31/25D	27. 9.42	19.10.42	12. 5.45	12. 5.45(a)
123	ALJ997	Sunbeam MS2	12092T	B.T-H. 201	Park Royal (3660)	H31/25D	6.10.42	2.12.42	22. 1.43	1. 3.43(b)
145	BEL830	Sunbeam MS2	12114T	B.T-H. 201	Park Royal (3682)	H31/25D	9.10.42	1.12.42	30. 4.45	5. 5.45(a)

(a) Returned to Bournemouth Corporation Transport
(b) Transferred to South Shields Corporation Transport

DISPOSALS OF TROLLEYBUS ROLLING STOCK

Fleet No.	Reg. No.	Disposal	Date	Fleet No.	Reg. No.	Disposal	Date
310	BVK800	Cohen	28. 6.49	341	DTN141	Tremble	25.11.50
311	BVK801	Tremble	31.10.50	342	DTN142	Tremble	25.11.50
312	BVK802	Cohen	28. 6.49	343	DTN143	Cohen	28. 6.49
313	BVK803	Tremble	31.10.50	344	DTN144	Cohen	28. 6.49
314	BVK804	Cohen	28. 6.49	345	DTN145	Cohen	28. 6.49
315	BVK805	Cohen	28. 6.49	346	DTN146	Cohen	26. 7.49
316	BVK806	Cohen	28. 6.49	347	ETN47	Cohen	28. 6.49
317	BVK807	Cohen	28. 6.49	348	ETN48	Cohen	26. 7.49
318	BVK808	Tremble	17. 2.50	349	ETN49	Cohen	26. 7.49
319	BVK809	Cohen	28. 6.49	350	ETN50	Cohen	26. 7.49
320	BVK810	Cohen	28. 6.49	351	ETN51	Cohen	26. 7.49
321	BVK811	Tremble	31.10.50	352	ETN52	Tremble	17. 2.50
322	BVK812	Cohen	26. 7.49	353	ETN53	Tremble	17. 2.50
323	BVK813	Tremble	17. 2.50	354	ETN54	Tremble	31.10.50
324	BVK814	Tremble	17. 2.50	355	ETN55	Tremble	25. 7.50
325	BVK815	Tremble	17. 2.50	356	ETN56	Douglas	20. 3.56
326	BVK816	Cohen	28. 6.49	357	ETN57	Cohen	28. 6.49
327	BVK817	Tremble	17. 2.50	358	ETN58	Cohen	26. 7.49
328	BVK818	Tremble	17. 2.50	359	ETN59	Cohen	26. 7.49
329	BVK819	Tremble	31.10.50	360	ETN60	Cohen	28. 6.49
330	BVK820	Cohen	28. 8.49	361	ETN61	Cohen	26. 7.49
331	BVK821	Cohen	28. 8.49	362	ETN62	Cohen	26. 7.49
332	BVK822	Cohen	28. 8.49	363	ETN63	Cohen	26. 7.49
333	BVK823	Cohen	28. 8.49	364	ETN64	Cohen	26. 7.49
334	BVK824	Cohen	28. 8.49	365	ETN65	Cohen	26. 7.49
335	BVK825	Cohen	28. 8.49	366	ETN66	Cohen	26. 7.49
336	BVK826	Cohen	28. 8.49	367	ETN67	Tremble	25. 4.50
337	BVK827	Cohen	28. 8.49	368	ETN68	Cohen	28. 6.49
338	BVK828	Cohen	28. 8.49	369	ETN69	Tremble	25. 4.50
339	BVK829	Cohen	28. 8.49	370	ETN70	Tremble	17. 2.50
340	CVK52	Tremble	25.11.50	371	ETN71	Tremble	25. 4.50

Fleet No.	Reg. No.	Disposal	Date
372	ETN72	Tremble	25. 7.50
373	ETN73	Tremble	25. 7.50
374	ETN74	Tremble	25. 7.50
375	ETN75	Tremble	25. 7.50
376	ETN76	Cohen	28. 6.49
377	ETN77	Tremble	25. 7.50
378	FBB78	Cohen	28. 6.49
379	FVK79	Tremble	31.10.50
380	FVK80	Richardson	31.10.50
381	FVK81	Richardson	31.10.50
382	FVK82	Tremble	7.50
383	FVK83	Tremble	25. 7.50
384	FVK84	Tremble	25. 7.50
385	FVK85	Tremble	25. 7.50
386	FVK86	Tremble	17. 2.50
387	FVK87	Tremble	17. 2.50
388	FVK88	Tremble	17. 2.50
389	FVK89	Tremble	17. 2.50
390	FVK90	Tremble	25. 7.50
391	FVK91	Tremble	25. 4.50
392	FVK92	Cohen	28. 6.49
393	FVK93	Cohen	28. 6.49
394	FVK94	Tremble	31.10.50
395	FVK95	Tremble	17. 2.50
396	FVK96	Tremble	25. 7.50
397	FVK97	Tremble	31.10.50
398	FVK98	Tremble	31.10.50
399	FVK99	Tremble	17. 2.50
400	FVK100	Cohen	28. 6.49
401	FVK101	Tremble	17. 2.50
402	FVK102	Tremble	17. 2.50
403	FVK103	Tremble	17. 2.50
404	FVK104	Cohen	28. 6.49
405	FVK105	Tremble	17. 2.50
406	FVK106	Tremble	17. 2.50
407	FVK107	Tremble	25. 4.50
408	FVK108	Cohen	28. 6.49
409	FVK109	Cohen	28. 6.49
412	DHP112	Tremble	31.10.50
413	HVK113	Tremble	31.10.50
414	HVK114	Richardson	31.10.50 (a)
415	HVK115	Tremble	25. 7.50
416	HVK116	Richardson	31.10.50
417	HVK117	Richardson	31.10.50
418	HVK118	Tremble	25. 7.50
419	HVK119	Tremble	31.10.50
420	HVK120	Tremble	31.10.50
421	HVK121	Tremble	31.10.50
422	HVK122	Tremble	31.10.50
423	HVK123	Tremble	31.10.50
424	HVK124	Tremble	31.10.50
301	KW9461	Ashman	25. 2.49 (b)
302	KW9463	Tremble	18. 3.49 (b)
303	KW9453	Tremble	18. 3.49 (b)
304	KW9454	Hope	?
305	KW9455	Tremble	18. 3.49 (b)
(6)	KW6063	Tremble	18. 3.49
307	KW6060	Tremble	18. 3.49 (b)
(8)	KW6656	Shaw	25. 4.45
(9)	KW6655	Shaw	25. 4.45
(0)	KW9464	Tremble	18. 3.49 (b)
425	JTN955	Autowreckers	27.10.53

Fleet No.	Reg. No.	Disposal	Date	Fleet No.	Reg. No.	Disposal	Date
426	JTN956	Autowreckers	27.10.53	456	LBB56	Dunston	4.63
427	JTN957	Autowreckers	27.10.53	457	LBB57	Dunston	4.63
428	JTN958	Autowreckers	27.10.53	458	LBB58	Dunsmore	6.64
429	JTN959	Autowreckers	27.10.53	459	LBB59	Dunsmore	6.64
430	JTN960	Autowreckers	27.10.53	460	LBB60	Dunston	4.63
431	JTN961	Douglas	20. 3.56	461	LBB61	Dunsmore	6.64
432	JTN962	Douglas	20. 3.56	462	LBB62	Dunsmore	6.64
433	JTN963	Douglas	20. 3.56	463	LBB63	Dunsmore	6.64
434	JTN964	Douglas	20. 3.56	464	LBB64	Dunsmore	6.64
435	JTN965	Douglas	20. 3.56	465	LBB65	Dunsmore	6.64
436	JTN966	Douglas	20. 3.56	466	LBB66	Dunsmore	6.64
437	JVK277	Autowreckers	27.10.53	467	LBB67	Dunsmore	6.64
438	JVK278	Autowreckers	27.10.53	468	LBB68	Dunsmore	6.64
439	JVK279	Autowreckers	27.10.53	469	LBB69	Dunston	4.63
440	JVK280	Autowreckers	27.10.53	470	LBB70	Dunsmore	6.64
441	JVK281	Autowreckers	27.10.53	471	LBB71	Dunsmore	6.64
442	JVK282	Autowreckers	27.10.53	472	LBB72	Dunsmore	6.64
443	LBB43	Dunsmore	6.64	473	LBB73	Dunston	4.63
444	LBB44	Dunston	4.63	474	LBB74	Dunsmore	6.64
445	LBB45	Dunston	4.63	475	LBB75	Dunsmore	6.64
446	LBB46	Dunston	4.63	476	LBB76	Dunsmore	6.64
447	LBB47	Dunston	4.63	477	LBB77	Dunsmore	6.64
448	LBB48	Breaker, Laisterdyke Bradford	7.63	478	LBB78	Dunston	4.63
449	LBB49	Dunstone	4.63	479	LTN479	Colbro	7.65
450	LBB50	Dunsmore	6.64	480	LTN480	Colbro	7.65
451	LBB51	Dunston	4.63	481	LTN481	Colbro	7.65
452	LBB52	Dunsmore	6.64	482	LTN482	Colbro	7.65
453	LBB53	Dunsmore	6.64	483	LTN483	Colbro	7.65
454	LBB54	Dunston	4.63	484	LTN484	Colbro	7.65
455	LBB55	Dunsmore	6.64	485	LTN485	Colbro	7.65
				486	LTN486	Colbro	7.65

Fleet No.	Reg. No.	Disposal	Date	Fleet No.	Reg. No.	Disposal	Date
487	LTN487	Colbro	7.65	514	LTN514	Colbro	7.65
488	LTN488	Colbro	7.65	515	LTN515	Colbro	7.65
489	LTN489	Colbro	7.65	516	LTN516	Colbro	7.65
490	LTN490	Colbro	7.65	517	LTN517	Colbro	7.65
491	LTN491	Colbro	7.65	518	LTN518	Colbro	7.65
492	LTN492	Colbro	7.65	519	LTN519	Colbro	7.65
493	LTN493	Colbro	7.65	520	LTN520	Colbro	7.65
494	LTN494	Colbro	7.65	521	LTN521	Colbro	7.65
495	LTN495	Colbro	7.65	522	LTN522	Colbro	7.65
496	LTN496	Colbro	7.65	523	LTN523	Colbro	7.65
497	LTN497	Colbro	7.65	524	LTN524	Colbro	7.65
498	LTN498	Colbro	7.65	525	LTN525	Colbro	7.65
499	LTN499	Colbro	7.65	526	LTN526	Colbro	7.65
500	LTN500	Colbro	7.65	527	LTN527	Colbro	7.65
501	LTN501	Retained for preservation; then to Laing Art Gallery, Newcastle upon Tyne. (On display at North East Open Air Industrial Museum, Beamish, Co. Durham.)		528	LTN528	Colbro	7.65
				529	LTN529	Dunsmore	6.64
				530	LTN530	Dunsmore	6.64
				531	LTN531	Dunsmore	6.64
				532	LTN532	Dunsmore	6.64
502	LTN502	Colbro	7.65	533	LTN533	Dunsmore	6.64
503	LTN503	Colbro	7.65	534	LTN534	Dunsmore	6.64
504	LTN504	Colbro	7.65	535	LTN535	Dunsmore	6.64
505	LTN505	Colbro	7.65	536	LTN536	Dunsmore	6.64
506	LTN506	Colbro	7.65	537	LTN537	Dunsmore	6.64
507	LTN507	Colbro	7.65	538	LTN538	Dunsmore	6.64
508	LTN508	Colbro	7.65	539	LTN539	Dunsmore	6.64
509	LTN509	Colbro	7.65	540	LTN540	Dunsmore	6.64
510	LTN510	Colbro	7.65	541	LTN541	Dunsmore	6.64
511	LTN511	Colbro	7.65	542	LTN542	Dunsmore	6.64
512	LTN512	Colbro	7.65	543	LTN543	Dunsmore	6.64 (c)
513	LTN513	Colbro	7.65	544	LTN544	Dunsmore	6.64

Fleet No.	Reg. No.	Disposal	Date
545	LTN545	Dunsmore	6.64 (c)
546	LTN546	Dunsmore	6.64
547	LTN547	Dunsmore	6.64
548	LTN548	Dunsmore	6.64
549	LTN549	Dunsmore	6.64
550	LTN550	Dunsmore	6.64
551	LTN551	Dunsmore	6.64
552	LTN552	Dunsmore	6.64
553	LTN553	Dunsmore	6.64
554	LTN554	Dunsmore	6.64
555	LTN555	Dunsmore	6.64
556	LTN556	Dunsmore	6.64
557	LTN557	Dunsmore	6.64
558	LTN558	Dunsmore	6.64
559	LTN559	Dunsmore	6.64
560	LTN560	Dunsmore	6.64
561	LTN561	Dunsmore	6.64
562	LTN562	Dunsmore	6.64
563	LTN563	Dunsmore	6.64
564	LTN564	Dunsmore	6.64
565	LTN565	Dunsmore	6.64
566	LTN566	Dunsmore	6.64
567	LTN567	Dunsmore	6.64
568	LTN568	Dunsmore	6.64
569	LTN569	Dunsmore	6.64
570	LTN570	Dunsmore	6.64
571	LTN571	Dunsmore	6.64
572	LTN572	Dunsmore	6.64
573	LTN573	Dunsmore	6.64
574	LTN574	Dunsmore	6.64
575	LTN575	Dunsmore	6.64
576	LTN576	Dunsmore	6.64
577	LTN577	Dunsmore	6.64
578	LTN578	Dunsmore	6.64
579	NBB579	Colbro	7.65
580	NBB580	Autospares	2.67
581	NBB581	Colbro	7.65
582	NBB582	Autospares	2.67
583	NBB583	Autospares	2.67
584	NBB584	Colbro	7.65
585	NBB585	Autospares	2.67
586	NBB586	Autospares	2.67
587	NBB587	Autospares	2.67
588	NBB588	Colbro	7.65
589	NBB589	Autospares	2.67
590	NBB590	Autospares	2.67
591	NBB591	Autospares	.67
592	NBB592	Colbro	7.65
593	NBB593	Autospares	.67
594	NBB594	Autospares	2.67
595	NBB595	Autospares	2.67
596	NBB596	Autospares	2.67
597	NBB597	Autospares	2.67
598	NBB598	Colbro	7.65
599	NBB599	Autospares	2.67
600	NBB600	Colbro	7.65
601	NBB601	Colbro	7.65
602	NBB602	Colbro	7.65
603	NBB603	Autospares	2.67
604	NBB604	Autospares	2.67
605	NBB605	Autospares	2.67
606	NBB606	Autospares	2.67

Fleet No.	Reg. No.	Disposal	Date
607	NBB607	Autospares	2.67
608	NBB608	Colbro	7.65
609	NBB609	Autospares	2.67
610	NBB610	Colbro	7.65
611	NBB611	Autospares	2.67
612	NBB612	Autospares	2.67
613	NBB613	Autospares	2.67
614	NBB614	Autospares	2.67
615	NBB615	Autospares	2.67
616	NBB616	Autospares	2.67
617	NBB617	Autospares	2.67

Fleet No.	Reg. No.	Disposal	Date
618	NBB618	Autospares	2.67
619	NBB619	Autospares	2.67
620	NBB620	Autospares	2.67
621	NBB621	Autospares	2.67
622	NBB622	Autospares	12.66
623	NBB623	Autospares	2.67
624	NBB624	Autospares	2.67
625	NBB625	Autospares	2.67
626	NBB626	Autospares	2.67
627	NBB627	Autospares	2.67
628	NBB628	Autospares 2.67 then to LTPS. 2.67	

NOTES: (a) In yard in Dudley Road, Oldbury, 7.58.
(b) One of these vehicles survived to become a caravan at Low Hauxley on the Northumberland coast (date unknown).
(c) Also reported as Unknown breaker, Laisterdyke, Bradford (see also No. 448).

The full titles of purchasers are as follows:—

Ashman   E. G. Ashman (breaker) unknown location.
Autospares   Autospares (breakers) Bingley, Yorkshire.
Autowreckers   Autowreckers (breakers) Dunston, Gateshead, Co. Durham.
Cohen   G. Cohen (breaker) Newcastle.
Colbro   Colbro (breaker) Rothwell, Yorkshire.
Douglas   I. Douglas (breaker) Newcastle.
Dunsmore   R. W. Dunsmore (breaker) Larkhall, Lanarks, Scotland.
Dunston   Dunston Autospares (breaker) Dunston, Gateshead, Co. Durham.
Hope   M. A. Hope (breaker) Bridge End, Hexham, Northumberland.
LTPS   London Trolleybus Preservation Society, Carlton Colville, Lowestoft, Suffolk.
Richardson   T. J. Richardson (breaker) Oldbury, Staffs.
Shaw   J. Shaw (breaker) West Hartlepool, Co. Durham.
Tremble   A. Tremble (breaker) Benton, Newcastle.

171

ANCILLARY VEHICLES

This revised Table now additionally gives information on earlier vehicles in the Ancilliary fleet. Certain vehicles were not exclusively used in connection with the trolleybus system.

Fleet No.	Reg. No.	Chassis Make	Use	Allocation	Into Serv.	Wdn.	Notes
901	JL6287	Bedford 3-ton	Haulage	Works	1.3.46	?	—
902	JX7971	Austin 3-ton	Haulage	Works	1.3.46	?	—
903	436ATN	Landrover (Petrol)	Runabout	Works	12.56	c.69	Ran with trailers.
904	907ETN	Landrover (Diesel)	Runabout	Works	9.58	c.69	Ran with trailers.
906	MBB869	Leyland Lynx	Haulage	Works	7.9.48	?	—
907	MBB870	Leyland Lynx	Haulage	—	7.9.48	?	—
908	MTN201	Leyland Lynx	Haulage	—	1.11.48	?	—
909	MTN202	Leyland Lynx	Haulage	—	1.11.48	?	—
910	UP6013	Leyland Hippo	Breakdown	Works	8.31	1.69	} Cranes to be used for recovery only (police orders) 911 was ex-W.D.
911	LVK661	A.E.C. Matador	Breakdown	Works	3.48	12.56	
912	LVK269	Foden 3-axle	Breakdown	Works	1.48	4.57	
918	TN1789	A.E.C. 411	Snow Plough	—	5.11.37	16.10.48	
919	TN1800	A.E.C. 411	Snow Plough	—	5.11.37	10.8.48	
951	ATN447	Herbert Morris	S.P. Crane	—	1.2.47	?	Used for overhead removals.
952	GXR213	Fordson	Wagon	Overhead	1.1.47	?	
(new 952?)	880 EBB	Thames Trader	Wagon	Works	8.58	c.70	
953	LVK662	Karrier CK3	Tower Wagon	Overhead	1.3.48	9.66	
954	TN1051	A.E.C. 411	Tower Wagon	Overhead	28.5.35	?	
955	TN1798	A.E.C. 411	Tower Wagon	Overhead	1.9.35	?	
956	TN1799	A.E.C. 411	Tower Wagon	Overhead	4.10.35	?	
957	TN1804	A.E.C. 411	Tower Wagon	Overhead	1.10.38	?	
958	TN1794	A.E.C. 411	Tower Wagon	Overhead	28.1.35	?	
960	NTN560	Karrier CK3	Tower Wagon	Overhead	11.49	10.66	
961	NTN561	Karrier CK3	Tower Wagon	Overhead	2.50	10.66	Power platform derelict Byker 5.72.
962	NTN562	Karrier CK3	Tower Wagon	Overhead	11.49	'64	Transferred to lighting '64.
963	NTN563	Karrier CK3	Tower Wagon	Overhead	11.49	'65	Transferred to lighting '65.
964	NTN564	Karrier CK3	Tower Wagon	Overhead	3.50	10.66	Transferred to lighting 10.66.
966	VK7088	Morris	Tower Wagon	Overhead	1.6.32	1.12.49	Tremble.
967	VK7089	Morris	Tower Wagon	Overhead	1.7.32	1.12.49	Tremble.
968	LTN80	Karrier CK3	Tower Wagon	Overhead	1.8.47	?	
969	TN1797	A.E.C. 411	Tower Wagon	Overhead	?	?	
970	TN12802	A.E.C. 411	Tower Wagon	Overhead	10.9.37	?	

The following vehicles were in the same livery and number series but were never in fact used by Newcastle Corporation Transport:

Fleet No.	Reg. No.	Chassis Make	Use	Allocation	Into Serv.	Wdn.	Notes
971	NTN371	Karrier CK3	Tower Wagon	Lighting	11.49	5.70	
972	NTN372	Karrier CK3	Tower Wagon	Lighting	11.49	6.67	
973	NTN373	Karrier CK3	Tower Wagon	Lighting	11.49	3.71	
976	391EVK	Karrier	Gully Emptier	Lighting	11.58	c.1970	Derelict at Byker until 1985.
977	GVK881	Karrier	Gully Emptier	Lighting	1.39	10.61	

BUT 9641T No. 606 being put through Newcastle Transport's unique trolleybus washer installed at Byker Depot in the early 1950s. The washer is thought to be the only one of its kind to be used in the U.K.

Tyne & Wear P.T.E.

A largely unnoticed side of a trolleybus system to the layman in the power distribution network. This section box, complete with City coat-of-arms, was still in situ at the north side of West Road at its junction with Two Ball Lonnen when photographed on 3rd September, 1972. In trolleybus days, feeder cables down the side of the traction pole would have connected it to the overhead lines.   Late D. Hanson

173

Coronation Year, 1953; the coronation of Queen Elizabeth II led to the decoration of four Newcastle Transport buses. One of them, BUT 9641T No. 596, spray painted gold and adorned with shields etc., poses at the Central Station terminus of service 31.

Newcastle Chronicle & Journal

The scene near Delaval Road, Benwell, on Friday, 13th February, 1959, after No. 612 had overturned following a collision with a traction pole. This vehicle was later rebuilt and returned to service.

Newcastle Chronicle & Journal

The tower of Benwell Church looms through the mist as No. 614 approaches the eastbound stop at Nichol Street reverser, Adelaide Terrace, Benwell on service 33A to Osborne Road, Jesmond.   A. N. Other

No. 604 is here seen westbound, crossing Byker Bridge on service 35A to Brighton Grove. The elaborately stayed overhead on the bridge is clearly seen in this late 1950's view.
                                                                                            R. F. Mack

New Bridge Street, beside St. Dominic's Priory, is the location for this photograph. No. 607 is about to pass under the junction of the Melbourne Street wires, closely followed by Sunbeam F4 No. 541. The stone setts in which the Melbourne Street tram tracks were let are visible under the BUT 6-wheeler. R. F. Mack

Three BUT 9641T 3-axle trolleybuses are seen inside Newcastle Transport's largest depot at Byker in the City's east end. A. N. Other

Stanhope Street, Arthurs Hill, in the City's west end saw trolleybuses from 1937 to the end in October 1966. No. 609 is seen eastbound in Stanhope Street on Sunday 1st September 1966.   N. Hanson

Byker Depot yard in May 1964 sees Sunbeam S7 511 being dewired. Although their bodywork was in poorer condition, these vehicles were retained in service after February 1964 in preference to the NCB-bodied 2-axle trolleys, which were withdrawn.   T. Steele

September 1964 sees BUT 3-axle 604 about to reverse at Wallsend Boundary. In the foreground, workmen are lifting Tyneside Tramways and Tramroads Company's track, buried unused for $34\frac{1}{2}$ years.   T. Steele

Journey to the scaffold: an NCB-bodied 4-wheeler about to depart from Byker Depot under tow to Dunsmore breakers, Larkhall, Lanarkshire. 23rd May 1964.   T. Steele

The condemned men line up for execution: the scene at Byker Depot, 23rd May 1964, as Sunbeam and BUT 2-axle trolleybuses are prepared for departure. Some already have towbars attached.   T. Steele

Fifteen condemned 2-axle trolleybuses seemingly huddle together for protection at Byker Depot, 22nd May 1964, after withdrawal. Front row, left to right, are 549, 551, 529, 537, and 532. Fleet names are painted out.   T. Steele

179

A resplendent preserved No. 628 at the East Anglia Transport Museum, Carlton Colville, Lowestoft. Summer 1976.   T. P. Canneaux

By contrast, the preserved Sunbeam S7 No. 501, is still undergoing extensive restoration at Beamish Open Air Museum in County Durham. In this 1979 view it is seen emerging from the small tram depot.   T. P. Canneaux

LIVERIES AND VEHICLE TYPES

With the introduction of trolleybuses in 1935, these vehicles were given their own distinctive livery. Trams had been predominantly maroon and white with yellow rocker panels. Motorbuses had always been blue and were thus known as 'The Blue Buses', a term that was used officially. The yellow rocker panels of the trams prompted the idea of using yellow as the main colour for the new trolley-buses. Vehicles were relieved with cream window surrounds and carried three chocolate bands, one below both upper and lower deck windows, and one extending from the top of the lower-deck windows to upper-deck floor level. The yellow panels were lined out in green. Fleet numbers were originally positioned on the rear lower panel only but in 1938 they were repositioned on the rear waist panel. The legend 'Newcastle Corporation Transport' was carried in gold lettering on the chocolate band under the lower deck side windows.

Internally, window surrounds were of polished wood, with black plastic-covered stanchions and rails, blue moquette seats on the lower-deck and blue leather seats on the upper-deck.

During the war, the livery was modified by painting roofs grey instead of yellow; later, repaints in an all-over grey livery became necessary and lettering was in yellow. The identity of vehicles painted grey remains unknown.

Immediately after the war, in 1946, and possibly at the time the trolleybus fleet was renumbered by the addition of 300 to existing fleet numbers, a new livery was introduced. The yellow became cadmium yellow and remained the dominant colour. It was relieved with cream window surrounds and roof and the bands became maroon. Wings and guard rails also became maroon, having previously been black. Black fleet numbers in Gill-Sans style were applied to the front dash panel, lower-deck side panels just aft of the front bulkhead, and rear lower panel, and a London Transport-style fleet-name was applied to the side panels below the lower-deck windows, incorporating the City coat-of-arms.

Internally, lower panels were red and ceilings cream, with bauxite floors, and stanchions and grab rails were usually black (one or two batches were white). Seats were covered in red leather.

About the early nineteen fifties, the front dash-panel fleet number position was abandoned.

The following list of rolling stock types gives, as far as possible, full details of each class of vehicle. Where question marks appear, readers are invited to fill in details if they are in possession of them, and to communicate such details to the publishers.

10—14 (BVK 800-804)   New 1935
(Renumbered 310—314 in 1946)
Chassis: Associated Equipment Company Ltd. 664T (three-axle)
Wheelbase: 18ft. 7 5/16ins.
Motor: English Electric type ? (80 n.h.p.)
Electrical Equipment: English Electric Co. Ltd.
Brakes: Regenerative and rheostatic both on the power pedal. In addition, they
    had air brakes.
Body: English Electric Co. Ltd. H33/27D
Length: 30ft. 0ins.   **Width:** 7ft. 6ins.
U.W.: 9 tons 2 cwt. 0 qtr.

The chassis of these vehicles and of 15-19 constituted the first batch of
A.E.C. 664T's to be ordered, had fully-floating rear axles and Timken roller
bearing hubs, and are understood to have been otherwise identical in most
respects to London Transport's C1 class vehicles which entered service at the
same time. The bodywork, on the other hand, by English Electric, draws obvious
comparison with five vehicles of similar dual entrance-exit layout delivered in
1934 to Bournemouth Corporation but seated two more on each deck than the
latter. However, the Newcastle vehicles were of metal construction.

Peters air-operated folding platform doors in two leaves were provided to the
front exit.

Facilities to operate on traction batteries were provided about 1936. Reports
have been received to the effect that at some unknown date No. 10 was involved
in an accident at Wingrove Depot, appearing to have been squashed between two
trams. The photograph now confirms this.

No. 13, from a photograph, appears to have been painted experimentally into
blue livery about 1937. Confirmation would be welcomed as to whether this was
so.

15—19 (BVK 805-809)   New 1935
(Renumbered 315-319 in 1946)
Chassis: Associated Equipment Company Ltd. 664T (three axle)
Wheelbase: 18 ft. 7 5/16ins.
Motor: English Electric type? (80 n.h.p.)
Electrical Equipment: English Electric Co. Ltd.
Brakes: Regenerative and rheostatic, both on the power pedal. In addition, they
    had air brakes.
Body: Brush Electrical Engineering Co. Ltd. H33/27D
Length: 30ft. 0ins.   **Width:** 7ft. 6ins.
U.W.: 9 tons 0 cwt. 7 lb.

These five vehicles with Brush bodywork can be considered to have been
built to the same standard specification as the preceding batch but incorporating
the body builder's own minor attention to detail—the nearside cab window, for
example, having a curved head, the maroon band under the upper-deck windows
being shallower, and the body gracefully tapering inwards from ground to roof

level. The front removable towing panel was horizontally fluted, and the front dash panel independently lined out, divided horizontally at the top of the towing panel and fitted with the combined A.E.C./E.E.C. winged badge. Again, metal construction was employed.

No. 19 was used to carry the official party after inauguration of the system on 1st October 1935.

Facilities to operate on traction batteries were provided about 1936.

20—29 (BVK 810-819)   New 1935
(Renumbered 320-329 in 1946)
Chassis: Karrier Motors Ltd. E6A (three-axle)   **Wheelbase:** 17ft. 9ins.
Motor: Metropolitan-Vickers Electrical Co. Ltd. MV 202Z (80 n.h.p.)
Electrical Equipment: Metropolitan-Vickers
Brakes: Regenerative and rheostatic brakes, both on the power pedal. Also air
        brakes.
Body: Metropolitan-Cammell Carriage & Wagon Co. H33/27D
Length: 30ft. 0ins.   **Width:** 7ft. 6ins.
U.W.: 9 tons 0 cwt. 1 qtr.

The Karrier E6A was an entirely new design of three-axle trolleybus chassis which, though numbered by the manufacturers in the E6 series, was more orthodox in construction than the existing E6 type. As it turned out, the marque was unique to Newcastle. The bogie was a Kirkstall product suspended on single centrally-pivoted springs on each side. Marles cam and roller steering was fitted. The traction motor was mounted admiships, drive being to underslung worm-driven units on each axle, offset to the offside.

Bodywork, again of metal construction, was this time by M.C.C.W., which was squarer than the preceding design, and providing a raking head to the cabside windows. The towing panel was not fluted and the lining out extended round the sides and over the front wheel arches. No makers' badge was fitted to the front but the concave dished front wheel rings fitted when new were indicative of the make.

Facilities to operate on traction batteries were provided about 1936.

30—39 (BVK 820-829)   New 1935
(Renumbered 330-339 in 1946)
Chassis: Guy Motors Ltd. BTX (three-axle)   **Wheelbase:** 18ft. 2½ins.
Motor: British Thomson-Houston Co. Ltd. type? (80 n.h.p.)
Electrical Equipment: British Thomson Houston
Brakes: Regenerative brakes on the power pedal, and rheostatic on the brake
        pedal. Also air brakes. Later the regenerative brakes were removed.
Body: Metropolitan-Cammell Carriage & Wagon Co. H33/27D
Length: 30ft. 0ins.   **Width:** 7ft. 6ins.
U.W.: ? tons ? cwt. ? qtrs.

The bodywork of these vehicles was identical to that fitted to the Karrier E6A's but the front towing panel was provided with an irregular-shaped aperture on the offside to facilitate towing without removal of the panel, using a screw-in towing eye on the end of the chassis frame. The towing panel carried the Guy badge. The Guy BTX chassis employed the use of a forward-mounted traction motor right under the cab floor with a consequently long propeller shaft but improved ventilation. Regenerative control was provided.

Facilities to operate on traction batteries were provided about 1936.

When new, as with all preceding deliveries, rainshields were provided over the lower-deck side windows and the side and front windows of the upper-deck. In later years, some vehicles were altered losing rainshields (except over opening windows) either on the lower-deck only or on both decks.

40 (CVK 52)   New 1935
(Renumbered 340 in 1946)
Chassis: Karrier Motors Ltd. E6A (three-axle)   **Wheelbase:** 17ft. 9ins.
Electrical Equipment: Metropolitan-Vickers
Motor: Metropolitan-Vickers Electrical Co. Ltd. MV202 Z (? n.h.p.)
Brakes: Regenerative and rheostatic brakes both on the power pedal. In addition, this vehicle had air brakes.
Body: Metropolitan-Cammell Carriage & Wagon Co. H33/27D
Length: 30ft. 0ins.   **Width:** 7ft. 6ins.
U.W.: ? tons ? cwt. ? qtrs.

This vehicle is believed to have been identical to 20-29 except that traction batteries were provided from new. 40 was reported to have a chromed chassis in its early days and was definitely the trolleybus at the 1935 Commercial Motor Show.

41—43 (DTN 141-143)   New 1936
(Renumbered 341-343 in 1946)
Chassis: Karriers Motors Ltd. E6A (three-axle)   **Wheelbase:** 17ft. 9ins.
Motor: Metropolitan-Vickers Electrical Co. Ltd. MC202 Z (? n.h.p.)
Electrical Equipment: ?
Brakes: Regenerative brakes and rheostatic brakes on the power pedal. In addition, they had air brakes.
Body: Metropolitan-Cammell Carriage & Wagon Co. H33/27D
Length: 30ft. 0ins.   **Width:** 7ft. 6ins.
U.W.: ? tons ? cwt. ? qtrs.

A repeat order of three, believed identical to earlier 20-29.

44—46 (DTN 144—146)   New 1939
(Renumbered 344-346 in 1946)
Chassis: Guy Motors Ltd. BTX (three-axle)   **Wheelbase:** 18ft. 2½ins.
Motor: English Electric Co. Ltd. (? n.h.p.)
Electrical Equipment: British Thomson-Houston Co. Ltd.
Brakes: Regenerative brakes on the power pedal and rheostatic on the brake pedal. Also air brakes. Later the regenerative brakes were removed.
Body: Metropolitan-Cammell Carriage & Wagon Co. H33/27D
Length: 30ft. 0ins.   **Width:** 7ft. 6ins.
U.W.: ? tons ? cwt. ? qtrs.

A repeat order for three vehicles thought to be identical to 30-39 except that English Electric motors were fitted in lieu of the B.T-H units provided in 30-39. B.T-H controllers and other electrical equipment were otherwise retained.

The batch was delivered and entered service at the same time as the preceding trio of Karrier E6As.

47—56 (ETN 47-56)   New 1937
(Renumbered 347-356 in 1946)
Chassis: Karrier Motors Ltd. E6A (three-axle)   **Wheelbase:** 17ft. 9ins.
Motor: Metropolitan-Vickers Electrical Co. Ltd. MV202 Z (? n.h.p.)
Electrical Equipment: ?
Brakes: Sames as Nos. 41-43
Body: Metropolitan-Cammell Carriage & Wagon Co. H33/27D
Length: 30ft. 0ins.   **Width:** 7ft. 6ins.
U.W.: ? tons ? cwt. ? qtrs.

A further repeat order similar to earlier M.C.C.W.-bodied Karrier E6As.

57—66 (ETN 57-66)   New 1937
(Renumbered 357-366 in 1946)
Chassis: Guy Motors Ltd. BTX (three-axle)   **Wheelbase:** 18ft. $2\frac{1}{2}$ins.
Motor: English Electric Co. Ltd. type ? (? n.h.p.)
Electrical Equipment: British Thomson-Houston Co. Ltd.
Brakes: Same as Nos. 44-46
Body: Metropolitan-Cammell Carriage & Wagon Co. H33/27D
Length: 30ft. 0ins.   **Width:** 7ft. 6ins.
U.W.: 9 tons 9 cwt. 2 qtrs.

A further repeat order for Guy BTX chassis and M.C.C.W. all-metal bodies, incorporating English Electric traction motors and B.T-H control and other electrical equipment.

These vehicles were delivered and entered service at the same time as the preceding batch of Karrier E6As.

No. 65 ran away in Westgate Road at a date unknown and crashed into a traction pole at the junction of Westgate Road and Fenkle Street (Cowen's Monument). Further details would be welcomed.

No. 60 was the last vehicle in the old livery c.1946/7.

66—77 (ETN 67-77)   New 1937
(Renumbered 367-377 in 1946)
Chassis: Associated Equipment Company Ltd. 664T (three-axle)
Wheelbase: 18ft. 7 5/16ins.
Motor: English Electric Co. Ltd. EE406 (95 n.h.p.)
Electrical Equipment: ?
Brakes: Same as Nos. 10-14 with one exception: Rheostatic brakes on the brake
        pedal only.
Body: Metropolitan-Cammell Carriage & Wagon Co. H33/27D

Length: 30ft. 0ins. **Width:** 7ft. 6ins.
U.W.: 9 tons 1 cwt. 0 qtrs.

A further repeat order for AEC 664T chassis and M.C.C.W. all metal frames, these vehicles were delivered and entered service at the same time as the preceding batches of Karrier E6A and Guy BTX vehicles.

No. 69 was the runaway trolleybus on Westgate Road in 1942.

No. 73 was either delivered in, or very shortly afterwards experimentally painted in, motorbus blue livery (see illustration on page 32). The authors would welcome further details.

78 (FBB 78)   New 1937
(Renumbered 378 in 1946)
Chassis: Guy Motors Ltd. BTX (three-axle)   **Wheelbase:** 18ft. 2½ins
Motor: English Electric Co. Ltd. type ? (? n.h.p.)
Electrical Equipment: British Thomson-Houston Co. Ltd.
Brakes: Same as Nos. 44-46
Body: Charles H. Roe Ltd. H34/26D
Length: 30ft. 0ins. **Width:** 7ft. 6ins.
U.W.: 9 tons 11 cwt. 3 qtrs.

The bodywork on this vehicle was a departure from the hitherto-standard metal M.C.C.W. body in being of composite construction and manufactured by Charles H. Roe Ltd. of Leeds, the complete vehicle being constructed to Newcastle Transport standard design by the manufacturers for exhibition at the 1937 Commercial Motor Show. Afterwards the vehicle was offered to Newcastle Transport at a reduced price and the offer accepted. The use of the Roe patent safety staircase caused one seat from the lower-deck to be lost to the upper-deck, overall capacity remaining the same. As had occurred of late with other batches of Guy trolleybuses, English Electric traction motors were provided although the remainder of the electrical equipment, including the controller, was by B.T-H.

79—84 (FVK 79-84)   New 1938
(Renumbered 379-384 in 1946)
Chassis: Associated Equipment Ltd. 664T (three-axle)
Wheelbase: 18ft. 7 5/16ins.
Motor: English Electric Ltd. EE406 (95 n.h.p.)
Electrical Equipment: English Electric series dynamic
Brakes: Rheostatic on the power pedal.
Body: Charles H. Roe Ltd. H34/26D
Length: 30ft. 0ins. **Width:** 7ft. 6ins.
U.W.: 8 tons 19 cwt. 2 qtrs.

The bodies on these vehicles were of composite construction as opposed to the all-metal construction previously favoured and were constructed by Roe following success of No. 78, the Roe patent safety staircase again being employed.

No. 83 was possibly the first of the prewar fleet to be repainted in postwar livery.

85—98 (FVK 85-98)   New 1938
(Renumbered 385-398 in 1946)
Chassis: Karriers Motors Ltd. E6A (three-axle)   **Wheelbase:** 17ft. 9ins.
Motor: Metropolitan-Vickers Ltd. MV202 BG
Electrical Equipment: ?
Brakes: Same as the A.E.C.'s.
Body: Metro-Cammell Carriage & Wagon Co. H33/27D
Length: 30ft. 0ins.   **Width:** 8ft. 6ins.
U.W.: 9 tons 7 cwt. 0 Qtrs.

Delivered and entering service about the same time as the preceding Roe-bodied AEC 664Ts, these vehicles constituted a repeat order of previous Karrier E6A's bodied by M.C.C.W. with all-metal construction.

99—108 (FVK 99-108)   New 1938
(Renumbered 399-408 in 1946)
Chassis: Guy Motors Ltd. BTX (three-axle)   **Wheelbase:** 18ft. 2½ins.
Motor: English Electric Co. Ltd. type ? (? n.h.p.)
Electrical Equipment: British Thomson-Houston Co. Ltd.
Brakes: Sames as Nos. 44-46
Body: Metropolitan-Cammell Carriage & Wagon Co. H33/27D
Length: 30ft. 0ins.   **Width:** 7ft. 6ins.
U.W.: 9 tons 9 cwt. 2qtrs.

These vehicles constituted yet another repeat order for Guy BTX chassis and M.C.C.W. all-metal bodies and they were delivered and entered service at the same time as the preceding batch of Karrier E6As.

No. 104 was the first in an experimental livery c.1946/7 with no centre chocolate band.

109 (FVK 109)   New 1938
(Renumbered 409 in 1946)
Chassis: Guy Motors Ltd. BTX (three-axle)   **Wheelbase:** 18ft. 2½ins.
Motor: English Electric Co. Ltd. type ? (? n.h.p.)
Electrical Equipment: British Thomson-Houston Co. Ltd.
Brakes: Regenerative brakes on the power pedal and rheostatic on the brake pedal. In addition 109 had air brakes. Later the regenerative brakes were removed.
Body: Northern Coachbuilders Ltd. H33/27D
Length: 30ft. 0ins.   **Width:** 7ft. 6ins.
U.W.: 9 tons 9 cwt. 3 Qtrs.

The chassis only of this vehicle was exhibited as the 1937 Commercial Motor Show, following which it was offered to Newcastle Transport. It was accepted and arrangements were made for a body to standard Newcastle specification to be built by Northern Coachbuilders Ltd., whose premises were local. The resulting vehicle incorporated certain minor variations to the standard design, which included raised waistbands below upper and lower-deck windows, a flatter front dome to the roof and an unusual treatment of the rear offside lower-

187

deck side windows as illustrated, lack of continuous rainshields, and the provision of stouter pillars to carry the trolley gantry. 109 also had a hand operated front-exit door.

112 (DHP 112)   New 1938
(Renumbered 412 in 1946)
Chassis: Daimler Commercial Vehicles Ltd. CTM6 (three-axle)
Wheelbase: ?ft. ?ins.
Motor: Metropolitan-Vickers Electrical Co. Ltd. type MV202Y (? n.h.p.)
Electrical Equipment: Metropolitan-Vickers
Brakes: This vehicle had no air brakes
Body: Metropolitan-Cammell Carriage & Wagon Co. H33/27D
Length: 30ft. 0ins.   **Width:** 7ft. 6ins.
U.W.: 9 tons 3 cwt. 0 qtrs.

In the absence of suitable views of the vehicle there is little to suggest that it was in any way different from Nos. 99-108 in appearance. A Wingrove Depot based trolley, it had a hand operated front-exit door.

113—118 (HVK 113-118)   New 1939/40
(Renumbered 413-418 in 1946)
Chassis: Karrier Motors Ltd. E6A (three-axle)   **Wheelbase:** 17ft. 9ins.
Motor: Metropolitan-Vickers Electrical Co. Ltd. MV202
Electrical Equipment: Nos. 116, 117 were experimentally fitted with 35v lighting
                     and traction batteries c.1946/47. Remainder had 24v.
Brakes: Same arrangement as the prewar AECs.
Body: Charles H. Roe Ltd. H34/26D
Length: 30ft. 0ins.   **Width:** 7ft. 6ins.
U.W.: 9 tons 7 cwt. 0 qtrs.

These vehicles, delivered after the outbreak of war, reverted to composite Roe bodywork similar to that fitted to Nos. 78-84.

119—124 (HVK 119—124)   New 1940
(Renumbered 419-424 in 1946)
Chassis: Karrier Motors Ltd. E6A (three-axle)   **Wheelbase:** 17ft. 9ins.
Motor: Metropolitan-Vickers Electrical Co. Ltd. MV202
Electrical Equipment: ?
Brakes: Sames as Nos. 113-118
Body: Metropolitan-Cammell Carriage & Wagon Co. H33/27D
Length: 30ft. 0ins.   **Width:** 7ft. 6ins.
U.W.: 9 tons 7 cwt. 0 qtrs.

This batch of vehicles which entered service towards the end of 1940 had M.C.C.W. all-metal bodies once again, and were the last to be delivered in the pre-war dual entrance-exit layout, being otherwise similar to previous M.C.C.W. bodied deliveries.

Nos. 113-124 were fitted with skids for the opening of the Elswick Road route in 1944. Formerly had trolley wheels.

1—9/0 (KW 9461/3/53-5/6063*/9460/6656*/5*/9464)　　　New 1929/31
(Some renumbered in 1946—see below)

Chassis: English Electric Co. Ltd. E11 (three-axle)　　**Wheelbase:** ?ft. ?ins
Motor: English Electric DK122 (100 n.h.p.) series/parallel
　　(Vehicles marked * English Electric DK122 (80 n.h.p.))
Electrical Equipment: English Electric. Electrically-operated contactor controller operated by left foot through a lightly balanced centre-pivoted pedal having eight positions. Centre trip pedal requiring actuating after braking to reconnect power. (Vehicles marked * had a 9-notch mechanical controller actuated by foot from centre pedal).
Brakes: Single foot-operated right foot pedal, the first two notches actuating an electric brake, then air. Hand brake for parking acting on rear wheels only. (Vehicles marked *, being older, had a right foot pedal operating a Westinghouse air brake system which acted on four wheels, whilst a four notch electric brake was actuated by a left foot pedal).
Body: English Electric H30/26D
Length: 28ft. 0ins.　　**Width:** 7ft. 6ins.
U.W.: 8 tons 7 cwt. 0 qtrs.

Originally new to Bradford Corporation Tramways these vehicles were purchased by Newcastle Transport as a stop-gap measure and the following relevant dates are given.

Reg. No.	Bradford Fleet No.	Bradford into	Service out of	Transfer out of Newcastle	Newcastle Fleet No.	Newcastle service into	out of
KW9461	592	9. 6.31	31. 7.42	30.11.42	1	11. 4.43	31.12.48
KW9463	594	1. 5.31	19. 6.42	4.12.42	2	5. 3.43	31.12.48
KW9453	584	5. 2.31	31. 7.42	11.12.42	3	9. 4.43	31.12.48
KW9454	585	13. 2.31	31. 7.42	8.12.42	4	6. 3.43	—
KW9455	586	6. 3.31	29. 9.42	10.12.42	5	4. 3.43	31.12.48
KW6063	573	4.12.29	18.12.42	19.12.42	6	—	—
KW9460	591	7. 7.31	31.11.42	3.12.42	7	1.3. 43	31.12.48
KW6656	580	2.11.29	29. 9.42	16.12.42	8	—	—
KW6655	579	26.10.29	31.10.42	17.12.42	9	—	—
KW9464	595	4.5. 31	29. 6.42	2.12.42	0	—	—

These vehicles were drawn from two batches put into service in Bradford, 572-83 (KW6062—7/6654—9) dating from 1929 and 584-596 (KW9453—64/KY1360) dating from 1931.The two batches differed to a slight degree in appearance but both batches nevertheless somewhat ungainly, and are reported to have been very heavy to steer. High voltage lighting from the traction supply was provided.

KW9464 was purchased for spares only. The fleet number 0 was apparently allocated as this appears in official Byker depot records. The remaining nine were prepared for (and were available for) service but 6, 8, and 9, remained unused (i.e. those with the 80 n.h.p. motors). The remainder, 1-5 and 7 were still in service at the time of the 1946 renumbering and were therefore renumbered 301-5/7.

In Newcastle these vehicles ran in Bradford blue livery, mainly during the peak-hours, though at least one was repainted in wartime grey.

The ten vehicles were purchased for £2,000 and sold at approximately £10 each!

Bodywork was of composite construction and of seven-bay layout with projecting full-width cab and overhanging peak at the front of the domed roof. The vehicles drawn from the 1929 batch (6, 8 and 9) had a simple flat upper deck front, slightly raked, whilst the remainder were rounded on plan. The rear-opposed to being the more usual panel, those on the 1929 stock being square cornered and on the 1931 stock square-cornered but with the rear-most top corner radiused. Opening windows were full-drop. Three fixed panes were provided across the front upper-deck. A single-line ultimate destination indicator was provided at the front only, positioned over the nearside cab windscreen below cab roof level. Black Doverite plastic-covered stanchions and grab-rails were provided.

125—136 (JTN 955-966)   New 1943/44
(Renumbered 425-436 in 1946)
Chassis: Karrier Motors Ltd. W4 (two-axle)   **Wheelbase:** 16ft. 3ins.
Motor: Metropolitan-Vickers Electrical Co. Ltd. type 207C1 (85 n.h.p.)/English
      Electric type ?
Electrical Equipment: Metropolitan Vickers/English Electric
Brakes: ?
Body: Park Royal Vehicles Ltd. UH30/26R
Length: 26ft 0ins.   **Width:** 7ft. 6ins.
U.W.: 7 tons 18 cwt. 0 qtrs.

These trolleybuses were the first Newcastle Transport trolleybuses to be built on two axles, and were of the Karrier W4 type, designed and built to stringent wartime utility standards, the only type of trolleybus available for purchase during the latter part of the war. The end-product was therefore similar in most respects to the many other utility trolleybuses built for service elsewhere in this country, of composite construction using unseasoned timber and steel panelling, aluminium being at a premium for aircraft production during the war.

Nos. 125-131 had M.V. motors and electrical equipment, plus traction batteries and low voltage lighting.

Nos. 132-136 had English Electrical equipment, and possibly motors. They had low voltage lighting and no traction batteries.

137—138 (JVK 277-278)   New 1945
(Renumbered 437-438 in 1946)
Chassis: Karrier Motors Ltd. W4 (two-axle)
Wheelbase: 16ft. 3ins.
Motor: Metropolitan-Vickers Electrical Co. Ltd. type 207C1 (85 n.h.p.)
Electrical Equipment: Metropolitan-Vickers
Brakes: ?
Body: Weymann Motor Bodies Ltd. UH30/26R
Length: 26ft. 0ins.   **Width:** 7ft. 6ins.
U.W.: 27 tons 18 cwt. 0 qtrs.

This pair were of similar utility specification to 125-136 but with Weymann bodywork. They had M.V. motors and equipment as 125-131, but were fitted with line voltage lighting, and did not have traction batteries.

139—142 (JVK 279-282)   New 1945
(Renumbered 439-422 in 1946)
Chassis: Karrier Motors Ltd. W4 (two-axle)   **Wheelbase:** 16ft. 3ins.
Motor: Metropolitan-Vickers Electrical Co. Ltd. type 207C1 (85 n.h.p.)
Electrical Equipment: Metropolitan-Vickers
Brakes: ?
Body: Park Royal Vehicles Ltd. UH30/26R
Length: 26ft. 0ins.   **Width:** 7ft 6ins.
U.W.: 7 tons 10 cwt. 2 qtrs.

These four vehicles were a further delivery of vehicles to utility specification. Bodywork was again by Park Royal and sliding opening windows were provided to the first, third and fifth bays on each side of the upper deck and second and fourth on each side of the lower deck, with "pull-in" hopper ventilator windows to the front upper-deck. Only the opening windows were fitted with rainshields, and the rear emergency window was glazed.

They had M.V. motors and equipment, but were fitted with line voltage lighting, and did not have traction batteries.

443—478 (LBB 43-78)   New 1948/49
Chassis: Sunbeam Commercial Vehicles Ltd. F4 (two-axle)   **Wheelbase:** ?
Motor: Metropolitan-Vickers Electrical Co. Ltd. type 209 (95 n.h.p.)
Electrical Equipment: Metropolitan-Vickers
Brakes: ?
Body: Metropolitan-Cammell Carriage & Wagon Co. H30/26R
Length: 26ft. 0ins.   **Chassis Width:** 7ft. 6ins. Note: These vehicles had 8ft. wide bodies: the axles were extended to accommodate the extra 6ins.
U.W.: 8 tons 3 cwt. 0 qtrs.

These 36 vehicles, although not delivered until 1948/9, were numerically Newcastle's first postwar batch of new trolleybuses. They were not, however, the first postwar delivery.

The following batch Nos. 479-498 entered service in 1948, and 499-528 about the same time this batch was being delivered. Bodywork of M.C.C.W. metal construction was typical of this manufacturer's design at this time, but features such as the belled-out skirt panels, and sliding ventilator windows exposed the connections the firm had with Weymann, although such typically Weymann characteristics as rainshields over side and front upper-deck windows were missing. Window panes had small-radius corners both top and bottom and those to the front upper-deck were fixed glass. A Sunbeam badge was carried on the front dash panel and at some stage a red triangular illuminated stop sign was fitted to the rear lower panel (possibly from new). In latter days these did not function. The bamboo retriever pole was located along the interior near side of the body but tubes under the vehicle were later provided to carry them. In spite of their stream-lined appearance these vehicles seemed to be under-powered.

No. 468 was exhibited at the 1948 Commercial Motor Show, for which purpose it was fitted with a window on the stairs which was later removed.

These, and all subsequent four-wheel vehicles, were nicknamed "doodlebugs" by crews after the German VI pilotless bomb.

479—498 (LTN 479-498)   New 1948
Chassis: British United Traction Co. Ltd. 9641T (three-axle)
Wheelbase: 18ft. 5ins.
Motor: English Electric Co. Ltd. type 410 (120 n.h.p.)
Electrical Equipment: English Electric. 11 notch controller
Brakes: Westinghouse air brakes and rheostatic
Body: Metropolitan-Cammell Carriage & Wagon Co. H40/30R
Length: 30ft. 0ins.   **Width:** 8ft. 0ins.
U.W.: 9 tons 19 cwt. 0 qtrs.

These vehicles were originally on order for London Transport (Q1 class) but by negotiation with the manufacturers and the Ministry of Transport they came to Newcastle. (The vehicles which actually went to London had Metropolitan-Vickers motors and electrical equipment). The chassis make was new to Newcastle, the builders being a unification of A.E.C. and Leyland trolleybus interests which took place in 1946. Bodywork was generally identical to the London deliveries apart from the seat upholstery, and it is said that traces of London Transport green paint could be detected under the red-painted interior panels. Indicator windows were inscribed LPTB and the floors had wooden slat floor strips in London fashion. The postwar London-type continuous ceiling style bell cord was also provided and the most noticeable feature was the London style of destination display, at front, side, and rear. These were larger in size than normal for Newcastle. The ultimate destination was shown in the centre of the main box, the top and bottom of the glass being painted out black, notwithstanding the fact that it would have been possible to have shown intermediate destinations. Route number indicators at the front and rear were originally provided with full width blinds showing the route number in the centre third. In later years the glass each side was painted out black. Some vehicles (it is not known which) had the rear number indicator painted out completely on delivery. In the mid-nineteen fifties, a few vehicles (identities unknown) had metal plates fitted to blank out both route number and ultimate destination windows instead of the glass being painted black. This modification was carried out rather haphazardly as some vehicles had the front and rear screens altered and rear route number boxes covered over whilst some had only the front and side boxes altered; others were altered only at the rear. None had every box altered.

About 1960, certain vehicles were fitted experimentally with destination and number blinds lettered in yellow in lieu of white in the hope that they would show up better in the dark. This was not a success. After conversion of service 34 on 1st June 1963 some vehicles received new ultimate and route number blinds, the latter having broader characters.

When new, rainshields were provided over the side windows to both decks and to the front upper-deck windows. Later, most were altered (somewhat haphazardly) retaining rainshields only over individually opening windows on both decks, or altered on one or other deck only, usually the lower-deck, the upper-deck remaining original. The upper-deck front was never changed.

The opening windows were half-drops, a departure from Newcastle's sliding type, the first, third and fifth opening on the upper-deck and the first and third on the lower-deck.

The all-metal body was built to the newly-permitted 8ft. wide dimension, thus allowing extra comfort by providing seats 1 in. wider and gangways 4 ins. wider, and was of five-bay construction. All prewar three-axle vehicles had been of six-bay construction. Improved ventilation was afforded in the front of the upper-deck and particular consideration was given to the comfort of crews. The rear platform was spacious and single sheet rubber-covered, and enabled the conductor to stand right under the stairs. Coat hooks and lockers were provided and both driver and conductor had food boxes.

These vehicles were fitted with "Syndromic" automatic chassis lubrication and a feature peculiar to Newcastle was the shielding of the Walsh resistances mounted in two banks under the body. This virtually boxed them in to keep out snow and slush, an adequate airflow being ducted from slots over the windscreens. The 11-notch controller, to Newcastle specification, gave smooth acceleration and an overload relay was provided to eliminate unnecessary operation of circuit breakers.

Other features of note were the provision of an interior mirror for the driver enabling him to view the whole of the lower deck, a B.U.T. badge in the centre of the front dash panel, and rubber wings all round, those at the front projecting below the body line and those at the rear "dipping" between the two wheels. 497 had metal rear wings like those fitted on 499-528, which were cut to the wheels but "straight across" at the top.

Finally, these vehicles were the first trolleybuses in Newcastle to be equipped with fog lamps. Although the later-delivered 443-478 did not have them, all subsequent deliveries did. Always known to crews as the "Gosforth Trolleys", these vehicles spent most of their life working from Newcastle Central Station to Gosforth via the Great North Road, and most were withdrawn on 30th May 1965 after a year on other routes subsequent to the Gosforth routes being converted to motorbus operation.

499—528 (LTN 499-528)   New 1948
Chassis: Sunbeam Commercial Vehicles Ltd. S7 (three-axle)
Wheelbase: ?ft. ?ins.
Motor: Metropolitan-Vickers Electrical Co. Ltd. type 210AG20 (115 n.h.p.)
Electrical Equipment: Metropolitan-Vickers
Body: Northern Coachbuilders Ltd. H39/31R
Length: 30ft. 0ins.   **Width:** 7ft. 6ins.
U.W.: 9 tons 19 cwt. 0 qtrs.

Delivered and entering service towards the end of 1948, these vehicles were bodied by the local firm of Northern Coachbuilders Ltd., on a three-axle chassis of a new design by Sunbeam designated type S7.

The solid looking body design was later used for batches of two-axle trolley-buses for Newcastle and Maidstone and a batch of prewar vehicles rebodied for Bradford. Six-bay all-metal construction was employed and the most notable features of the design and finish were the fixed pane upper deck front windows, having larger radiused corners to the top outside corners, the lack of rainshields over any windows, sliding ventilators fitted to the first, third and fifth bays of each deck, provision of an outward-opening nearside window to the driver's cab instead of a door, and white-plastic-covered stanchions and grab-rails.

The mudguards to the rear bogie were dressed between the wheels, but the top edge carried straight over. Nearside foglamps were again provided. Three indicator boxes were provided at the front. Offset towards the offside was a single-line ultimate destination indicator (though two lines were often squashed in), under which was a double-line intermediate point indicator. A single-track route number box was fitted towards the nearside. Single-line ultimate destination boxes were positioned over the platform and at the bottom of the rear upper-deck panel. 512 was exhibited at the 1948 Commercial Motor Show.

501 was retained by Newcastle Transport for inclusion in the Newcastle Museum of Science and Engineering and was stored for some years at Byker Depot. Its latest destination is the Beamish Open Air Museum. During 1973 the vehicle was at an army camp in County Durham being given an electrical over-haul by Byker Depot electricians.

506 was involved in an accident on the West Road, Denton Burn (near Slatyford Lane junction) whilst westbound for Denton Square, 2nd November 1953. The trolleybus ran backwards when the driver was believed to have blacked out. The vehicle demolished railing and ran into a house. A report 15 days later said the driver was found dead in bed.

522 was fitted with 4in. skid, experimentally. Non standard.

523 was fitted with short skids of a later pattern than 425s. This vehicle was reputed to have been involved in an accident on Fenham Hall Drive on 4th May 1965. Further details would be appreciated.

The odd number of seats on each deck is explained by the provision of a single seat on the offside of each deck, that on the upper deck being at the top of the stairs and that on the lower deck forward of the inward facing bench seat over the rear bogie wheel arch.

Most vehicles carried the retriever pole under the vehicle in a tube, but at some stage certain vehicles had them in a tube along the inside nearside lower-deck, access being from the platform. Some vehicles are understood to have run with polished front wheel rings, unusual for Sunbeam trolleybuses. Sunbeam badges were carried, fixed to the top of the front dash panel.

These vehicles were known to crews as "Coffins", as they were "long and thin".

194

529—553 (LTN 529-553)   New 1949/50
Chassis: Sunbeam Commercial Vehicles Ltd. F4 (two-axle)
Wheelbase: ?ft. ?ins.
Motor: Metropolitan-Vickers Ltd. type 209 (95 n.h.p.)
Electrical Equipment: Metropolitan-Vickers
Brakes: Rheostatic and Westinghouse air brakes
Body: Northern Coachbuilders Ltd. H30/26R
Length: 26ft. 0ins.   **Width:** 7ft. 6ins.
U.W.: 7 tons 19 cwt. 0 qtrs.

These 25 vehicles delivered in the latter part of 1949 and early months of 1950 were a two-axle version of the NCB bodied Sunbeam S7's mounted on the type F4 chassis. Five-bay construction was employed and sliding ventilator windows were provided to the first, third and fifth bays each side on the upperdeck and second and fourth bays each side on the lower-deck. Black plastic-covered stanchions and grab-rails were used instead of white as on the S7's and a Sunbeam badge was again provided at the top of the front dash panel. Rubber rear wings were fitted. The trolley booms on these vehicles appeared to be longer than necessary.

546 on service 41 northbound on Friday 30th September 1960 ran into a pile of gravel in Northumberland Street and hit the canopy of Fenwick's department store, injuring nine people.

On Monday 17th December 1951, at 5 p.m. 552, fully laden, ran away forwards from Bewick Street terminus across Neville Street and collided with a sand bin in front of the Central Station.

554—578 (LTN 554-578)   New 1949
Chassis: British United Co. Ltd. 9611T (two-axle)
Wheelbase: 16ft. 4ins.
Motor: English Electric Co. Ltd. type 410 (120 n.h.p.)
Electrical Equipment: English Electric
Brakes: Rheostatic and Westinghouse air brakes
Body: Northern Coachbuilders Ltd. H30/26R
Length: 26ft. 0ins.   **Width:** 7ft. 6ins.
U.W.: 7 tons 19 cwt. 0 qtrs.

This batch of 25 vehicles entered service in the summer of 1949, before Nos. 529-553. The bodywork of these vehicles, five-bay all-metal construction by NCB, was identical in all respects to that described for 529-553. The B.U.T. 9611T chassis was a two-axle equivalent to the B.U.T. 9641T three-axle vehicles already in service although Newcastle's 9611T's were only 7ft. 6ins. wide. These vehicles carried B.U.T. badges at the top of the front dash panel and were fitted with front wheel rings.

579—628 (NBB 579-628)   New 1950
Chassis: British United Traction Co. Ltd. 9641T (three-axle)
Wheelbase: 18ft. 5ins.
Motor: English Electric Co. Ltd. type 410 (120 n.h.p.)
Electrical Equipment: English Electric; Series Dynamic control gear
Brakes: Rheostatic and Westinghouse air brakes

Body: Metropolitan Cammell Carriage & Wagon Co. H40/30R
Length: 30ft. 0ins.   **Width:** 8ft. 0ins.
U.W.: 9 tons 19 cwt. 0 qtrs.

The final delivery of trolleybuses to Newcastle took place in 1950 when a repeat order for 50 London-type vehicles was built. In many respects, this batch was identical to the twenty vehicles diverted from London in 1948. However, the destination blind display was to standard Newcastle layout. Seats were tubular steel finished in leather with Dunlopillo cushions. The bodywork was constructed with tubular steel pillars and inner rivetted steel truss panels; the aluminium outer panels were screw fixed to timber fillets. Unlike the diverted London order, this batch of vehicles had 'Slide-a-Vent' windows to the first, third and fifth bays each side on the upper-deck and the first and third each side on the lower-deck mounted in 'Simplastic' pans. The vehicles had enclosed-type trolley gantries of Metro-Cammell-Weymann patented construction insulated from the body in respect of both electricity and sound by rubber.

628 was exhibited at the 1950 Commercial Motor Show, and was demonstrated at Tees-side whilst on its delivery run to Newcastle. In early 1967, negotiations were made between London Trolleybus Preservation Society and Messrs. Autospares of Bingley, who purchased most of the batch for breaking, with a view to purchasing 628 for preservation prior to its removal from Byker Depot. These were successful and 628 was towed south initially to Uxbridge, Middlesex, then to Pluckley, Kent. 628 has since been transferred to Carlton Colville, near Lowestoft, where the East Anglian Transport Museum Society have a working transport museum at which the L.T.P.S. have constructed a small trolley system, and work in restoring 628 to its former glory is virtually complete.

612 overturned in Benwell Lane whilst on service 33A from Delaval Road on 13th February 1959 as a result of hitting a traction pole. The vehicle was repaired and returned to service with shorter metal front wings instead of rubber ones, and also lost its air intake slots over the windscreens (which ducted air to cool the resistances) and its upper-deck side windows rainshields.

591 ran backwards out of control down Grainger Street between Bigg Market traffic lights and Westgate Road on 12th May 1959, the driver having collapsed and died at the wheel, and was halted by crashing into a car at the foot of Grainger Street.

592 had shorter rubber front wings cut to the same height above ground as the front dash panels.

596 was painted in gold livery and decorated in connection with the Coronation of Queen Elizabeth II on 2nd June 1953.

Unlike the 1948 batch, rainshields, when later removed, were removed completely from above the lower-deck side windows only. It is thought that most, if not all, vehicles received this treatment during the nineteen fifties. Only 612 lost those to the upper-deck side windows due to repairs following the overturning accident mentioned above.

In spite of the conversion to motorbuses being well under way by 1964, certain vehicles received late repaints including 579, 588, 589, 597, 604, 607, 616, 617, 619 and 625.

196

DEMONSTRATORS

CNE 474   New 1936
Chassis: Crossley Motors Ltd. TDD6 (three-axle)   **Wheelbase:** 18ft. 7ins.
Motor: Metropolitan-Vickers Electrical Co. Ltd. type 206 (? n.h.p.)
Electrical Equipment: Metropolitan-Vickers
Brakes: ?
Body: Crossley Motors Ltd. H38/30R
Length: 30ft. 0ins.   **Width:** 7ft. 6ins.
U.W.: 9 tons 0 cwt. 0 qtrs. 7 lbs.

This vehicle, which was finished in the blue, white and red livery of Ashton-under-Lyne Corporation and carried their fleet number 58, appears to have visited Newcastle for a two-week period prior to entering service in Ashton, on loan from the manufacturer. It was eventually purchased by Ashton-under-Lyne Corporation in June 1938 and continued to run in service until withdrawn in January 1955. This vehicle, together with a two-axle example, was originally built by Crossley as a prototype demonstrator.

CWK 67   New 1937
Chassis: Transport Vehicles (Daimler) Ltd. CTM4 (two-axle)
Wheelbase: ?ft. ?ins.
Motor: Metropolitan-Vickers Electrical Co. Ltd. type ? (80h.p.)
Electrical Equipment: Metropolitan-Vickers contractor control
Brakes: Rheostatic and air on brake pedal; regenerative on power pedal
Body: Willowbrook H28/24R
Length: 26ft. 0ins.   **Width:** 7ft. 6ins.
U.W.: 7 tons 12 cwt. 0 qtrs.

This vehicle, which was finished in a red-and-cream livery reminiscent of Huddersfield, spent nine weeks in Newcastle during the autumn of 1936, apparently at the instigation of the manufacturers. It was eventually placed in service in nearby South Shields in 1938 and subsequently purchased by that undertaking. Its original body was destroyed by enemy action on 30th September 1941, and the vehicle was rebodied by Roe to utility specification in 1942, and ran until January 1959.

During its demonstration career, for which purpose it was first licensed by Daimler on 5th June 1937, it is believed also to have visited Derby and West Hartlepool. By the time it first ran in South Shields, the seating capacity had been increased to H30/26R. The vehicle was the first attempt by Daimler at trolleybus production and served as a demonstrator and prototype.

The composite body by Willowbrook was of pleasing proportions, having belled-out skirt panels and convex-shaped lower-deck waistrail panels, rainshields over the upper-deck front and side windows and lower-deck side windows. Fixed panes were provided to the front upper-deck and half drop opening windows to the first, third and fifth bays on each side of the upper-deck and the second and fourth bays on each side of the lower-deck. A rather small front towing panel was fitted which was grilled. Both windscreens opened. A large single-line ultimate

197

destination box was provided at both front and rear surmounted by a square centrally-positioned route number indicator box, whilst at the side a single-line indicator box was positioned over the platform.

WARTIME LOANS

FUF 11—15 New 1939
Chassis: Associated Equipment Company Ltd. 661T (two-axle)
Wheelbase: 16ft. 3ins.
Motor: Crompton Parkinson Ltd. type C400B2 (80 n.h.p.)
Electrical Equipment: Allen West and Company Ltd. 9-notch controller
Brakes: Rheostatic series dynamic and Westinghouse air brakes with coasting brake set for 14 m.p.h. and run-back brake set for 2 m.p.h.
Body: Weymann Motor Bodies Ltd. H30/24R
Length: 26ft.0ins.   **Width:** 7ft. 6ins.
U.W.: 7 tons 6 cwt. 0 qtrs.

These vehicles, which had entered service in Brighton in June 1939, were part of a batch of 44 vehicles introduced to replace the trams. The Weymann metal-framed bodies were of five-bay construction with half-drop windows provided to the first, third and fifth bays each side on upper-deck and first and third bays each side on the lower-deck. No nearside cab door was provided. A large two-blind destination box was provided front and rear, the ultimate blind being at the top, the boxes projecting from the raking front and rear. A destination box was also provided over the platform. These vehicles had belled-out skirt panels in true Weymann tradition, twin ventilator slots over the front upper-deck windows, a fluted removable towing panel, low set headlamps, and "dustbin-lid" front wheel rings.

The Brighton Corporation livery was red relieved with cream upper and lower-deck window surround areas and roof. During the war, the roofs of vehicles were painted grey whilst some unidentified vehicles received an all-over grey livery. It is not known in which livery the Brighton vehicles appeared in Newcastle. Internally, these vehicles had Alhambrinal coverings to ceilings, green-painted lower panels, and red stairs and platforms. Window frames were varnished wood. Seats were tubular framed and upholstered in moquette, whilst stanchions and grab-rails were black plastic-covered.

Their stay in Newcastle was brief. This was probably due to reasons given in Chapter 13. At the same time as they were being returned to Brighton Bournemouth three-axle vehicles were being placed in service, and shortly after that the temporary second-hand purchases from Bradford arrived.

It is believed that whilst in Newcastle three vehicles saw service on Service 9 (Central Station—Osborne Road). No view of these vehicles in service in Newcastle has been traced, and the authors would be pleased if any reader is able to help in locating one.

AEL 400/1/5—7/10   New 1934/35
ALJ 63/997
BEL 830
Chassis: Sunbeam Commercial Vehicles Ltd. MS2 (three-axle)
Wheelbase: ?ft. ?ins.
Motor: British Thomson-Houston Co. Ltd. type 201 (80 n.h.p.)
Electrical Equipment: British Thomson-Houston; scissors-type controller
Brakes: Regenerative and Westinghouse air brakes
Body: AEL400/1/5: Park Royal Vehicles Ltd. H31/25D
       AEL406/7/10: English Electric Co. Ltd. H31/25D
       ALJ 63/997: Park Royal Vehicles Ltd. H31/25D
       BEL 830: Park Royal Vehicles Ltd. H31/25D
Length: 28ft. 6ins.   **Width:** 7ft. 6ins.
U.W.: 8 tons 12 cwt. 0 qtrs.

These vehicles were perhaps the nearest possible type to their own stock which Newcastle was able to borrow, for Bournemouth also favoured a front exit in addition to the rear platform. The six-bay body was of composite construction and the two-leaf front exit doors were manually-operated by a lever in the driver's cab. The similarity to Newcastle stock was carried a stage further, for the Bournemouth livery was also yellow and maroon, although not, of course, identical. Internally, the vehicles had brown leather seats on tubular steel frames, varnished wood window frames, brown interior panels, and Alhambrinal ceilings.

Bournemouth initially loaned some of its trolleybuses to London Transport and they were put into service in the Ilford area of east London. The placing in service of some new trolleybuses originally destined for export to South Africa enabled the Bournemouth stock to be released, whereupon these nine vehicles travelled north to Newcastle. Four of these were surplus to Newcastle's requirements once the second-hand stock from Bradford had been acquired, and they passed on to South Shields where they were referred to as "Newcastle Trolleys". The other five were returned direct to Bournemouth in 1945, at the end of the war. As with the Brighton vehicles, no photographs have come to light of these vehicles in service in Newcastle, and the authors would be pleased to hear if readers have traced any.

One of the Bournemouth vehicles, identity unknown, is reported to have fallen into one of the tram pits at Wingrove Depot on a date unknown.

BEL 830 (Bournemouth 145) was an exhibit at the 1935 Commercial Motor Show.

DESTINATION BLINDS

It is now possible to give details of earlier blinds for both the prewar and "Q1" trolleybuses. First let us deal with the prewar vehicle screens, from drawings dated 1947.

Front Destination Screens

There are six separate blinds depending on Route Allocation:—

Service 4

WALLSEND
via Westgate Rd
Arcade City Rd
St Anthonys

WALKER
via Westgate Rd
Arcade City Rd
St Anthonys

ST NICHOLAS
CATHEDRAL

DENTON RD
via Westgate Rd
Fergusons Lane

DENTON SQUARE
via Westgate Rd
Denton Bank

FOX & HOUNDS
via Westgate Rd

WINGROVE
Depot

BYKER

RESERVED

BRIGHTON GROVE
via Welbeck Rd
Stanhope St

Service 5

CHURCH ST
via Shields Rd

WELBECK RD
via Shields Rd

WALLSEND
via Welbeck Rd

PILGRIM ST
via Shields Rd

BRIGHTON GROVE
via Stanhope St

DENTON SQUARE
via Stanhope St
Denton Bank

WALLSEND
Boundary
via Shields Rd

WESTBOURNE AV
via Welbeck Rd

WINGROVE
DEPOT

ST JAMES
PARK

BYKER

RESERVED

Services 6-12

WESTERHOPE
via Barrack Rd
Fenham

FENHAM
via Barrack Rd

CENTRAL
Railway Stn

OSBORNE RD
via Jesmond Stn

PILGRIM ST

HAYMARKET

WINGROVE
DEPOT

ST JAMES
PARK

BYKER

RESERVED

WALLSEND
BOUNDARY
via Shields Road

DENTON Rd

Services 3-5c	Service 31	Service 36
CHURCH ST via Shields Rd	GOSFORTH PARK via North Road	BENTON PARK Rd via North Road Matthew Bank
WELBECK RD via Shields Rd	POLWARTH DRIVE via North Road	BENTON PARK Rd via Jesmond Road
WESTBOURNE AV via Shields Rd	GOSFORTH vis North Road	Benton Road
PILGRIM ST via Shields Rd	CENTRAL STATION via North Road	BENTON Rd (Swarland Av) via Westgate Road Jesmond Road
DENTON RD via Elswick Rd	CENTRAL STATION via Percy Street	MATTHEW BANK via North Road
DELAVAL RD via Elswick Rd	PILGRIM ST via North Road	TOWN MOOR via North Road
BENWELL CHURCH via Elswick Rd	BYKER	MONUMENT via Matthew Bank North Road Percy St
OSBORNE RD via Jesmond Station	HAYMARKET WINGROVE	MONUMENT via Jesmond Road Percy Street
WALLSEND via City Rd	RESERVED *HOLLYWOOD AVE via North Road	DENTON ROAD via Jesmond Rd West Rd Ferguson's Lane
BYKER		
WINGROVE DEPOT	*GRANGE ESTATE via North Road	CENTRAL RAILWAY Stn
RESERVED	*added 4.6.48	BYKER DEPOT
		HAYMARKET
		WINGROVE DEPOT

Route Nos.	Rear and Side Screens
3	*HOLLYWOOD AVE
3A	*POLWARTH DRIVE
3B	*GOSFORTH
4	*GOSFORTH PARK
4A	*GRANGE ESTATE
4B	WALLSEND
5	WALKER
5A	St NICHOLAS
5B	WESTBOURNE Av
5C	Denton Road
	Fergusons Lane
6	Denton Square
	Denton Bank
6A	FOX & HOUNDS
12	CHURCH ST
12A	WELBECK Rd
31	PILGRIM ST
31A	BRIGHTON GROVE
31B	WESTERHOPE
32	FENHAM
33	CENTRAL Stn
33A	OSBORNE Rd
33B	BYKER
34	HAYMARKET
34A	WINGROVE DPT
34B	RESERVED
35	ST JAMES PARK
35A	DENTON RD TERM
35B	DELAVAL Rd
35C	NICHOL STREET
36	MONUMENT
	MATTHEW BANK
	BENTON PARK Rd
	*Benton Road
	Swarland Av
	*TOWN MOOR
	*Added 4.6.48

The original 1935 blinds were as follows:—

Route Nos. | **Front Destination Screens**

Route Nos.			
4	WALLSEND	DENTON BURN	FOX & HOUNDS
4A	via Westgate Rd	via Westgate Road	via City Rd
4B	Arcade City Rd	Denton Bank	St Anthony's Arcade
4C	St Anthony's		Westgate Rd
4D			
	WALKER	DENTON BURN	ST NICHOLAS
	via Westgate Rd	via Westgate Road	Cathedral
	Arcade City Rd	Ferguson's Lane	via City Rd
	St Anthony's		St Anthony's
	ST NICHOLAS	DENTON BURN	FOX & HOUNDS
	Cathedral	Boundary	via Westgate Road
	via Westgate Road	via Westgate Road	
			WINGROVE DEPOT
			via Westgate Road
			RESERVED

Details of the "Q1" Screens (Front, Rear and Side)

Route Numbers	Destination Screens
31	DENTON ROAD
31A	DELAVAL Rd
31B	BENWELL
	CHURCH
32	WALLSEND
32a	Park Road
33	St NICHOLAS
	CATHEDRAL
33A	WALLSEND
33B	BOUNDARY
34	DENTON
34A	SQUARE
34B	WEST ROAD
35	FOX & HOUNDS
35A	HAYMARKET
35B	WINGROVE
35C	Depot
36	BYKER DEPOT
36A	RESERVED
37	ST JAMES
37A	PARK
37B	BRIGHTON
38	GROVE
38A	CHURCH ST
39	WELBECK RD
39A	PILGRIM ST
40	WESTBOURNE
40A	AVENUE
41	WESTERHOPE
41	FENHAM
41A	CENTRAL STN
plus 10 others	OSBORNE RD
	MATTHEW BANK
	GOSFORTH
	POLWARTH DRIVE
	HOLLYWOOD AVE
	GOSFORTH PARK
	*GRANGE ESTATE
	*BENTON PARK Rd
	*BENTON ROAD
	Swarland Av
	*TOWN MOOR
	*MONUMENT
	*COAST ROAD

*Added 4.6.48

Ultimate Destination Blind
DENTON ROAD TERMINUS
DELAVAL ROAD
BENWELL CHURCH
MONUMENT
WALLSEND (PARK ROAD)
WALKER
ST. NICHOLAS CATHEDRAL
DENTON BURN
WALLSEND BOUNDARY
DENTON SQUARE
WEST ROAD (FOX AND HOUNDS)
HAYMARKET
SLATYFORD LANE DEPOT
COWEN'S MONUMENT
WINGROVE DEPOT
BYKER
BYKER DEPOT
RESERVED
ST. JAMES PARK
BRIGHTON GROVE
CHURCH STREET
WELBECK ROAD
PILGRIM STREET
WESTBOURNE AVENUE
WESTERHOPE
FENHAM
CENTRAL STATION
OSBORNE ROAD
BENTON
GOSFORTH
NORTH GOSFORTH
GOSFORTH PARK
LOW FELL
GATESHEAD
MATTHEW BANK
BENTON PARK ROAD
POLWARTH DRIVE

HOLLYWOOD AVENUE
BENTON PARK ROAD
BENTON ROAD (SWARLAND AVE.)
TOWN MOOR
HEATON ROAD
COAST ROAD
MONUMENT
DENTON ROAD TERMINUS
NEWGATE ST.
GATESHEAD STATION
DUNSTON

Intermediate Destination Blind

ELSWICK ROAD
WESTGATE ROAD AND CITY ROAD
CITY ROAD AND WESTGATE ROAD
WESTGATE ROAD
WESTGATE ROAD AND FERGUSON'S LANE
WESTGATE ROAD AND DENTON BANK
SHIELDS ROAD
SHIELDS ROAD AND WELBECK ROAD
STANHOPE ST. AND DENTON BANK
STANHOPE STREET
BARRACK ROAD, FENHAM
BARRACK ROAD
JESMOND STATION
OSBORNE ROAD AND SOUTH GOSFORTH
JESMOND ROAD AND BENTON ROAD
NORTHUMBERLAND STREET
PERCY STREET
PERCY STREET, CENTRAL STATION
PERCY STREET AND HIGH LEVEL BRIDGE
PERCY ST., NORTH ROAD AND MATTHEW BANK
NORTH ROAD AND MATTHEW BANK
JESMOND ROAD, WEST ROAD AND FERGUSON'S LANE
NORTH ROAD
HIGH LEVEL BRIDGE
COAST ROAD
WESTGATE ROAD AND JESMOND ROAD

Note the inclusion of ultimate destinations which were never used, due to trolleybuses never operating to those districts. Similarly, the intermediate point blind exposures "High Level Bridge" and "Coast Road" were never used.

The route number blind carried numbers 31 to 50, several with A, B or C suffixes. 45 to 50 were never used, having been provided for use on the projected routes crossing the River Tyne to Gateshead, which were never implemented.

SYNOPSIS OF ROUTES OPERATED

I — PREWAR, WARTIME AND EARLY POSTWAR PERIOD

The service numbers allocated were based originally on the assumption that all tram routes would be converted to trolleybus operation, for they were numbered in a clockwise sequence related to the various main roads radiating from the City, for example 1 — Scotswood Road, 2 — Westmorland Road, 3 — Elswick Road, 4 — Westgate Road.

4   **NEW SERVICES:** DENTON BURN
4A   BOUNDARY (4B) (having turned via Denton
4B   Loop consisting of Denton Road, Whickham View,
4C   Fergusons Lane, Tower View and Fox-and-
4D   Hounds Lane OR REVERSE) — West Road —
FOX & HOUNDS (4) (4A) (4C) (reverser) — West Road — Westgate Road — Collingwood Street — St. Nicholas Square — ST. NICHOLAS CATHEDRAL (turning via loop Collingwood Street — St. Nicholas Street — Westgate Road) (4B) (4C) (4D) — Mosley Street — Pilgrim Street — City Road — Glasshouse Bridge — Walker Road to WALKER (CHURCH STREET) (foot of) (turning circle) (4A) (4D) or via Station Road — White Street — Fisher Street — Neptune Road — Buddle Street — Hadrian Road — WALLSEND PARK ROAD (Vine Street) (reverser) (4) (4D) and return
4, 4A, 4B operated daily.
4C, 4D operated Mon. — Fri. peak hours only

2.10.35—23.4.38

5A   **NEW SERVICE:** BRIGHTON GROVE (loop
5B   via Dilston Road — Callerton Place — Brighton
5C   Grove) (5A) (5B) — Crossley Terrace — Stanhope Street — Barrack Road — Gallowgate — Blackett Street — PILGRIM STREET (loop via New Bridge Street — Pilgrim Street — Market Street) (5C) — New Bridge Street — Byker Bridge — Shields Road West — Shields Road — Union Road — Bothal Street — Welbeck Road — WELBECK ROAD (east end of) (turning circle) (5B) (5C) — Church Street — WALKER (CHURCH STREET) (foot of) (turning circle) (5A) and return

207

5A, 5B operated daily
5C operated Mon. — Fri. Peak hours only

ADDITIONAL JOURNEYS OPERATED:

PILGRIM STREET — Market Street — New Bridge Street — Byker Bridge — Shields Road West — Shields Road — Union Road — Bothal Street — Welbeck Road — WALKER (WEST-BOURNE AVENUE) (reverser) and return entering Pilgrim Street from New Bridge Street. Operated Mon. — Sat. part day extras and as a special service covering Greyhound and Dirt Track Race Meetings at Brough Park Stadium.

19.9.37—31.10.48

4   **EXISTING SERVICES EXTENDED:**
4A   DENTON BURN BOUNDARY (existing
4B   reverser removed) and route extended via West
4C   Road to DENTON SQUARE (Copperas Lane)
4D   (turning circle). Service 4B extended over the new section and section also used by a peak hour only service running PILGRIM STREET — DENTON SQUARE.

24.4.38—31.10.48

5   **NEW SERVICE:** DENTON SQUARE (Copperas Lane) (turning circle) — West Road — *Fox & Hounds* — Westgate Road — Brighton Grove — Crossley Terrace — Stanhope Street — Barrack Road — Gallowgate — Blackett Street — and as 5 group to WALKER (CHURCH STREET) and return. Operated daily

24.4.38—31.10.48

6   **NEW SERVICE:** FENHAM (Two Ball Lonnen) (reverser) — Fenham Hall Drive — Ponteland Road — Barrack Road — Gallowgate — Blackett Street — Grainger Street — Grainger Street West — Neville Street — CENTRAL STATION thence loop Bewick Street — Clayton Street West — Neville Street and return. Operated daily.

1.8.38—29.6.41

9   **NEW SERVICE:** OSBORNE ROAD (Jesmond) (having turned via Tavistock Road and Lonsdale Terrace) — Osborne Road — Jesmond Road — Barras Bridge — Northumberland Street — Pilgrim Street — Market Street — Grainger Street — Grainger Street West — Neville Street — CENTRAL STATION thence loop Bewick

Street — Clayton Street West — Neville Street and return.
Operated daily.

2.9.38—31.10.48

12 **NEW SERVICE: WALLSEND BOUNDARY** (Walkerville) (Oak Tree Gardens) (reverser) — Shields Road — Shields Road West — Byker Bridge — New Bridge Street — Blackett Street — Grainger Street — Grainger Street West — Neville Street — CENTRAL STATION thence loop Bewick Street — Clayton Street West — Neville Street and return
Operated daily.
ADDITIONAL JOURNEYS OPERATED: WALLSEND BOUNDARY (Walkerville) (Oak Tree Gardens) (reverser) — Shields Road — Shields Road West — Byker Bridge — New Bridge Street — PILGRIM STREET returning via Market Street — New Bridge Street

2.9.38—29.6.41

12 **EXISTING SERVICE EXTENDED:** WALLSEND BOUNDARY (Walkerville) (Oak Tree Gardens) (reverser) —- CENTRAL STATION as above extended via Grainger Street? — Westgate Road — West Road — *Fox & Hounds*—Fox-and-Hounds Lane —Tower View — Ferguson's Lane — Whickham View — — DENTON ROAD TERMINUS (junction of Denton Road and Whickham View) (turning circle) and return
Operated daily.

30.6.41—10.6.44

6 **EXISTING SERVICE EXTENDED:** FENHAM (Two Ball Lonnen) reverser removed and route extended via Netherby Drive to FENHAM (Bingfield Gardens) (reverser).

23.11.41—31.10.48

3 **NEW SERVICES: DENTON ROAD**
3A TERMINUS (junction of Denton Road and
3B Whickham View) (turning circle) (3) Whickham View — DELAVAL ROAD (junction of Benwell Lane with Delaval Road) (3A) Benwell Lane—BENWELL CHURCH (reverser at junction of Adelaide Terrace and Nichol Street) (3B) — Adelaide Terrace — Elswick Road — Westgate Road — Clayton Street — MONUMENT (Eldon Square) (3) (3A) (3B) and return via Grainger Street to Westgate Road
Operated daily.

11.6.44—31.10.48

12 **SHORTENED SERVICE:** Section between
DENTON ROAD TERMINUS and *FOX &
HOUNDS* withdrawn, the service then running
FOX & HOUNDS   —   WALLSEND
BOUNDARY (Walkerville)
Operated daily.

11.6.44—30.7.44

12 **REINSTATED SERVICE:** Section between
DENTON ROAD TERMINUS and *FOX &
HOUNDS* reinstated following adverse public
reaction to cutting back of service on 11.6.44

31.7.44—31.10.48

31 **NEW SERVICES:** CENTRAL STATION (31)
31A (31A) — Neville Street — Grainger Street West
— Grainger Street — Market Street — Pilgrim
Street — Northumberland Street — Barras Bridge
— Great North Road — Gosforth High Street —
Great North Road — GOSFORTH PARK (31)
(turning circle) or POLWARTH DRIVE (31A)
(turning circle) and return.
Operated daily.

18.4.48—31.10.48

31B **NEW SERVICE:** CENTRAL STATION —
Neville Street — Grainger Street West —
Grainger Street —Newgate Street — Percy Street
— Haymarket — Barras Bridge — Great North
Road — Gosforth High Street — Great North
Road — HOLLYWOOD AVENUE (elongated
turning circle with siding in layby in Hollywood
Avenue itself) and return.
Operated weekdays only.

18.4.48—31.10.48

The 31 Group of services were so numbered as a prelude to the re-numbering
of all trolleybus services to bring the service numbers into a single common series
for both motorbus and trolleybus routes.

II — LATER POSTWAR PERIOD

Apart from the 31 Group of services all existing trolleybus services were
re-numbered and re-organised with effect from 1st November 1948 including
extensions and introduction of new routes.

31 **SERVICES AS EXISTING:** CENTRAL
31A STATION (31) (31A) and as before to GOS-
FORTH PARK (31) (4.80 miles) or
POLWARTH DRIVE (31A) (4.00 miles) and
return
Operated daily.

1.11.48—27.10.51

210

31B **SERVICE AS EXISTING:** CENTRAL STATION and as before to HOLLYWOOD AVENUE (3.20 miles) and return. Operated weekdays only

1.11.48—27.10.51

32 **NEW SERVICE:** FENHAM (Bingfield Gardens) (reverser) — Netherby Drive — Fenham Hall Drive — Ponteland Road — Barrack Road — Gallowgate — Blackett Street — New Bridge Street — Byker Bridge — Shields Road West — Shields Road — WALLSEND BOUNDARY (Walkerville) (Oak Tree Gardens) (reverser) (5.80 miles) and return. Operated daily.

1.11.48—29.5.65

ADDITIONAL JOURNEYS OPERATED: PILGRIM STREET — Market Street — New Bridge Street — Byker Bridge — Shields Road West — Shields Road — WALLSEND BOUNDARY (Walkerville) (Oak Tree Gardens) (reverser) and return Operated Mon. — Sat. Early mornings and peak hours.

33   **RENUMBERED AND EXTENDED**
33A   **SERVICES (based on former 3):** DENTON
33B   ROAD TERMINUS (junction Denton Road and Whickham View) (turning circle) (33) — Whickham View — DELAVAL ROAD (junction of Benwell Lane with Delaval Road) (33A) Benwell Lane — BENWELL CHURCH (reverser at junction of Adelaide Terrace and Nichol Street) (33B) — Adelaide Terrace — Elswick Road — Westgate Road — Grainger Street — Market Street — Pilgrim Street — Northumberland Street — Barras Bridge — Jesmond Road — Osborne Road — and via turning loop Tavistock Road — Lonsdale Terrace — OSBORNE ROAD (Jesmond) (33) (5.60 miles) (33A) (4.80 miles) (33B) (4.20 miles) and return Operated Daily

ADDITIONAL JOURNEYS OPERATED:

Service 33B from DELAVAL ROAD (Junction of Benwell Lane with Delaval Road) — Benwell Lane — Adelaide Terrace — Elswick Road — Westgate Road — Clayton Street — MONUMENT (Eldon Square) and return via Grainger Street to Westgate Road. Operated Mon. —Sat.

early mornings and Mon. - Fri. peak hours only.

1.11.48—29.5.65

34   **SERVICES RE-NUMBERED (former 4, 4A,**
34A   **4B):** DENTON SQUARE (junction of West
34B   Road and Copperas Lane) (turning circle) (34B)
— West Road —*FOX & HOUNDS* (34), (34A)
— West Road — Westgate Road — Collingwood
Street—St. Nicholas Square—ST. NICHOLAS
CATHEDRAL (turning via loop Collingwood
Street — St. Nicholas Street — Westgate Road)
(34B) — Mosley Street — Pilgrim Street — City
Road — Glasshouse Bridge — Walker Road to
WALKER (CHURCH STREET) (foot of)
(turning circle) (34A) or via Station Road —
White Street — Fisher Street — Neptune Road —
Buddle Street — Hadrian Road — WALLSEND
PARK ROAD (Vine Street) (reverser) (34)
(8.30 miles) and return. Operated Mon. — Sat.
On Sundays a through DENTON SQUARE —
WALLSEND/PARK ROAD service was
operated with additional journeys operated ST.
NICHOLAS CATHEDRAL — WALKER
(CHURCH STREET) and return.

1.11.48—31.7.55

35   **RE-NUMBERED AND EXTENDED SER-**
35A   **VICES:** DENTON SQUARE (junction of West
35B   Road and Copperas Lane) (35) — West Road
— Westgate Road — BRIGHTON GROVE
(35A) (35B) — Crossley Terrace — Stanhope
Street — Barrack Road — Gallowgate —
Blackett Street — New Bridge Street — Byker
Bridge — Shields Road West — Shields Road
— Union Road — Bothal Street — Welbeck Road
— WELBECK ROAD (east end of) (turning
circle) (35) (35B) (4.60 miles) OR thence
Church Street — WALKER (CHURCH
STREET) (foot of) (turning circle) (35) (35A)
(7.00 miles) (4.70 miles) and return.
Operated daily.

1.11.48 $\left\{ \begin{array}{l} 21.8.65 \ (35B) \\ 22.8.65 \ (35) \ (35A) \end{array} \right.$

35C   **NEW SERVICE:** DELAVAL ROAD (junction
of Benwell Lane and Delaval Road) — Benwell
Lane — Adelaide Terrace — Elswick Road —
Westgate Road — Grainger Street — Market
Street — New Bridge Street — Byker Bridge —
Shields Road West — Shields Road — Union
Road — Bothal Street — Welbeck Road —
WALKER (WESTBOURNE AVENUE)

212

(reverser) (6.40 miles) and return.
Operated daily.

ADDITIONAL JOURNEYS OPERATED:
BENWELL CHURCH (reverser at junction of
Adelaide Terrace and Nichol Street) — Adelaide
Terrace — Elswick Road — Westgate Road —
Clayton Street — MONUMENT (Eldon
Square) and return via loop Blackett Street —
Grainger Street — Westgate Road.
Operated Mon. - Fri. Peak hours only

ADDITIONAL JOURNEYS OPERATED:
WALKER (WESTBOURNE AVENUE)
(reverser) — Welbeck Road — Bothal Street —
Union Road — Shields Road — Shields Road
West — Byker Bridge — New Bridge Street —
PILGRIM STREET returning via Market Street
— New Bridge Street.

Operated weekdays morning peaks only.

1.11.48—29.5.65

36 **SERVICE RE-NUMBERED (former 6):**
CENTRAL STATION — Neville Street —
Grainger Street West — Grainger Street —
Blackett Street — Gallowgate — Barrack Road
— Ponteland Road — Fenham Hall Drive —
Netherby Drive — FENHAM (Bingfield
Gardens) (reverser) (3.20 miles) and return.
Operated daily.

1.11.48—29.5.65

38 **NEW SERVICE:** DENTON ROAD
TERMINUS (junction of Denton Road and
Whickham View) (turning circle) — Whickham
View—Ferguson's Lane—Fox-and-Hounds Lane
— West Road — Westgate Road — Grainger
Street — Market Street — Pilgrim Street —
Northumberland Street — Barras Bridge —
Jesmond Road — Benton Bank — Stephenson
Road — Benton Road — BENTON ROAD
(SWARLAND AVENUE) (turning circle)
(7.00 miles) and return.
Operated daily.

1.11.48—1.2.64

39 **NEW SERVICE:** MONUMENT (Eldon
Square) — Blackett Street — Northumberland
Street — Barras Bridge — Jesmond Road —
Benton Bank — Stephenson Road — Benton
Road — Benton Park Road — Haddrick's Mill
Road — Matthew Bank — Jesmond Dene Road

213

— Great North Road — Barras Bridge —
Haymarket — Percy Street — MONUMENT
(Eldon Square) (7.50 miles) — CIRCULAR
SERVICE OPERATED IN BOTH
DIRECTIONS.
Operated daily.

1.11.48—15.1.49

III — SUBSEQUENT REVISIONS AND NEW ROUTES

37 **NEW SERVICE:** DENTON ROAD
TERMINUS (junction of Denton Road and
Whickham View) (turning circle) — Whickham
View—Ferguson's Lane—Fox-and-Hounds Lane
— West Road — Westgate Road — Grainger
Street — Blackett Street — New Bridge Street
— Byker Bridge — Shields Road West — Shields
Road — Heaton Road — Stephenson Road —
Benton Road — BENTON ROAD (SWAR-
LAND AVENUE) (turning circle) (7.40 miles)
and return.
Operated daily.

16.1.49—c.56

39 **REVISED SERVICE:** CENTRAL STATION
— Neville Street — Grainger Street West —
Grainger Street — Market Street — Pilgrim
Street — Northumberland Street — Barras Bridge
— Jesmond Road — Benton Bank — Stephenson
Road — Benton Road — Benton Park Road —
Haddrick's Mill Road — Matthew Bank —
Jesmond Dene Road — Great North Road —
Barras Bridge — Northumberland Street —
Pilgrim Street — Market Street — Grainger
Street — Grainger Street West — Neville Street
CENTRAL STATION (7.50 miles). CIRCU-
LAR SERVICE OPERATED IN ONE
DIRECTION ONLY AS ABOVE.
Operated daily.

16.1.49—31.3.62

40 **NEW SERVICE:** CENTRAL STATION —
Neville Street — Grainger Street West —
Grainger Street — Market Street — Pilgrim
Street — Northumberland Street — Barras Bridge
— Great North Road — Jesmond Dene Road —
Matthew Bank—Haddrick's Mill Road—Benton
Park Road — Benton Road — Stephenson Road
— Benton Bank — Jesmond Road — Barras
Bridge — Northumberland Street — Pilgrim

Street — Market Street — Grainger Street —
Grainger Street West — Neville Street —
CENTRAL STATION (7.50 miles).
CIRCULAR SERVICE OPERATED IN ONE
DIRECTION ONLY AS ABOVE.
Operated daily.

16.1.49—31.3.62

41 **NEW SERVICE:** CENTRAL STATION —
Neville Street — Grainger Street West —
Grainger Street — Market Street —Pilgrim Street
— Northumberland Street — Barras Bridge —
Jesmond Road — Benton Bank — Stephenson
Road — Heaton Road — Shields Road — Shields
Road West — Byker Bridge — New Bridge
Street — Market Street — Grainger Street —
Grainger Street West — Neville Street —
CENTRAL STATION (5.20 miles) —
CIRCULAR SERVICE OPERATED IN ONE
DIRECTION ONLY AS ABOVE.
Operated daily.

16.1.49—31.3.62

42 **NEW SERVICE:** CENTRAL STATION —
Neville Street — Grainger Street West —
Grainger Street — Blackett Street — New Bridge
Street — Byker Bridge —- Shields Road West —
Shields Road — Heaton Road — Stephenson
Road — Benton Bank — Jesmond Road — Barras
Bridge — Northumberland Street — Pilgrim
Street — Market Street — Grainger Street —
Grainger Street West — Neville Street —
CENTRAL STATION (5.20 miles) —
— CIRCULAR SERVICE OPERATED IN
ONE DIRECTION ONLY AS ABOVE
Operated daily.

16.1.49—31.3.62

31A **REVISED SERVICE:** Service diverted along new
wiring in Broadway West to GRANGE ESTATE
(junction of Broadway West and Kielder Way)
(turning circle) as a separate route instead of
working to POLWARTH DRIVE virtually as a
"short" 31. (3.90 miles).
Operated daily.

28.10.51—1.2.64

31 **SERVICE AS EXISTING:** CENTRAL
STATION — GOSFORTH PARK
Operated daily.

28.10.51—1.2.64

215

31B   **EXTENDED SERVICE:** Service extended along Great North Road and along new wiring in Broadway West to GRANGE ESTATE (junction of Broadway West and Kielder Way) (turning circle) in lieu of turning at HOLLYWOOD AVENUE.
Operated weekdays only.

28.10.51—c 57

NOTE: Turning facilities retained at Hollywood Avenue for use by all day extras and Stadium Specials.

31 **REVISED ROUTE:** Following construction of a
31A roundabout at the junction of Neville Street and
31B Clayton Street West these services turned around
36 same in lieu of travelling the square of streets
39 surrounding St. Mary's R.C. Cathedral.
40
41
42

c 10.53

34 **EXTENDED SERVICE:** Service extended to operate DENTON SQUARE — WALKER (CHURCH STREET) OR WALLSEND PARK ROAD.
Operated daily.

1.8.55—1.6.63

ADDITIONAL JOURNEYS OPERATED:

FOX & HOUNDS — WALKER (CHURCH STREET) OR WALLSEND PARK ROAD numbered 34A and 34B Monday — Saturday.
ADDITIONAL JOURNEYS OPERATED (Sundays only) ST. NICHOLAS CATHEDRAL —WALKER (CHURCH STREET).

43/44 **NEW SERVICES:** CENTRAL STATION (departures showing 44 — FENHAM) —Neville Street — Grainger Street West — Grainger Street — Blackett Street — Gallowgate — Barrack Road — Ponteland Road — Fenham Hall Drive — Netherby Drive (blind then changed to 33 — OSBORNE ROAD) — Silver Lonnen — Denton Road — Whickham View — Benwell Lane — Adelaide Terrace — Elswick Road — Westgate Road — Grainger Street — Market Street — Pilgrim Street — Northumberland Street — Barras Bridge — Jesmond Road — Osborne Road turning via loop Tavistock Road — Londsdale Terrace — OSBORNE ROAD (Returning vehicles then showed 43—DENTON

ROAD TERMINUS as far as Delaval Road/ Whickham View and blinds were then turned to 36 — CENTRAL STATION) (9.80 miles) Operated daily.

ADDITIONAL JOURNEYS OPERATED: In effect short workings of the above numbered 33 operated DENTON ROAD TERMINUS — OSBORNE ROAD and short workings of the above numbered 36 operated CENTRAL STATION — FENHAM

21.10.56—29.5.65

37 **REVISED SERVICE:** The service as introduced 16.1.49 continued to run as set out earlier but vehicles running into the city from Benton Road (Swarland Avenue) were revised to run via New Bridge Street — Market Street — Grainger Street.

c.56—1.2.64

31B **REVISED SERVICE:** Service introduced 28.10.51 altered from CENTRAL STATION — GRANGE ESTATE to run CENTRAL STATION—POLWARTH DRIVE still traversing Newgate Street — Percy Street — Haymarket — Barras Bridge (Monday — Friday) but running via Market Street — Pilgrim Street — Northumberland Street (Saturdays only). Operated weekdays only.

c 57—1.2.64

ADDITIONAL JOURNEYS OPERATED: Special services when required were operated as 31B to HOLLYWOOD AVENUE for Greyhound Racing and TOWN MOOR for "The Hoppings". At this time HOLLYWOOD AVENUE ceased to be used as a regular all day terminus.

39 **REVISED SERVICE:** NEWGATE STREET — Grainger Street — Market Street — Pilgrim Street — Northumberland Street — Barras Bridge — Jesmond Road — Benton Bank — Stephenson Road — Benton Road — Benton Park Road — Haddrick's Mill Road — Matthew Bank — Jesmond Dene Road — Great North Road — Percy Street — NEWGATE STREET — CIRCULAR SERVICE OPERATED IN ONE DIRECTION ONLY AS ABOVE. Operated daily.

1.4.62—1.2.64

217

40   **REVISED SERVICE:** NEWGATE STREET—
      Grainger Street — Market Street — Pilgrim
      Street — Northumberland Street — Barras Bridge
      — Great North Road — Jesmond Dene Road —
      Matthew Bank — Haddricks Mill Road — Benton
      Park Road — Benton Road — Stephenson Road
      — Benton Bank — Jesmond Road — Barras
      Bridge — Haymarket — Percy Street — NEW-
      GATE STREET — CIRCULAR SERVICE
      OPERATED IN ONE DIRECTION ONLY AS
      ABOVE.
      Operated daily.

                                                    1.4.62—1.2.64

41   **REVISED SERVICE:** NEWGATE STREET—
      Grainger Street — Market Street — Pilgrim
      Street — Northumberland Street — Barras
      Bridge — Jesmond Road — Benton Bank —
      Stephenson Road — Heaton Road — Shields
      Road — Shields Road West — Byker Bridge —
      New Bridge Street — Market Street — Grainger
      Street — Neville Street — CENTRAL
      STATION and depart as 42 below.
      Operated daily.

                                                    1.4.62—29.5.65

42   **REVISED SERVICE:** CENTRAL STATION—
      Neville Street — Grainger Street West —
      Grainger Street — Blackett Street — New Bridge
      Street — Byker Bridge — Shields Road West —
      Shields Road — Heaton Road — Stephenson
      Road — Benton Bank — Jesmond Road — Barras
      Bridge — Haymarket — Percy Street — NEW-
      GATE STREET and depart as 41 above.
      Operated daily.

                                                    1.4.62—29.5.65

33   **VARIED   TERMINAL   ARRANGEMENT:**
37   DENTON ROAD TERMINUS altered from
38   junction of Denton Road and Whickham View to
      Castlenook Place — otherwise no change.

                                                    c.4.62

34   ABANDONED AND COVERED BY MOTOR-
34A   BUS OPERATION
34B

                                                    2.6.63

218

31 31A 31B 37 38 39 40	ABANDONED AND COVERED BY MOTOR- BUS OPERATION	
		2.2.64
32 33 33A 33B 36 41 42 43 44	ABANDONED AND COVERED BY MOTOR- BUS OPERATION	
		30.5.65
35C	**VARIED SERVICE:** DELAVAL ROAD — WALKER (WESTBOURNE AVENUE) changed from operating daily to operating Satur- days only and irregularly on weekdays.	
		1.6.65—1.10.66
35	**EXISTING SERVICE EXTENDED:** DENTON SQUARE (junction of West Road and Copperas Lane) — WELBECK ROAD (east end of) extended via Welbeck Road — White Street — Walker Road — Proctor Street to WALKER CHURCH STREET and return Operated daily.	
		22.8.65—1.10.66
35A	**SHORTENED SERVICE:** BRIGHTON GROVE — WALKER (CHURCH STREET) (foot of) cut back to WALKER (WEST- BOURNE AVENUE). Operated daily.	
		22.8.65—1.10.66
35B	ABANDONED	21.8.65
35 35A 35C	ABANDONED AND COVERED BY MOTOR- BUS OPERATION	
		2.10.66

TICKETS

Bell Punch machines were used, as on the trams, until 1948. The only geographical fare stage ticket known to have been produced for trolleybuses was in 1935, for the original route, Denton—Wallsend. Later, on other routes, tramway fare stage tickets were used and later still, "Blue Bus" fare stage tickets, for instance on the Gosforth route in April 1948. 1d. parcel tickets were issued for the trolleybuses, pre-war.

One interesting ticket is a "Racegoer's Special Fare", issued for use on trams working race specials into Gosforth Park, and in this context to be used on trolleybuses after April 1948, as it is inscribed on the reverse "for use by passengers returning from the Course by Trolleybus". Such passengers were allowed to walk along the Gosforth Park Light Railway to the West Gates trolleybus terminus.

In pre-war days, tickets were headed variously "Newcastle Corp. Tramways", and "Newcastle Corporation Trans. Services", but by the 1940's it had become "Newcastle Corp. Trans". In 1949-50, experiments were conducted from Wingrove Depot using Ultimate ticket machines and on the demise of the trams Ultimates became standard and remained so until the end in 1966. Acknowledgment is here due to Mr. G. S. Hearse for an opportunity to inspect his collection of tickets and for his useful comments and information.

STOP SIGNS

Right from 1935, Newcastle Transport had standardised on an enamel plate design of stop sign about one foot square attached to traction poles by straps. Trolleybus stop signs were the same size as those for motorbuses except that they were chrome yellow instead of white. They were inscribed:—

TROLLEY
BUS
STOP

The word "Trolley" was in slightly smaller-sized lettering than "Bus Stop". In smaller lettering at the bottom was either "Fare Stage" or "By Request". Motorbus stop signs had "Newcastle Corporation Transport" in lieu of "Trolley". Strangely, the style of lettering used was not of the Gill Sans face which was in general use by the Undertaking on vehicles and most notices. In the City centre and at important boarding points in the suburbs, larger signs were provided about two feet by one foot, which gave route numbers, services, and details of intermediate points of use to intending passengers. For example, in Westgate Road in the City centre, signs at stops for West Road services carried such information as "All services from this stop pass General Hospital" and "Service 34 passes the Crematorium".

Where traction poles were not conveniently situated, the stop signs were carried on 3ins. diameter tubular poles as used on the motorbus services.

New stop signs were being provided on the Fenham route a few weeks before conversion to motorbus operation in May 1965.

It may be of interest to readers, especially those from Newcastle, that several examples of Newcastle trolleybus stop sign do still exist, together with some of the instruction notices to drivers which were fitted to traction poles to indicate the position of frogs and crossings etc. These are in the care of the London Trolleybus Preservation Society, owners of former Newcastle trolleybus 628, at their museum premises at Carlton Colville near Lowestoft.

OPERATING STATISTICS

We have been able to compile virtually a complete table which we consider is of great interest as it shows the overall picture of Newcastle's trolleybus system, giving details of the spiralling operating costs per mile over the years, corresponding revenue, and the rise and fall in the numbers of passengers carried. It could perhaps be said to be typical of a British trolleybus system and explains the demise of this form of transport after the mid-nineteen fifties.

Year ending	Operating cost per mile	Passengers carried	Revenue
31/3/36 (6 months)	10.759d	7,162,800	£41,827
31/3/37	10.930d	15,968,612	£94,082
31/3/38	11.463d	25,037,350	£143,517
31/3/39	11.494d	39,281,180	£222,793
31/3/40	12.381d	42,295,414	£242,297
31/3/41	13.844d	45,066,350	£259,366
31/3/42	15.130d	51,144,785	£292,561
31/3/43	16.494d	55,103,398	£315,200
31/3/44	Not available	57,440,899	£328,299
31/3/45	Not available	64,630,219	£367,005
31/3/46	18.754d	67,925,192	£388,668
31/3/47	20.038d	71,116,044	£411,730
31/3/48	24.034d	70,856,025	£416,771
31/3/49	24.808d	82,737,382	£585,576
31/3/50	23.114d	85,822,140	£694,649
31/3/51	22.324d	83,709,871	£675,750
31/3/52	23.739d	84,236,376	£715,476
31/3/53	24.170d	84,552,744	£732,018
31/3/54	24.973d	84,723,607	£735,296
31/3/55	25.930d	84,553,258	£730,218
31/3/56	27.746d	84,719,475	£759,167
31/3/57	29.861d	83,979,141	£802,276
31/3/58	31.923d	78,459,657	£901,026
31/3/59	33.054d	76,366,178	£906,108
31/3/60	33.350d	75,290,529	£892,213
31/3/61	35.542d	71,705,117	£934,452
31/3/62	38.488d	68,249,768	£991,303
31/3/63	39.278d	62,977,017	£995,197
31/3/64	42.110d	50,271,628	£806,154
31/3/65	48.054d	34,522,841	£531,729
31/3/66	55.087d	16,287,461	£292,207
31/3/67 (to 1/10/66)	57.896d	6,124,106	£111,090

DEPOT STATISTICS

Depot	Opened	Closed	Maximum Capacity	Size	Structure
Byker	1901	Extant	100 Trolleybuses (80 Trams)	13 Acres (14.5 Acres with motorbus garage)	
Handysides (Morden Street)	1958	Extant	12 Trolleybuses 18 Motorbuses		
Haymarket	1902	1957	15 Trolleybuses 20 Motorbuses		
Slatyford	1956	Extant	60 Trolleybuses 60 Motorbuses	4.6 Acres + 4.6 Acres of spare ground	2 bays of 80ft. 1 bay of 90ft. all 360ft. long
Wingrove	1903	1956	70 Trolleybuses (60 Trams)	1.7 Acres	2 bays of 37ft. 6ins. 335ft. long+yard 200ft. x 75ft.

SUBSTATIONS

The following substations served the Newcastle trolleybus system, the figure after each indicating the Newcastle postal district.

1. Manors (former generating station), Newcastle 1
2. Byker (at depot), Newcastle 6
3. Westgate (West Road), Newcastle 4
4. Barrack Road, Newcastle 4
5. Diana Street, (Arthur's Hill), Newcastle 4
6. Northbourne Street, (Elswick), Newcastle 4
7. Slatyford, (at depot), Newcastle 5
8. Vine Street, (in City Centre), Newcastle 1
9. Cartington Terrace, (North Heaton), Newcastle 6
10. Matthew Bank, Newcastle 2
11. Broadway West, (Gosforth), Newcastle 3
12. Ministry, (Benton Park Road), Newcastle 3
13. St. Peter's, (in Glasshouse Street), Newcastle 6
14. Welbeck Road, (at eastern end), Newcastle 6
15. Walker Road, (near Crown & Anchor Hotel, Fisher Street), Newcastle 6

NOTE: Manors, Byker, and Westgate were originally rotary-converters. Manors controlled other "slave" stations in the suburbs.
The total length of High Tension Feeders was 30,619 yards.

REMOVAL OF OVERHEAD INSTALLATIONS

KEY: n.o. — night of   w.e. — weekend of

w.e. 8/9.6.63	Eastbound running wire east end of St. Nicholas' Square to foot of Melbourne Street removed.
7.63	Eastbound running wire removed from west end of Collingwood Street to St. Nicholas' Square; east and west bound running wire removed along Walker Road from St. Nicholas' Square to foot of Church Street.
29.2.64	Running-wire removed both directions along North Road northwards from Jesmond Road to Jesmond Dene Road.
4.64	Running wire removed both directions along North Road northwards from Jesmond Dene Road junction to Gosforth Park, (Broadway West not removed until June 1964).
May/June 64	Running wire removed both directions along Jesmond Dene Road, Matthew Bank and Benton Park Road to Swarland Avenue.
8.64	Running wire removed both directions from *"Corner House"* (top of Heaton Road) along Stephenson Road to Benton Road (Swarland Avenue).
By Autumn 64	Traction poles outside City boundary removed on North Road — Gosforth Park Route. Traction poles also removed at this time along Jesmond Dene Road, Matthew Bank, Benton Park Road and Benton Road south to City boundary.
n.o. 8/9.6.65	Reverser at Fenham (Bingfield Gardens) dismantled.
6.65	Running wire from eastern end of Welbeck Road to Wallsend (Park Road) removed.
8.65	Running wires removed in Northumberland Street, Haymarket, Percy Street north of Morden Street, Jesmond Road, Osborne Road, Benton Bank, Stephenson Road and Heaton Road.
8.65	Running wires removed in Shields Road from Byker Depot to Wallsend Boundary. Westbound running wires removed in Shields Road from Byker Depot to Fossway junction.
w.e. 11/12.9.65	Running wire removed in Pilgrim Street but not inner road of wiring on east side.
w.e. 23/24.10.65	Heaton Road Junction frogs removed on Shields Road.
10.65	Running wire removed in Fox-and-Hounds Lane, and from Pendower Way junction along Ferguson's Lane to Whickham View junction.
10.65	Left hand connection from Blackett Street to Northumberland Street removed.
6/7.11.65	Running wire removed from Fenham Hall Drive west from Convent Road, and along Netherby Drive, to Silver Lonnen junction; also Silver Lonnen to West Road roundabout except

	Netherby Drive/Silver Lonnen junction frogs and wiring to depot entrance.
20/21.11.65	Running wire removed from remainder of Fenham Hall Drive
n.o. 27/28.11.65	Running wire removed along Ponteland Road, from Fenham Hall Drive junction eastwards to Brighton Grove.
w.e. 4/5.12.65	Running wire removed along Barrack Road, from Brighton Grove junction to four poles short of Stanhope Street junction.
19.12.65	St. Nicholas' turning loop eastwards from Stephenson's Monument dismantled.
12.65	Netherby Drive/Silver Lonnen junction frogs removed.
15/16.1.66	Left hand connection from Percy Street, and siding in Blackett Street dismantled. Running wire removed along Clayton Street from Westgate Road junction to two poles short of Blackett Street junction, including frogs and connections at Newgate Street junction.
?5/6.2.66	Turning circle Neville Street East—Stephenson's Monument dismantled and running wire removed from Bewick Street. Frogs in Neville Street removed.
By 2.66	Remaining running wire removed from Fox-and-Hounds Lane together with connections on West Road including bracket arms.
?26/27.2.66	Remaining wiring at Neville Street roundabout dismantled. Running wire also removed from Bewick Street, Clayton Street West, and Grainger Street West.
2.66	Remaining running wire removed in Melbourne Street leaving some spans.
w.e. 12/13.3.66	Inner (eastbound) road of wiring removed in Westgate Road from Blenheim Street to Clayton Street junction.
By 4.66	Running wire removed from Whickham View from about 200 yds. west of Delaval Road, and Denton Road (including terminus wiring in Castlenook Place) to West Road roundabout including removal of bracket arms, but leaving bracket arms and eastbound wiring in Whickham View from Blind Workshops to Delaval Road.
4.66	All traction poles removed on perimeter of South African War Memorial in Haymarket due to pavement being cut back.
By 30.4.66	All traction poles removed in Silver Lonnen from West Road roundabout to Netherby Drive junction together with depot approach poles in Slatyford Lane.
1-14.5.66	All traction poles removed from Netherby Drive.
8.66	All traction poles removed from south side of Stephenson Road, from Chillingham Road Ends to junction with King Edward Road, due to motorway works.
Summer 66	All traction poles removed in Wallsend east from City Boundary to Wallsend Park Road.

Between Summer 1965 and Summer 1966	All running wire removed along Fossway and Coutts Road together with bracket arms but excluding depot exit wiring.
n.o. 14/15.10.66	All running wire removed from east end of Welbeck Road, White Street, Station Road and Proctor Street.
w.e. 22/23.10.66	All running wire removed from Welbeck Road westwards to Scrogg Road junction.
w.e. 29/30.10.66	All running wire removed from remainder of Welbeck Road, together with Byker reverser, and wiring along Bothal Street and Union Road (to link to Byker Depot) and link to Fossway for Depot.
w.e. 12/13.11.66	All running wire removed from Pilgrim Street terminus, inner road of west bound wiring from crossover, in front of Dex Garage, and New Bridge Street to Pilgrim Street junction. All wiring was removed from Pilgrim Street to Market Street junction.
19/20.11.66	Remainder of wiring removed from Percy Street, and Newgate Street and whole length of Market Street together with left-hand connections from Grainger Street to Blackett Street and Blackett Street to Grainger Street, and inner road of south-bound wiring in Grainger Street (from Gas Board to St. John's Church) used by services to Central Station.
During week 20-26.11.66	Wiring removed from Eldon Square siding and outer road of eastbound wiring to Monument used by Service 36 to Central Station. Also right-hand connection Grainger Street— Monument — Blackett Street. Running wire only removed from whole length of Grainger Street, and left-hand connection from Westgate Road to Grainger Street.
11.66	Tram wires (used as feeders) removed from lower Pilgrim Street.
During week 27.11.66—3.12.66	Span wires removed in Grainger Street.
n.o. 2/3.12.66	Running wire removed from St. James' Park loop, Barrack Road.
By 5.12.66	Running wire removed from remainder of Union Road together with Byker depot and associated wiring. Also removed from Shields Road, Shields Road West, Byker Bridge (leaving gantries) and New Bridge Street to $\frac{1}{4}$ mile east of Market junction.
n.o. 5.12.66	Remaining running wire removed from Pilgrim Street terminal loop in New Bridge Street.
w.e. 3/4.12.66	Running wire removed from Brighton Grove terminal loop in Dilston Road and Callerton Place together with siding in Brighton Grove.
6-8.12.66	Running wire removed in Stanhope Street from Barrack Road junction frogs to Brighton Grove junction.

by 9.12.66	Remaining running wire removed in New Bridge Street westwards to Dex Garage.
w.e. 10/11.12.66	Running wire removed from Blackett Street and Gallowgate to about 50 yards west of Newgate Street junction leaving some span wires.
17/18.12.66	Remainder of running wire removed from Gallowgate, and Barrack Road to Stanhope Street junction, together with Brighton Grove from Stanhope Street junction to Westgate Road junction.
w.e. 31.12.66 1.1.67	Eastbound running wire removed from Benwell Lane, Adelaide Terrace, and in Elswick Road from Delaval Road to Elswick.
n.o. 5/6.1.67	Eastbound running wire removed in Elswick Road from Elswick to Big Lamp.
w.e. 7/8.1.67	Westbound running wire removed in Elswick Road from Big Lamp to Elswick leaving span wires in situ.
w.e. 14/15.1.67	Span wires removed from the whole length of Elswick Road.
Winter 1966/67	Terminal wiring at *Fox-&-Hounds* removed.
During week 11/27.1.67	Westbound running wire removed from Westgate Road and in West Road from Stephenson's Monument to Denton Square (?)
During period 29.1.67-8.2.67	Eastbound running wire removed from Westgate Road and West Road from Denton Square (?) to Big Lamp.
8-11.2.67	FINAL WIRING REMOVAL: Eastbound running wire in Westgate Road between Big Lamp and Stephenson's Monument.
by 28.2.67	Span wires removed from Westgate Road and West Road.
n.o. 9.3.67	Cross gantries and bracing wires removed from Byker Bridge.
w.e. 11/12.3.67	Bracket arms removed from St. James' Park loop.
n.o. 16.3.67	Gantries removed from Westgate Road at foot of Westgate Hill
16.3.67-9.67	Traction poles removed along Welbeck Road working east to west.
During 1967	Cross gantries and bracket arms removed from Westgate Road.
4.67	Ditto West Road.
6.67	Surplus poles for removal in City centre marked with white squares.
During 1967	Traction poles removed from Westgate Hill.
Early 1968	Traction poles removed from Barras Bridge, and in Great Road at Grandstand Road/Jesmond Dene Road junction.
Summer 1968	Traction poles removed from Osborne Road, Denton Burn roundabout.
11.68	Traction poles removed in Neville Street in connection with one way traffic scheme.
3.69	Traction poles removed from Collingwood Street.
1968/9	Traction poles removed in Whickham View from just East of junction with Ferguson's Lane to Denton Road. Also Tower View and Ferguson's Lane from Pease Avenue junction to Benwell Lane junction.
April/May 1969	Traction poles removed from Byker Bridge on erection of crash barriers.

228

1970	Traction poles removed in City Centre from Bewick Street, St. Thomas' Street, and Westgate Road.
2.71	112 Traction poles in Heaton Road.
Late May/1st week June 1971	99 Traction poles in Fenham Hall Drive.
First week of Feb. 1972	Traction poles removed from junction of Percy Street and Blackett Street due to widening of junction.
2.72	Traction poles removed in Gallowgate at about 50 yards west from Newgate Street junction and west to Strawberry Place.
6.72	Traction poles removed from virtually whole length of Melbourne Street east from City Road junction.
8.72 onwards	Traction poles removed in West Road, from Condercum Road east to Benwell Grove junction.
12.72—1.73	Traction poles removed in Great North Road from about 50ft. north of Grandstand Road junction northwards to City Boundary.
Winter 1972/73	Traction poles removed from North end of Clayton Street north of Newgate Street junction, Newgate Street and Percy Street.
1.73	Traction poles removed from Westgate Road at junction with Brighton Grove ("The Brighton").
2.73	Traction poles removed from south side of Blackett Street, from Monument to Gallowgate.
3.73	Traction poles removed from Adelaide Terrace, Benwell.
Autumn 1973	Traction poles removed from junction of Stanhope Street and Barrack Road.
Winter 1973/4	Traction poles removed from Grainger Street from Westgate Road to Market Street.
Pre-May 1974	Traction poles removed (some) from south side of Stanhope Street.
June 1974	Traction poles removed from Dilston Road and Callerton Place.
13.5.76	Traction poles removed from Barrack Road and Ponteland Road, from Strawberry Place to Fenham Hall Drive.
April/May 77	Traction poles removed from New Bridge Street from Central Motorway East to Byker Bridge.
8.12.77	Traction poles removed from section of New Bridge Street near Broadcasting House.
July 1979	Traction poles removed from West Road/Westgate Road from Hoyle Avenue to Wingrove Depot.
1979	Traction poles removed from Jesmond Road, from Barras Bridge to Central Motorway East.
pre-1980	Traction poles removed from West Road from Denton Burn Roundabout to Denton Square.
pre-1980	Traction poles removed from Fossway.
pre-1980	Traction poles removed from Westgate Road between Wingrove Depot and Big Lamp.

pre-1980	Traction poles removed from City Road (east of Crawhall Road), Glasshouse Bridge and sections of Walker Road to City boundary.
1983	Traction poles removed from Benton Bank.
1983	Traction poles removed from Wingrove Road (two poles).
?	Traction poles removed from Great North Road between Barras Bridge and just short of Grandstand Road junction.
Spring 1985	Traction poles removed from Denton Road, from Whickham View to Denton Burn Roundabout. …the job continues